Partnership Taxation

Partnership Taxation

EIGHTH EDITION

Stephen Schwarz
Professor of Law Emeritus
University of California, Hastings College of the Law

Daniel J. Lathrope
Distinguished E.L. Wiegand Professor of Law
University of San Francisco School of Law

Brant J. Hellwig
Dean and Professor of Law
Washington and Lee University School of Law

BLACK LETTER SERIES®

WEST
ACADEMIC
PUBLISHING

Summary of Contents

CAPSULE SUMMARY 1

Perspective **25**

Chapter I. Introduction **29**
A. Forms of Business Organizations 30
B. Conceptual Taxation Models 31
C. Overview of Taxing Regimes Under the Code 32
D. Influential Policies 33
E. Pervasive Judicial Doctrines 34

Chapter II. Classification **37**
A. Introduction 38
B. Existence of a Separate Entity 39
C. Classification of Business Entities 42
D. Choice of Entity Considerations 45
E. Review Questions 46

Chapter III. Formation of a Partnership **47**
A. Introduction 48
B. Contributions of Property 48
C. Treatment of Liabilities 51
D. Organization and Syndication Expenses 54
E. Review Questions 54

Chapter IV. Partnership Operations: General Rules **57**
A. Aggregate and Entity Theories of Partnership Taxation 58
B. Taxing Partnership Operations 58
C. Review Questions 67

Chapter V. Partnership Allocations: § 704(b) **69**
A. Partnership Allocations: Substantial Economic Effect 70
B. Allocations Attributable to Nonrecourse Liabilities 83
C. Review Questions 87

Chapter VI. Partnership Allocations: Income-Shifting Safeguards **89**
A. Allocations with Respect to Contributed Property 90
B. Partnership Interests Created by Gift or Acquired by Purchase from Family
    Member 100
C. Allocations Where Partners' Interests Vary During the Year 101
D. Review Questions 104

Chapter VII. Partnership Liabilities **105**
A. Introduction 106

B. Economic Risk of Loss..106
C. Nonrecourse Liabilities...109
D. Special Rules 113
E. Review Questions..114

Chapter VIII. Compensating the Service Partner **115**
A. Payments for Services: General Rules...116
B. Partnership Equity Issued in Exchange for Services 121
C. Policy Issues: Carried Interests 126
D. Review Questions..127

Chapter IX. Property Transactions Between Partnerships and Partners **129**
A. Introduction...130
B. § 707(a)(1) Property Transactions..130
C. Guaranteed Payments: § 707(c) 131
D. Sales and Exchanges of Property Between Partners and Partnerships: General Rules 132
E. Disguised Sales Between Partners and Partnerships: § 707(a)(2)(B) 132
F. Review Questions..133

Chapter X. Sales and Exchanges of Partnership Interests...............................**135**
A. Introduction...136
B. Tax Consequences to the Selling Partner 136
C. Tax Consequences to the Buying Partner 143
D. Review Questions..148

Chapter XI. Operating Distributions **151**
A. Consequences to the Partner 152
B. Consequences to the Partnership 158
C. Mixing Bowl Transactions..161
D. Distributions Which Shift the Partners' Interests in § 751 Assets: § 751(b) 164
E. Review Questions..168

Chapter XII. Liquidating Distributions and Terminations **169**
A. Liquidation of a Partner's Interest 170
B. Liquidation of the Entire Partnership..179
C. Review Questions..184

Chapter XIII. Death of a Partner **185**
A. Introduction...186
B. The Deceased Partner's Distributive Share in the Year of Death..........................186
C. Estate Tax, Income in Respect of a Decedent, and Basis Consequences 186
D. Review Questions..189

Chapter XIV. Partnership Anti-Abuse Rule...**191**
A. Introduction...192
B. Abuse of Subchapter K Rule 192
C. Abuse of Partnership Entity 195
D. Review Questions..195

Chapter XV. S Corporations **197**
A. Introduction...198

B.   Eligibility for S Corporation Status...198
C.   Election, Revocation, and Termination of Subchapter S Status.............203
D.   Tax Treatment of S Corporation Shareholders.................................205
E.   Distributions to Shareholders...215
F.   Taxation of the S Corporation...218
G.   Coordination of Subchapter S with Subchapter C and Other Tax Provisions.........221
H.   Review Questions...223

Appendix A. Answers to Review Questions...**225**

Appendix B. Practice Examination..**237**

Appendix C. Glossary..**241**

TABLE OF CASES..249

TABLE OF INTERNAL REVENUE CODE SECTIONS...251

TABLE OF TREASURY REGULATIONS...255

TABLE OF REVENUE RULINGS AND PROCEDURES...259

INDEX...261

Table of Contents

Capsule Summary 1

Perspective **25**

Chapter I. Introduction **29**
A. Forms of Business Organizations 30
   1. Sole Proprietorship 30
   2. Corporation...30
   3. Partnership...30
      a. General Partnership 30
      b. Limited Partnership..30
      c. Limited Liability Partnership 30
      d. Publicly Traded Partnership 30
      e. Joint Venture..31
   4. Limited Liability Company 31
   5. Demography 31
B. Conceptual Taxation Models...31
   1. Aggregate Concept 31
   2. Entity Concept 31
   3. Hybrid Concepts..31
C. Overview of Taxing Regimes Under the Code 32
   1. Subchapter C 32
   2. Subchapter K...32
   3. Subchapter S 32
   4. Specialized Tax Regimes 33
D. Influential Policies..33
   1. The Double Tax 33
   2. Rate Structure...33
   3. Preferential Rates on Capital Gains and Qualified Dividends 34
   4. Nonrecognition of Gain or Loss 34
E. Pervasive Judicial Doctrines...34
   1. Substance over Form 35
   2. Step Transactions 35
      a. The Binding Commitment Test..35
      b. The End Result Test 35
      c. The Interdependence Test 35
      d. Application by Courts and IRS..35
   3. Business Purpose 36
   4. Sham Transaction 36
   5. Economic Substance 36
   6. Codification of the Economic Substance Doctrine 36

Chapter II. Classification **37**
A. Introduction...38
   1. Impact of Classification 38
   2. The Role of State Law 38

      3.   Principal Classification Issues 38
  B. Existence of a Separate Entity...39
      1.   In General...39
      2.   Joint Profit Motive 39
      3.   Separate Entity vs. Co-ownership of Property..........................40
          a.   In General 40
          b.   Fractional Interests in Rental Real Property.....................40
          c.   Section 761(a) Election...40
          d.   Section 761(f): Husband-Wife Qualified Joint Venture 41
      4.   Separate Entity vs. Expense Sharing, Employment, Loan, and Other
          Relationships 41
  C. Classification of Business Entities 42
      1.   Introduction..42
      2.   The "Check-the-Box" Classification Regulations 43
          a.   Introduction 43
          b.   Entities with Two or More Members 43
          c.   Business Entities with One Owner....................................43
          d.   Series LLCs...43
          e.   Entity Owned as Community Property 44
          f.   Foreign Entities..44
          g.   Election 44
          h.   Existing Entities...44
      3.   Publicly Traded Partnerships 44
      4.   Trusts...44
  D. Choice of Entity Considerations..45
      1.   Publicly Traded Businesses 45
      2.   Closely Held Businesses 45
          a.   In General...45
          b.   C Corporations...45
          c.   S Corporations..45
          d.   Limited Liability Companies 46
          e.   Limited Partnerships 46
          f.   Converting from Corporation to Pass-Through Entity 46
          g.   State Tax Considerations..46
  E. Review Questions 46

Chapter III. Formation of a Partnership **47**
  A. Introduction...48
  B. Contributions of Property..48
      1.   General Rules 48
      2.   Related Issues 48
          a.   Recapture Provisions 48
          b.   Installment Obligations..48
          c.   Investment Partnerships 49
          d.   Noncompensatory Options...49
              1) In General..49
              2) Noncompensatory Option Defined 49
              3) Applicability of Section 721 to Noncompensatory Options 49
          e.   Debt-for-Equity Exchanges..49
      3.   Basis and Holding Period 50
          a.   "Outside" and "Inside" Bases...50

  b. Holding Period...50
C. Treatment of Liabilities..51
  1. Impact on Partner's Outside Basis 51
    a. Introduction...51
    b. Classification of Liabilities and Partners' Shares of Partnership
      Liabilities..51
    c. Economic Risk of Loss..52
  2. Contributions of Property Encumbered by Recourse Liabilities 53
D. Organization and Syndication Expenses 54
  1. General Rule..54
  2. Deduction and Amortization of Organization Expenses 54
  3. Syndication Expenses 54
E. Review Questions..54

Chapter IV. Partnership Operations: General Rules **57**
A. Aggregate and Entity Theories of Partnership Taxation............58
B. Taxing Partnership Operations 58
  1. Partnership Level Determination of Tax Results....................58
    a. Partnership Accounting Method 58
    b. Partnership Taxable Year 58
      1) Mechanical Rules 58
      2) Business Purpose 59
      3) Fiscal Year Election 59
    c. Partnership Taxable Income 60
      1) In General..60
      2) Separately Stated Items 60
    d. Tax Elections 60
  2. Tax Consequences to the Partners 60
    a. Timing and Character of Pass Through Items...........60
    b. Basis Adjustments 61
  3. Limitations on Partnership Losses 62
    a. Basis Limitation...62
    b. At-Risk Limitation 63
      1) Introduction 63
      2) At-Risk Amount: In General...........................63
      3) Qualified Nonrecourse Financing....................63
      4) Other Nonrecourse Debt 64
      5) Limited Partner Guarantees and Other Partner Obligations............64
      6) Adjustments to Amount at Risk and Carryover of Suspended
        Losses 65
    c. Passive Activity Loss Limitation.............................65
      1) Introduction 65
      2) Material Participation.....................................66
      3) Definition of "Activity" 66
      4) Later Use of Suspended Losses 66
C. Review Questions..67

Chapter V. Partnership Allocations: § 704(b) **69**
A. Partnership Allocations: Substantial Economic Effect 70
  1. Introduction...70

2. Special Allocations 70
   a. Introduction 70
   b. Partnership Accounting: The Basics 70
   c. Economic Effect 72
      1) Introduction 72
      2) Basic Test: "The Big Three" 72
      3) Alternate Test for Economic Effect 74
      4) Economic Effect Equivalence 76
   d. Substantiality 77
      1) Introduction 77
      2) General Rule for Substantiality 77
      3) Shifting and Transitory Allocations 78
         a) Shifting Allocations 78
         b) Transitory Allocations 79
      4) The Baseline for Testing Substantiality 80
      5) Presumption Validating "Gain Chargeback" Provisions 80
   e. Partner's Interest in the Partnership 80
   f. Allocations of Depreciation Recapture 82
   g. Allocations of Tax Credits 82
   h. Target Allocations 83
B. Allocations Attributable to Nonrecourse Liabilities 83
  1. Introduction 83
  2. Partnership Minimum Gain 83
  3. Nonrecourse Deductions 83
  4. Safe Harbor Test for Respecting Allocations of Nonrecourse Deductions 84
  5. Minimum Gain Chargeback Requirement 84
  6. Refinancings and Distributions 86
C. Review Questions 87

Chapter VI. Partnership Allocations: Income-Shifting Safeguards 89
A. Allocations with Respect to Contributed Property 90
  1. § 704(c) Allocations: General Principles 90
  2. § 704(c) Allocation Methods 91
   a. In General 91
   b. The Ceiling Rule 91
   c. Sales and Exchanges of Contributed Property 91
      1) Traditional Method 91
      2) Traditional Method with Curative Allocations 93
      3) Remedial Method 93
   d. Depreciation and Depletion 94
      1) Traditional Method 94
      2) Traditional Method with Curative Allocations 95
      3) Remedial Method 96
  3. Application of § 704(c)(1)(A) Principles to the Entry of a New Partner 97
   a. Allocation of Preexisting Gains and Losses: In General 97
   b. Methods of Allocating Preexisting Gains and Losses 97
      1) Allocation in Partnership Agreement 97
      2) Revaluation and Restatement of Capital Accounts 97
  4. Distributions of Contributed Property Within Seven Years of Contribution 98

5. Characterization of Gain or Loss upon Partnership's Disposition of Contributed Property...98
    a. Unrealized Receivables..98
    b. Inventory Items...99
    c. Capital Loss Property 99
    d. Depreciation Recapture 100
6. Anti-Abuse Rule for Loss Property 100
B. Partnership Interests Created by Gift or Acquired by Purchase from Family Member..100
1. Purpose of § 704(e)...100
2. Definitions of Partnership and Partner...100
3. Determination of Distributive Share of Donee 100
C. Allocations Where Partners' Interests Vary During the Year 101
1. Introduction...101
2. Determination of Distributive Shares 101
    a. Permissible Allocation Methods 101
    b. Services Partnerships 102
    c. Allocation of Extraordinary Items 102
3. Distributive Shares of Allocable Cash Basis Items: § 706(d)(2) 102
    a. Determination on Per-Day, Per-Partner Basis........................102
    b. Items Attributable to Periods Not Within Taxable Year........103
4. Tiered Partnerships 103
D. Review Questions...104

Chapter VII. Partnership Liabilities..**105**
A. Introduction..106
B. Economic Risk of Loss 106
1. General Rules..106
2. The Relationship Between Economic Risk of Loss and Economic Effect........108
3. Proposed Regulations 109
C. Nonrecourse Liabilities 109
1. General Rules..109
2. Proposed Regulations 113
D. Special Rules 113
1. Part Recourse and Part Nonrecourse Liabilities 113
2. Tiered Partnerships 114
E. Review Questions...114

Chapter VIII. Compensating the Service Partner **115**
A. Payments for Services: General Rules 116
1. Services Rendered in a Nonpartner Capacity: § 707(a)(1) 116
    a. General Rules 116
    b. Tax Stakes 116
    c. Determination of Partner or Nonpartner Status 117
2. Disguised Payments for Services: § 707(a)(2)(A) 117
    a. Tax Planning Agenda..117
    b. Recharacterization Under § 707(a)(2)(A)................................117
    c. § 707(a)(2)(A) Factors...118
    d. Proposed Regulations...118
        1) Focus on Entrepreneurial Risk 118
        2) Application to Management Fee Waivers............................119

3) Breadth of Proposed Regulations 119
3. Guaranteed Payments for Services: § 707(c) 119
   a. Guaranteed Payment Defined 119
   b. Tax Consequences to the Service Partner 119
   c. Tax Consequences to the Partnership 120
   d. Treatment Under Other Code Provisions 120
   e. Calculation of Guaranteed Payments 120
      1) Current Approach of IRS 120
      2) Proposed Regulations 121
B. Partnership Equity Issued in Exchange for Services 121
  1. Introduction 121
  2. Capital Interest vs. Profits Interest 121
  3. Receipt of a Capital Interest for Services 122
   a. Tax Consequences to the Service Partner 122
   b. Tax Consequences to the Partnership 122
      1) Business Expense Deduction to the Partnership 122
      2) Taxable Event to Partnership 123
  4. Receipt of a Profits Interest for Services 124
   a. Tax Consequences to the Service Partner 124
      1) Historical Approach 124
      2) The *Diamond* Case 124
      3) Safe Harbor: Revenue Procedure 93–27 124
      4) Timing Issues: Revenue Procedure 2001–43 125
   b. Tax Consequences to the Partnership 125
  5. Proposed Regulations 126
C. Policy Issues: Carried Interests 126
  1. Tax Advantages of Carried Interests 126
  2. Criticisms of Current Tax Treatment 127
D. Review Questions 127

Chapter IX. Property Transactions Between Partnerships and Partners 129
A. Introduction 130
B. § 707(a)(1) Property Transactions 130
  1. In General 130
  2. Disguised Payments for the Use of Property: § 707(a)(2)(A) 130
   a. Tax Planning Agenda 130
   b. Recharacterization Under § 707(a)(2)(A) 130
   c. § 707(a)(2)(A) Factors 131
C. Guaranteed Payments: § 707(c) 131
D. Sales and Exchanges of Property Between Partners and Partnerships: General Rules 132
E. Disguised Sales Between Partners and Partnerships: § 707(a)(2)(B) 132
  1. Key Factors 132
  2. Debt-Financed Distributions 133
F. Review Questions 133

Chapter X. Sales and Exchanges of Partnership Interests 135
A. Introduction 136
B. Tax Consequences to the Selling Partner 136
  1. Computation of Gain or Loss 136
   a. Amount Realized 136

      b.   Adjusted Basis of Partnership Interest 136
  2. Characterization of Gain or Loss 137
      a.   General Rule: § 741 137
      b.   Definition of § 751 Assets 137
         1) Unrealized Receivables 137
         2) Inventory Items 138
      c.   Computation of § 751 Gain or Loss 138
      d.   Capital Gains Look-Through Rules 140
      e.   Holding Period 141
  3. Related Issues 142
      a.   Installment Sale of a Partnership Interest 142
      b.   Exchange or Conversion of Partnership Interests 143
         1) Exchanges of Partnership Interests 143
         2) Conversions of Partnership Interests 143
         3) Conversions into LLC or LLP Interests 143
C. Tax Consequences to the Buying Partner 143
  1. Introduction 143
  2. Operation of § 743(b) 144
      a.   Requirement of § 754 Election or Substantial Built-in Loss 144
         1) General Rules 144
         2) Special Rules 144
      b.   Adjustments to Inside Basis Under § 743(b) 144
         1) The Overall § 743(b) Adjustment 144
         2) Allocation of the Adjustment 146
      c.   Effect of § 743(b) Adjustment 148
      d.   Contributed Property with a Built-in Loss 148
D. Review Questions 148

Chapter XI. Operating Distributions **151**
A. Consequences to the Partner 152
  1. Cash Distributions 152
      a.   In General 152
      b.   Distributions of Marketable Securities 153
         1) General Rule 153
         2) Reduction for Distributee's Share of Partnership Net Gain 153
         3) Exceptions 154
  2. Property Distributions 154
      a.   Recognition of Gain or Loss 154
      b.   Basis Consequences 154
         1) General Rule: Transferred Basis 154
         2) Basis Limitation 154
         3) Allocation of Basis 155
         4) Holding Period 155
      c.   § 732(d) Election 157
  3. Dispositions of Distributed Property 157
      a.   General Rules: § 735 157
      b.   Depreciation Recapture 158
B. Consequences to the Partnership 158
  1. Nonrecognition of Gain or Loss 158
  2. Impact on Inside Basis 158
      a.   General Rule: No Adjustment to Inside Basis 158

		b.	§ 734(b) Adjustment	159
		c.	Allocation of Basis Adjustment	159
	3.		Adjustments to Capital Accounts	161
C.			Mixing Bowl Transactions	161
	1.		Introduction	161
	2.		Distributions of Contributed Property to Another Partner	162
		a.	The Attempted Strategy	162
		b.	General Rule of § 704(c)(1)(B)	162
		c.	Exceptions	163
	3.		Distributions of Other Property to the Contributing Partner	163
		a.	The Attempted Strategy	163
		b.	General Rule of § 737	163
		c.	Exceptions	164
D.			Distributions Which Shift the Partners' Interests in § 751 Assets: § 751(b)	164
	1.		Purpose and Scope of § 751(b)	164
	2.		§ 751(b) Assets	165
	3.		Operation of § 751(b)	165
	4.		Criticisms of § 751(b)	167
	5.		Proposed Regulations	167
E.			Review Questions	168

Chapter XII. Liquidating Distributions and Terminations **169**

A.			Liquidation of a Partner's Interest	170
	1.		Introduction	170
	2.		§ 736(b) Payments	170
		a.	Tax Consequences of § 736(b) Payments to the Partner	171
			1) Recognition of Gain	171
			2) Recognition of Loss	171
			3) Basis of Distributed Property: In General	171
			4) Allocation of Basis	171
			5) Holding Period	172
		b.	Tax Consequences of § 736(b) Payments to the Partnership	172
			1) General Rules	172
			2) § 754 Election	172
		c.	Interaction of § 736 and § 751(b)	173
	3.		§ 736(a) Payments	175
		a.	Definition of § 736(a) Payments	175
		b.	Tax Treatment of § 736(a) Payments	175
		c.	Timing of § 736(a) Payments: In General	175
		d.	Special Treatment for Partnership Goodwill	175
	4.		Allocation and Timing of § 736 Installment Payments	176
		a.	Allocation	176
		b.	Timing	176
	5.		Liquidation vs. Sale	178
		a.	In General	178
		b.	Abandonment of a Partnership Interest	179
B.			Liquidation of the Entire Partnership	179
	1.		Voluntary Liquidation	179
		a.	In General	179
		b.	Incorporation of a Partnership	179

  c. Partnership Mergers and Divisions 180
   1) Merger or Consolidation 180
   2) Divisions...181
 2. Termination Forced by Statute 181
  a. Sale or Exchange of 50% or More of Total Interests in Capital or Profits: § 708(b)(1)(B) 181
  b. Effect of Termination 182
C. Review Questions...184

Chapter XIII. Death of a Partner **185**
A. Introduction..186
B. The Deceased Partner's Distributive Share in the Year of Death...........186
C. Estate Tax, Income in Respect of a Decedent, and Basis Consequences 186
 1. Federal Estate Tax..186
 2. Income in Respect of a Decedent ("IRD") 186
  a. In General..186
  b. Distributive Share in Year of Death 187
  c. Income in Respect of a Decedent in a Sale at Death or Continuing Interest...187
  d. Income in Respect of a Decedent in a Liquidation of a Partnership Interest...187
 3. Outside and Inside Basis 187
D. Review Questions...189

Chapter XIV. Partnership Anti-Abuse Rule **191**
A. Introduction..192
B. Abuse of Subchapter K Rule 192
 1. In General..192
  a. "Common Law" Requirements of Subchapter K 192
  b. Administrative Convenience Exception...........................192
  c. Impermissible Tax Reduction Purpose 193
 2. Facts and Circumstances Analysis 193
  a. In General..193
  b. Specific Factors...193
  c. Examples 194
 3. Commissioner's Power to Recast Transactions........................194
C. Abuse of Partnership Entity 195
D. Review Questions...195

Chapter XV. S Corporations **197**
A. Introduction..198
B. Eligibility for S Corporation Status..198
 1. Ineligible Corporations and Subsidiaries 198
  a. In General..198
  b. Wholly Owned Subsidiaries 198
 2. 100-Shareholder Limit...199
 3. Restrictions on Types of Shareholders 199
  a. In General..199
  b. Nonresident Alien Restriction...200
  c. Trusts as Eligible Shareholders 200
  d. Qualified Subchapter S Trusts..200

		e.	Electing Small Business Trusts	201
	4.	One-Class-of-Stock Requirement		201
		a.	In General	201
		b.	Buy-Sell and Redemption Agreements	201
		c.	Obligations Treated as Equity Under General Principles	202
		d.	Straight Debt Safe Harbor	202
			1) Background	202
			2) Straight Debt Defined	202
			3) Treatment of Straight Debt for Other Purposes	202
			4) Treatment of Converted C Corporation Debt	202

C. Election, Revocation, and Termination of Subchapter S Status.....203
   1. Electing S Corporation Status.....203
      a. In General.....203
      b. Timing and Effective Date of Election.....203
   2. Revocation and Termination of S Corporation Status.....204
      a. Revocation.....204
      b. Termination.....204
         1) Ceasing to Be a Small Business Corporation.....204
         2) Passive Income Limitation for Certain S Corporations.....204
      c. S Termination Year.....205
      d. Inadvertent Terminations.....205

D. Tax Treatment of S Corporation Shareholders.....205
   1. Introduction.....205
   2. Corporate Level Determination of Tax Results.....206
      a. Accounting Method.....206
      b. Taxable Year.....206
         1) In General.....206
         2) Natural Business Year.....206
         3) § 444 Fiscal Year Election.....207
      c. S Corporation Taxable Income.....207
         1) In General.....207
         2) Separately Stated Items.....208
         3) Charitable Contributions.....208
         4) No Dividends Received Deduction.....208
         5) Organizational Expenses.....209
      d. Tax Elections.....209
   3. Tax Consequences to Shareholders.....209
      a. Timing and Character of Pass-Through Items.....209
      b. Determining Each Shareholder's Pro Rata Share.....210
         1) In General.....210
         2) Special Rule for Termination of a Shareholder's Interest.....210
         3) Special Rule for a Family Group.....210
      c. Limitations on Losses.....211
         1) § 1366(d) Basis Limit.....211
         2) Basis of Indebtedness of S Corporation to a Shareholder.....212
         3) Basis Credit for Shareholder Guarantee of S Corporation Debt.....212
         4) No Basis Credit for Entity Debt.....212
         5) Use of Suspended Losses After Termination of S Corporation Status.....213
         6) Related Provisions.....213
      d. Basis Adjustments.....213

  e. Sale of S Corporation Stock 214
E. Distributions to Shareholders 215
 1. S Corporations Without E & P 215
 2. S Corporations with E & P 215
  a. In General 215
  b. The Accumulated Adjustments Account 216
 3. Distributions of Property 217
 4. Ordering of Basis Adjustments 217
 5. Distributions Following Termination of S Corporation Status 218
F. Taxation of the S Corporation 218
 1. § 1374 Tax on Built-In Gains 218
  a. Policy of Built-In Gains Tax 218
  b. Operation of § 1374 218
  c. Treatment of Substituted Basis Properties 219
  d. Installment Sales and § 1374 220
 2. § 1375 Tax on Excessive Passive Investment Income 220
G. Coordination of Subchapter S with Subchapter C and Other Tax Provisions 221
 1. Subchapter C 221
 2. Other Tax Provisions 221
 3. Employment Taxes 222
  a. Background 222
  b. S Corporation Tax Avoidance Strategy 222
 4. Net Investment Income Tax 222
  a. Background 222
  b. Application to S Corporation Shareholders 223
  c. Sale of S Corporation Stock 223
H. Review Questions 223

Appendix A. Answers to Review Questions **225**

Appendix B. Practice Examination **237**

Appendix C. Glossary **241**

TABLE OF CASES 249

TABLE OF INTERNAL REVENUE CODE SECTIONS 251

TABLE OF TREASURY REGULATIONS 255

TABLE OF REVENUE RULINGS AND PROCEDURES 259

INDEX 261

Capsule Summary

I. INTRODUCTION

A. Forms of Business Organization

The most common forms for a business organization in the United States are:

1. Sole proprietorships, which are businesses owned and operated by a single individual.

2. Corporations, which are legal entities organized under state law that offer limited liability to their owners.

3. Partnerships, including general and limited partnerships, limited liability partnerships, and joint ventures. A small number of unincorporated businesses, known as publicly traded partnerships, have ownership interests that may be traded on an established securities market.

4. Limited liability companies, a popular business entity form that provides limited liability for all of its members.

B. Conceptual Taxation Models

1. Aggregate Concept

The aggregate concept treats the assets of a business as owned directly by its individual owners, who are each responsible for a proportionate share of the liabilities of the business. The business organization itself is not a taxable entity.

2. Entity Concept

The entity concept treats a business organization as a taxable entity that is separate and apart from its owners. Transactions between the owners and the entity are generally taxable events.

3. Hybrid Concepts

Some taxing models adopt a hybrid approach, treating an organization as an entity for some purposes and an aggregate for others.

C. Overview of Taxing Regimes Under the Code

1. Subchapter C

Subchapter C embodies an entity approach by treating most corporations as separate taxable entities and by providing rules that govern transactions between corporations and their shareholders.

2. Subchapter K

Subchapter K applies a hybrid approach to partnerships and their partners. Partnerships do not pay taxes but pass through their income and deductions to their partners. A partnership is treated as an accounting entity, however, for purposes of determining its income and filing of returns. A modified entity approach is applied in various substantive contexts.

3. Subchapter S

Subchapter S is a hybrid model governing the treatment of eligible corporations that make an "S" election. S corporations are pass-through entities that generally are not subject to tax except in limited situations where they have a prior history as a C corporation.

4. Specialized Tax Regimes

The Code includes other specialized tax regimes tailored for particular industries, such as insurance companies, banks, mutual funds, real estate investment trusts, and cooperatives.

D. Influential Policies

The taxation of business organizations has been shaped by four broad tax policy decisions that influence taxpayer behavior. The relationship of these policies has changed as a result of periodic tax legislation enacted over many years.

1. The Double Tax

The double tax regime of Subchapter C often increases the cost of operating a business as a C corporation and may provide an incentive for taxpayers to choose partnerships, limited liability companies, or S corporations for business and investment activities.

2. Rate Structure

For most of our tax history, the maximum individual tax rate exceeded the highest corporate rate. This rate structure historically made the corporation a refuge from much steeper individual rates and provided an incentive to operate as a C corporation. When the maximum individual rate is the same as or, as now, only slightly higher than the top corporate rate, the choice of entity is not as clear. Many closely held businesses may prefer to operate as partnerships, limited liability companies, or S corporations to avoid the double tax. In some situations, however, C corporations will remain the entity of choice for businesses that are able to minimize their taxable income by paying out most of their earnings in a tax-deductible form, such as salary, interest or rent.

3. Preferential Rates for Capital Gains and Qualified Dividends

Whenever there is a significant capital gains rate preference, taxpayers are motivated to devise strategies to convert ordinary income into capital gains, such as "bailing out" C corporation profits at capital gains rates. The bailout strategy is much less significant, however, when dividends are taxed at the same rate as long-term capital gains, as they have been since 2003.

4. Nonrecognition of Gain or Loss

Many transactions involving partnerships and their partners qualify for nonrecognition treatment because they are regarded as mere changes in form which result in a continuity of investment.

E. Pervasive Judicial Doctrines

In addition to the language of the Code, the courts frequently apply various "common law" doctrines in determining the tax consequences of a transaction. The judicial doctrines have been invoked by the Service with increasing success to attack a variety of tax shelter transactions utilizing corporations and partnerships.

1. Substance over Form

The Supreme Court has admonished that the tax consequences of a transaction should be determined by economic substance rather than form. Despite this well accepted doctrine, the Code often permits a taxpayer to assure a desired tax result by utilizing a particular form.

2. Step Transactions

Under the step transaction doctrine, separate formal steps are combined into a single integrated transaction for tax purposes. The courts disagree as to how and when the doctrine should be applied.

3. Business Purpose

Under the business purpose doctrine, a transaction may be denied certain tax benefits, such as nonrecognition of gain, if it is not motivated by a corporate business purpose apart from tax avoidance. The doctrine has been extended through regulations to patrol against abusive partnership transactions and corporate tax shelters.

4. Sham Transaction

A sham is a transaction that never actually occurred or is devoid of substance. Sham transactions are not respected for tax purposes.

5. Economic Substance

Under the judicially created economic substance doctrine, tax benefits are denied for transactions that actually occur and may comply with the literal language of the statute but do not result in a meaningful change to a taxpayer's economic position apart from a reduction in taxes.

6. Codification of the Economic Substance Doctrine

Congress has codified the economic substance doctrine and enacted a strict liability penalty on transactions found to lack economic substance.

II. CLASSIFICATION

A. Introduction

1. Impact of Classification

The operation of many Code sections varies depending upon whether the taxpayer is an individual, a partnership, a corporation or some other type of entity. Thus, the classification of an organization for tax purposes may be extremely important.

2. The Role of State Law

The classification of entities for federal tax purposes is a matter of federal law and depends on standards in the Internal Revenue Code.

3. Principal Classification Issues

Classification issues generally arise in two settings:

a. Determining whether a separate entity exists for federal tax purposes, and

b.   Determining whether an entity with more than one owner should be classified as a corporation or partnership, or whether a single-owner entity should be disregarded for federal tax purposes or classified as a corporation.

B.   Existence of a Separate Entity

1.   In General

The regulations provide that a joint venture or other contractual arrangement may create a separate entity for federal tax purposes if the participants carry on a trade, business, financial operation, or venture and divide the profits therefrom. This definition is derived from case law distinguishing partnerships from less formal relationships.

2.   Joint Profit Motive

The existence of a joint profit motive may be difficult to determine and depends on the particular fact situation. A critical factor in determining whether a partnership exists is whether "the parties in good faith and acting with a business purpose intended to join together in the present conduct of the enterprise." Courts look at a list of factors to determine the intent of the parties. The most critical factor frequently is whether the parties have a joint profit motive.

3.   Separate Entity vs. Co-ownership of Property

The "mere co-ownership" of property which is maintained, kept in repair, and rented or leased does not create a separate entity. A separate entity exists if co-owners lease space and in addition provide services to the tenants either directly or through an agent. The IRS has specified conditions that must be met to receive a ruling that undivided fractional interests in rental property are a co-ownership rather than a partnership.

4.   Separate Entities vs. Expense Sharing, Employment, Loan, and Other Relationships

An expense sharing relationship does not constitute a separate entity for tax purposes. In situations where one person supplies services or capital to a business venture, the determination of whether there is a separate entity generally depends on whether the parties are sharing a joint profit as co-owners or co-proprietors. In limited circumstances, an unincorporated organization may make a statutory election to be excluded from partnership classification for tax purposes. A joint venture meeting certain requirements that is operated by a married couple also may qualify to elect to be excluded from partnership classification.

C.   Classification of Business Entities

1.   Introduction

The Code defines a corporation as including "associations, joint-stock companies, and insurance companies." The interpretation of this definition has a rich and textured history.

2. The "Check-the-Box" Classification Regulations

Historically, the regulations employed four corporate characteristics to classify a business organization as either an association taxable as a corporation or as a partnership. Since 1997, the regulations generally classify most unincorporated business entities as partnerships. A business entity organized under a state corporation statute is taxed as a corporation. An unincorporated business entity, such as a limited liability company or limited partnership, with two or more members is classified as a partnership. An unincorporated business entity with one owner, such as a single-member LLC, is disregarded and thus treated as a sole proprietorship, branch, or division of the owner for federal tax purposes. Every unincorporated entity has the option of electing to be taxed as a corporation.

3. Publicly Traded Partnerships

A "publicly traded partnership" ("PTP"), as defined in § 7704(b), is generally classified as a corporation for federal tax purposes, but a PTP is classified as a partnership if 90% or more of its gross income consists of certain types of passive investment income.

4. Trusts

The fact that a business is operated in a trust will not prevent it from being classified as a business entity. The critical question in determining whether a trust will be classified as a business entity is whether a business objective is present or whether the trust was established merely to protect and conserve trust property.

D. Choice of Entity Considerations

1. Publicly Traded Businesses

Virtually all publicly traded businesses are C corporations for tax purposes.

2. Closely Held Businesses

Many closely held businesses operate as pass-through entities to avoid two levels of tax. Limited liability companies provide the most flexibility, while S corporations offer simplicity, a familiar governance structure, and potential employment tax savings for owners who perform services for the business. A C corporation may be a tax efficient choice for corporations that can distribute most of their profits in a tax-deductible form (e.g., salary, interest, or rent) and limit their taxable income to amounts taxed at the lower marginal corporate tax rates. C corporations are also widely used by start-up companies financed by venture capital firms.

III. FORMATION OF A PARTNERSHIP

A. Introduction

Section 721 provides that no gain or loss is recognized by a partnership or any of its partners on a contribution of property to the partnership in exchange for a partnership interest.

B. Contributions of Property

1. General Rules

For purposes of § 721, "property" includes cash, inventory, accounts receivable, patents, installment obligations and goodwill.

2. Related Issues

Section 721 overrides the recapture provisions and also overrides § 453B so that gain is not recognized when installment obligations are contributed in exchange for a partnership interest.

3. Basis and Holding Period

A partner's "outside" basis in his partnership interest is equal to the sum of money and the adjusted basis of property contributed to the partnership. The partnership's "inside" basis in contributed property is equal to the property's basis in the hands of the contributing partner.

The holding period for the partner's partnership interest is tacked when capital or § 1231 assets are contributed and begins on the day of the exchange when any other property is contributed. A partner may have a split holding period when a combination of assets is contributed to a partnership. The partnership tacks the partner's holding period for all contributed property.

C. Treatment of Liabilities

1. Impact on Partner's Outside Basis

If a partner's share of partnership liabilities increases, that increase is treated as a contribution of money which increases the partner's outside basis. § 752(a). Partners share recourse liabilities according to which partner bears the economic burden of discharging the liability if the partnership is unable to do so. Partners generally share nonrecourse liabilities in proportion to their shares of partnership profits.

2. Contributions of Property Encumbered by Recourse Liabilities

If property subject to a liability is contributed to a partnership, the partnership is considered to have assumed the liability to the extent the liability does not exceed the property's fair market value. The partners' shares of recourse liabilities are determined under the economic risk of loss rules. A decrease in a partner's share of partnership liabilities is treated as a distribution of money which decreases a partner's outside basis. § 752(b).

D. Organization and Syndication Expenses

1. General Rule

Generally, no deduction is allowed for amounts paid or incurred to organize a partnership or to promote the sale of partnership interests.

2. Deduction and Amortization of Organization Expenses

An election may be made to deduct up to $5,000 of expenses incurred to organize a partnership. The $5,000 limit is reduced by the amount of the expenses exceeding $50,000. Expenses that are not deducted are amortized ratably over 180 months. Qualifying expenditures are those which (1) are incident to the creation of the partnership, (2) are chargeable to a capital account, and (3) are of a type which would be amortized over the life of a partnership having an ascertainable life.

3. Syndication Expenses

Expenses connected with issuing and marketing partnership interests may not be deducted or amortized even when the syndication effort is abandoned. Capitalized syndication expenses may be deducted as a capital loss on liquidation of the partnership.

IV. PARTNERSHIP OPERATIONS: GENERAL RULES

A. Aggregate and Entity Theories of Partnership Taxation

Depending on the circumstances, a partnership is treated as an aggregate of its partners or as an entity separate and apart from its partners.

B. Taxing Partnership Operations

1. Partnership Level Determination of Tax Results

Even though a partnership is not a taxable entity, a partnership must calculate its gross income and taxable income to determine tax results to its partners. The partnership elects its own accounting method and taxable year subject to limitations that may require the accrual method and a calendar year.

2. Tax Consequences to the Partners: In General

Certain partnership tax items must be separately stated to preserve their tax character as they pass through to the partners. Partners are required to take into account their distributive share of partnership items in the taxable year in which the partnership's taxable year ends.

A partner must increase his outside basis by his distributive share of partnership income and tax-exempt income and decrease it (but not below zero) by partnership distributions as provided in § 733 and his distributive share of partnership losses and expenditures which are neither deductible nor chargeable to a capital account.

3. Limitations on Partnership Losses

A partner's distributive share of loss is limited to the partner's outside basis at the end of the partnership year in which the loss occurred. A partner's share of loss also is limited by the at-risk and passive activity loss limitations. Disallowed losses are carried over indefinitely.

V. PARTNERSHIP ALLOCATIONS: § 704(b)

A. Partnership Allocations: Substantial Economic Effect

1. Introduction

Each partner is required to take into account his distributive share (determined under the partnership agreement) of separately stated items and nonseparately computed income or loss.

2. Special Allocations

In order to be recognized as valid, the regulations require partnership allocations to have "substantial economic effect." Partnership capital accounts are used to test that requirement.

To have economic effect, an allocation must be consistent with the underlying economic arrangement of the partners, and the economic benefit or burden must be borne by the partner receiving the allocation. This requirement can be met by satisfying any of the three tests set forth in the regulations: "The Big Three," the Alternate Test for Economic Effect, or the Economic Equivalence Test.

In order to be respected, the economic effect of an allocation must be "substantial," which requires that there be a reasonable possibility that the allocation will affect substantially the dollar amounts to be received by the partners from the partnership, independent of tax consequences. An allocation is not substantial if, at the time the allocation becomes part of the partnership agreement, (1) the after-tax consequences of at least one partner may be enhanced compared to the after-tax consequences if the allocation were not contained in the partnership agreement, and (2) there is a strong likelihood that the after-tax consequences of no partner will be substantially diminished compared to the after-tax consequences if the allocation were not contained in the partnership agreement. Specific rules apply to determine the substantiality of shifting and transitory allocations.

If either the partnership agreement is silent or the partnership allocations lack substantial economic effect, a partner's distributive share of partnership items is determined in accordance with the partner's interest in the partnership.

A new trend in partnership agreements is the use of a "target allocations" providing for tax items to be allocated so that they correspond to the partners' economic deal, usually measured by how they agree to distribute cash proceeds of the partnership's operations.

B. Allocations Attributable to Nonrecourse Liabilities

To be respected, allocations attributable to nonrecourse liabilities generally must correspond to any later gain attributable to such debt under a four-part safe harbor test.

VI. PARTNERSHIP ALLOCATIONS: INCOME-SHIFTING SAFEGUARDS

A. Allocations with Respect to Contributed Property

1. § 704(c) Allocations: General Principles

Section 704(c)(1)(A) provides that income, gain, loss and deduction with respect to property contributed by a partner to a partnership shall be allocated among the partners so as to take account of the variation between the inside basis of the property and its fair market value at the time of contribution. For example, the difference between the partnership's tax and book gain or loss on the disposition of a contributed asset is allocated to the contributing partner and any additional book gain or loss is allocated in accordance with the partnership agreement. Under a "ceiling rule," the total income or loss allocated to a partner under § 704(c) may not exceed the partnership's total income or loss with respect to the contributed property for the taxable year.

2. § 704(c) Allocation Methods

The regulations authorize three § 704(c) allocation methods: the traditional method, the traditional method with curative allocations and the remedial method. The latter two methods are designed to correct distortions resulting from the ceiling rule.

3. Application of § 704(c)(1)(A) Principles to Entry of a New Partner

When a new partner joins an existing partnership, the regulations apply § 704(c) principles to ensure that preexisting gains and losses are allocated to the continuing partners rather than the new partner.

4. Distributions of Contributed Property Within Seven Years of Contribution

If property contributed by one partner is distributed to another partner within seven years of the contribution, the contributing partner recognizes gain or loss in an amount equal to the gain or loss that would be allocated under § 704(c)(1)(A) if the property had been sold for its fair market value.

5. Characterization of Gain or Loss upon Partnership Disposition of Contributed Property

The characterization of partnership gains and losses is generally determined at the partnership level. Section 724, however, provides different rules for contributed unrealized receivables, inventory items, and capital loss property.

6. Anti-Abuse Rule for Loss Property

If a partner contributes property with a built-in loss to a partnership, the loss is taken into account only in determining items allocated to the contributing partner. In determining items allocable to the other partners, the partnership's basis in the contributed property is deemed to be its fair market value at the time of the contribution.

B. Partnership Interests Created by Gift or Acquired by Purchase from Family Member

Section 704(e) largely codifies the assignment of income doctrine and prevents the shifting of income among partners who might not be dealing at arm's length, such as family members and other donees.

C. Allocations Where Partners' Interests Vary During the Year

1. Introduction

If there are changes during the year in any partner's interest in the partnership (e.g. by entry of a new partner or partial liquidation of the partner's interest), each partner's distributive share of partnership items must be determined by taking into account the partner's varying ownership interests in the partnership during the year.

2. Determination of Distributive Shares

Where there is a change in a partner's capital interest in the partnership, the partners' distributive shares can be determined by either (1) prorating the partnership items over the year, or (2) through an interim closing of the partnership's books. The interim closing of the books method in the default rule, but the partners may elect to use the proration method.

3. Distributive Shares of Allocable Cash Basis Items: § 706(d)(2)

To prevent cash basis partnerships from using the interim closing of the books method to shift deductions related to certain items such as interest, taxes and payments for services, § 706(d)(2) requires these cash basis items to be allocated on a per-day, per-partner basis.

4. Tiered Partnerships

Tiered partnerships are subject to rules to prevent them from being used to shift income among their partners.

VII. PARTNERSHIP LIABILITIES

A. Introduction

Under § 752(a), an increase in a partner's share of partnership liabilities is considered a contribution of money which increases the partner's outside basis under § 722. A decrease in a partner's share of partnership liabilities is considered under § 752(b) to be a distribution of money to the partner which decreases the partner's outside basis (but not below zero).

B. Economic Risk of Loss

A partner bears the economic risk of loss for a partnership liability to the extent that the partner would bear the economic burden of discharging the obligation represented by the liability if the partnership were unable to do so. The regulations employ a "doomsday" liquidation analysis to determine whether a partner bears the economic risk of loss for a liability. The analysis assumes that all partnership assets are worthless, all liabilities are due and payable, and all assets are disposed of for no consideration in a taxable transaction.

C. Nonrecourse Liabilities

A liability is nonrecourse to the extent that no partner bears the economic risk of loss for the liability. A partner's share of nonrecourse liabilities is equal to the sum of:

1. the partner's share of "partnership minimum gain"; and

2. the amount of any taxable gain that would be allocated to the partner under § 704(c) if the partnership disposed of the property subject to nonrecourse liabilities for relief of such liabilities and no other consideration.

Any remaining partnership nonrecourse liabilities generally are shared by the partners in accordance with their shares in partnership profits.

D. Special Rules

The regulations include special rules to determine how partners bear the economic risk of loss in the case of part recourse and part nonrecourse liabilities and how to allocate liabilities in tiered partnerships.

E. Proposed Regulations

Proposed regulations would alter the manner in which both recourse and nonrecourse liabilities are allocated among partners.

VIII. COMPENSATING THE SERVICE PARTNER

A. Payments for Services: General Rules

1. Services Rendered in Nonpartner Capacity: § 707(a)(1)

Section 707(a)(1) generally adopts an entity theory for determining the tax consequences of services transactions between a partner and a partnership by providing that if a partner engages in a transaction with a partnership "other than in his capacity as a member of such partnership," the transaction is to be taxed as if it occurred between the partnership and a nonpartner unless a Code section provides otherwise.

2. Disguised Payments for Services: § 707(a)(2)(A)

Section 707(a)(2)(A) provides that a direct or indirect allocation and distribution received by a partner for services will be treated as a § 707(a)(1) payment if the performance of services and the allocation and distribution, when viewed together, are properly characterized as a transaction between the partnership and a nonpartner.

3. Guaranteed Payments: § 707(c)

Fixed payments to a partner for services performed as a partner are guaranteed payments taxable under § 707(c). A guaranteed payment is ordinary income under § 61 to the partner and is potentially deductible under § 162 by the partnership, subject to the capitalization requirement of § 263.

B. Partnership Equity Issued in Exchange for Services

1. Introduction

A partner who receives a partnership interest in exchange for services is being compensated for those services and is taxable under § 61 and § 83.

2. Capital Interest vs. Profits Interest

A capital interest is an interest in both the partnership's assets and future profits. A profits interest only entitles a partner to share in future partnership profits after the interest is acquired.

3. Receipt of a Capital Interest for Services

A partner who receives a capital interest in a partnership in exchange for services has gross income when the interest is transferable or is no longer subject to a substantial risk of forfeiture. If the services are not capital in nature, the partnership is entitled to a deduction for the services when the partner recognizes income.

4. Receipt of a Profits Interest for Services

A partner who receives a profits interest in a partnership in exchange for services generally is not taxable on receipt of the interest. But a service partner is taxable on the receipt of a profits interest when:

a.   the profits interest relates to a substantially certain and predictable stream of income from partnership assets,

b.   the partner disposes of the profits interest within two years, or

c.   the interest is in a publicly traded limited partnership.

5. Proposed Regulations

Proposed regulations would change the approach to taxing a transfer of a partnership interest in connection with the performance of services by providing a safe harbor election for valuation of a transferred partnership interest (whether capital or profits) and nonrecognition for the partnership.

C. Policy Issues: Carried Interests

Managers of investment funds typically are entitled to a preferred profit allocation known as a "carried interest." Carried interests are taxed as distributive shares rather than compensation, allowing the service partner to defer income from services and characterize it as capital gain. Proposed legislation would eliminate these tax benefits.

IX. PROPERTY TRANSACTIONS BETWEEN PARTNERSHIPS AND PARTNERS

A. Introduction

A property transaction involving a partner and a partnership may be characterized: (1) under § 707(a)(1) as a transaction between the partnership and an unrelated person; (2) as a guaranteed payment under § 707(c); or (3) as a distributive share.

B. § 707(a)(1) Property Transactions

1. In General

If a partner engages in a transaction with a partnership in a nonpartner capacity, the transaction generally is taxed under § 707(a)(1) as if it were a between the partnership and an unrelated party.

2. Disguised Payments for the Use of Property: § 707(a)(2)(A)

Disguised payments for the use of property that are properly treated as capital expenditures may be recharacterized under § 707(a)(2)(A), applying a list of factors set forth in the regulations.

C. Guaranteed Payments: § 707(c)

Fixed payments made to a partner as a return on contributed capital are taxed as guaranteed payments under § 707(c).

D. Sales and Exchanges Between Partners and Partnerships: General Rules

A sale of property between a partner and a partnership generally is treated in the same manner as a sale between the partnership and a nonpartner except that various provisions of the Code may disallow losses on sales or exchanges between related taxpayers.

E. Disguised Sales Between Partners and Partnerships: § 707(a)(2)(B)

Section 707(a)(2)(B) prevents sales of property between a partner and partnership from being structured as nontaxable contributions and distributions under § 721 and § 731.

X. SALES AND EXCHANGES OF PARTNERSHIP INTERESTS

A. Introduction

When a partner disposes of some or all of her partnership interest, she must determine the recognized gain or loss with reference to her amount realized and the adjusted basis of her partnership interest, and the gain or loss must be characterized. The buying partner ordinarily obtains a cost basis in the acquired interest.

B. Tax Consequences to the Selling Partner

1. Computation of Gain or Loss

A partner's amount realized on the disposition of a partnership interest includes the cash and the fair market value of any property received for the interest, and any decrease in the selling partner's share of partnership liabilities. The partner's adjusted basis includes his distributive share of partnership items for the taxable year of the sale. The partnership's taxable year only closes with respect to a partner who sells or exchanges his entire partnership interest.

2. Characterization of Gain or Loss

Section 751 provides that consideration received by a partner in exchange for his interest in unrealized receivables and inventory items shall be considered as realized from property producing ordinary income. The remainder of the transaction is treated under § 741 as gain or loss from the sale of a partnership interest and is a capital gain or loss. The regulations apply a capital gains look-through rule to characterize long-term capital gain. The partner's holding period for the partnership interest determines whether capital gain is long-term or short-term.

3. Related Issues

If a partner sells a partnership interest under the installment method, gain attributable to certain assets may not be deferred. An exchange of partnership interests cannot qualify for nonrecognition as a like-kind exchange.

C.   Tax Consequences to the Buying Partner

1.   Introduction

A buying partner will take a cost basis in the partnership interest, receiving full credit for the share of partnership liabilities attributable to the interest. The sale of a partnership interest generally has no impact on the bases of partnership property. § 743(a). But a partnership may elect to adjust the bases of its assets with respect to the buying partner under § 754. An inside basis adjustment also is required if the partnership has a substantial (more than $250,000) built-in loss immediately after the transfer.

2.   Operation of § 743(b)

If the partnership has a § 754 election in effect or it has a substantial built-in loss, § 743(b) requires that if there is a sale or exchange of a partnership interest the partnership shall adjust its inside basis by the difference between the buying partner's share of inside basis and his basis in his partnership interest. The process for allocating the § 743(b) adjustment among the partnership assets is prescribed by § 755.

XI.   OPERATING DISTRIBUTIONS

A.   Consequences to the Partner

1.   Cash Distributions

Under § 731(a) a partner generally does not recognize gain or loss on the receipt of a cash distribution from a partnership. But if the money distributed exceeds the partner's outside basis, the excess must be recognized as gain from the sale or exchange of the partner's partnership interest. For purposes of this rule, marketable securities are treated as money to the extent of their fair market value on the date of distribution, subject to several exceptions.

2.   Property Distributions

When a partnership distributes property to a partner in a nonliquidating distribution, generally neither the partner nor the partnership recognizes gain or loss. Under the general rule, a partner takes a transferred basis in property distributed by a partnership and the partner's outside basis is reduced by the basis of the distributed property.

3.   Dispositions of Distributed Property

Under § 735(a), any subsequent gain or loss recognized with respect to distributed "unrealized receivables" is characterized as ordinary and any subsequent gain or loss recognized with respect to "inventory items" within five years after the distribution is characterized as ordinary income.

B.   Consequences to the Partnership

1.   Nonrecognition of Gain or Loss

Under § 731(b), no gain or loss generally is recognized by a partnership when it distributes property (including money) to a partner. The principal exception is a distribution which is treated as a sale or exchange under § 751(b).

2. Impact on Inside Basis

Under § 734(a) the inside basis of the partnership's assets is not adjusted as a result of a property distribution by the partnership unless it has a § 754 election in effect. A downward adjustment to the basis of the partnership's assets may be required in the case of a liquidating distribution.

3. Adjustments to Capital Accounts

A partner's capital account is reduced by the fair market value of property received in a distribution from the partnership.

C. Mixing Bowl Transactions

1. Introduction

Subchapter K includes two provisions to combat "mixing bowl transactions," a technique used in the partnership setting to shift or defer recognition of precontribution gain on contributed property.

2. Distributions of Contributed Property to Another Partner

Under § 704(b)(1)(B), if property contributed by a partner is distributed to another partner within seven years of the contribution, the contributing partner must recognize gain or loss from the sale or exchange of the property in an amount equal to the § 704(c)(1)(A) gain that would have been allocated to that partner if the partnership had sold the property for its fair market value. To prevent double taxation, appropriate adjustments are made to the contributing partner's outside basis and the partnership's inside basis in the distributed property.

Exceptions are provided for distributions of contributed property back to the contributing partner and certain distributions of like-kind property within prescribed time limits.

3. Distributions of Other Property to the Contributing Partner

Under § 737, a contributing partner must recognize gain if she contributes appreciated property to a partnership and within seven years of the contribution the partnership distributes property other than money to that partner. In general, the amount of gain recognized is the value of the distributed property less the contributing partner's outside basis before the distribution, but in no event may the gain exceed the net precontribution gain on all property contributed to the partnership by that partner. Section 737 does not apply to the extent that § 751(b) applies.

D. Distributions That Shift the Partners' Interests in § 751 Assets: § 751(b)

1. Purpose and Scope of § 751(b)

Section 751(b) applies to both liquidating and nonliquidating distributions that shift the partners' interests in certain assets that, if sold, generate ordinary income. Section 751(b) is designed to prevent shifts of ordinary income and capital gain among partners through property distributions.

2. § 751(b) Assets

Section 751(b) assets are unrealized receivables and substantially appreciated inventory items.

3. Operation of § 751(b)

The operation of § 751(b) involves a complex four-step process that requires determining the tax consequences of various constructive transactions.

4. Criticisms of § 751(b)

Despite its complexity, § 751(b) does not reach all shifts in income among partners because it focuses on shifts in the values of § 751 property rather than the built-in gains and losses in such property at the time of the distribution. Because of its many deficiencies, the American Law Institute and other commentators have called for the repeal of § 751(b).

5. Proposed Regulations

The IRS has issued proposed regulations which would use a hypothetical-sale approach to determine if a distribution alters the partners' interests in § 751(b) property.

XII. LIQUIDATING DISTRIBUTIONS AND TERMINATIONS

A. Liquidation of a Partner's Interest

1. Introduction

Section 736 classifies payments received in a liquidation of a partner's interest in a partnership into two broad categories. The specific tax treatment of the payments is determined under other provisions of Subchapter K.

2. § 736(b) Payments

Under § 736(b), payments for a partner's interest in partnership property generally are treated as property distributions. Excluded from this treatment are payments for a general partnership interest in a partnership where capital is not a material income-producing factor if the payments are attributable to § 751(c) unrealized receivables and unstated goodwill. If a partner's interest in partnership property is determined in an arm's length agreement, that allocation generally is accepted. Section 736(b) payments may trigger § 751(b) because they are treated as partnership distributions. But § 736(b) does not apply to the distributee partner's share of unrealized receivables and unstated goodwill, two types of property which normally would have to be analyzed in applying § 751(b), when those payments are for a general partner's interest in a services partnership.

3. § 736(a) Payments

Section 736(a) payments are for three types of partnership property:

a. Amounts paid in addition to the partner's share of partnership property which are in the nature of a premium or mutual insurance; and

b. § 751(c) unrealized receivables (excluding recapture items) and goodwill (unless the partnership agreement expressly provides for payment of goodwill), but only when the payments are for a general partnership interest in a partnership where capital is not a material income-producing factor.

Section 736(a) payments produce ordinary income to the distributee partner and a reduction in the income of the other partners via either reduced distributive shares or a partnership deduction.

4. Allocation and Timing of § 736 Installment Payments

If liquidating distributions are made over more than one year, payments made in each year must be allocated between the § 736(b) portion and the § 736(a) portion. The regulations permit the distributee partner and partnership to agree on an allocation. If there is no agreement and the payments are fixed in amount and paid over a fixed number of years, the § 736(b) portion each year is equal to the agreed fixed payment for the year multiplied by a ratio of the total fixed payments under § 736(b) divided by the total fixed payments under § 736(a) and (b). If the payments are not fixed in amount they are first treated as § 736(b) payments to the extent of the partner's interest in partnership property and, thereafter, § 736(a) payments.

Section 736(a) payments which are considered a distributive share are included in income in the taxable year in which the partnership's taxable year ends. Section 736(a) payments which are considered a guaranteed payment are included in the year in which the partnership is entitled to a deduction.

5. Liquidation vs. Sale

The key difference between § 736 payments and the sale of a partnership interest is that § 736(a) liquidating distributions generally produce ordinary income to retiring partners and reduce the income reportable by the continuing partners, while a sale of an interest to the partners produces capital gain to the retiring partner and the continuing partners must capitalize the purchase price as part of their outside bases.

B. Liquidation of the Entire Partnership

1. Voluntary Liquidation

Section 736 does not apply to the liquidation of an entire partnership because that section contemplates payments by an ongoing partnership. Instead, the rules in § 731, § 732, § 735 and § 751(b) apply to distributions in complete liquidation of a partnership. The IRS permits the tax consequences of an incorporation of a partnership to be determined based on the form of the transaction. The tax treatment of partnership mergers, consolidations and divisions also vary depending on the form used for the transaction and various other factors.

2. Termination Forced by Statute

Under § 708(b)(1)(B) a partnership is considered to have terminated if within a 12-month period there is a sale or exchange of 50% or more of the total interests in partnership capital and profits. The partnership is then deemed to contribute its assets and liabilities to a new partnership in exchange for a partnership interest and then liquidate by distributing the partnership interest to the purchaser and other partners.

XIII. DEATH OF A PARTNER

A. Introduction

When a partner dies, three things may happen to his partnership interest:

1. the interest may pass to the partner's successor in interest who continues as a partner;

2. the interest may be sold at the partner's death pursuant to a preexisting buy-sell agreement; or

3. the interest may be liquidated pursuant to a preexisting agreement among the partners.

B. The Deceased Partner's Distributive Share in the Year of Death

When a partner dies, the partnership's taxable year closes with respect to the partner and the deceased partner's final return will include his distributive share of partnership income or loss for the short taxable year.

C. Estate Tax, Income in Respect of a Decedent, and Basis Consequences

1. Federal Estate Tax

The fair market value of a deceased partner's partnership interest, including any distributive shares earned prior to death, is includible in the partner's gross estate for federal estate tax purposes.

2. Income in Respect of a Decedent ("IRD")

In general, "income in respect of a decedent" is a right to income which was earned by the decedent but not previously taxed. The amount of § 736(a) payments (payments for a general partnership interest in a services partnership for unrealized receivables and unstated goodwill as well as premium payments made to liquidate any partner) are income in respect of a decedent. Payments attributable to depreciation recapture are not within § 736(a) and are not income in respect of a decedent. The courts also have held that an aggregate approach is used to determine whether items are income in respect of a decedent so a deceased partner's share of a cash method partnership's accounts receivable is income in respect of a decedent.

3. Outside and Inside Basis

The basis of a partnership interest acquired from a decedent is the fair market value of the interest at the date of her death or the alternate valuation date, increased by the successor's share of partnership liabilities and reduced by the value of items considered income in respect of a decedent. Section 743 cannot be applied to give the successor the benefit of an inside basis adjustment in items which are income in respect of a decedent.

XIV. PARTNERSHIP ANTI-ABUSE RULE

A. Introduction

The partnership anti-abuse regulation contains two main provisions. The first allows the IRS to recast a transaction as appropriate to achieve tax results consistent with the intent of Subchapter K. The second rule permits the IRS to treat a partnership as an aggregate of its partners as appropriate to carry out the purposes of the Code or regulations. In addition, the regulations under § 704(c)(1)(B) and § 737 have anti-abuse provisions.

B. Abuse of Subchapter K Rules

The partnership anti-abuse regulation generally requires that partnership transactions must satisfy business purpose, substance over form, and clear reflection of income requirements. The regulation also provides that if a partnership is formed or availed of in connection with a transaction a principal purpose of which is to reduce substantially the present value of the partners' aggregate federal tax liability in a manner inconsistent with Subchapter K, the IRS can recast the transaction to achieve appropriate tax results. The regulation employs an all facts and circumstances test to determine whether a partnership is formed or availed of for an impermissible purpose and illustrates the rule with several examples.

C. Abuse of Partnership Entity

Under the second anti-abuse rule, the Commissioner can treat a partnership as an aggregate of its partners in whole or in part as appropriate to carry out the purpose of any Code or regulation provision.

XV. S CORPORATIONS

A. Introduction

A Subchapter S election allows a "small business corporation" to avoid almost all corporate-level taxes. The shareholders of an S corporation are taxed directly on corporate-level profits, thereby avoiding the corporate double tax.

B. Eligibility for S Corporation Status

The special tax provisions of Subchapter S are available only to "small business corporations" making an election under § 1362(a). "Small business corporations" must meet all of the following requirements:

1. Ineligible Corporations and Subsidiaries

Ineligible corporations, as defined by § 1361(b)(2), do not qualify as small business corporations. The category includes certain types of banks and insurance companies. A corporation is not "ineligible" if it has a subsidiary.

2. 100-Shareholder Limit

A small business corporation may not have more than 100 shareholders. Spouses and their estates are considered one shareholder for purposes of the 100-shareholder limit. Members of a "family" (including spouses) also are treated as one shareholder. A family generally is defined to include up to six generations with a common ancestor plus spouses and former spouses.

3. Restrictions on Types of Shareholders

Small business corporations may not have shareholders who are not individuals except for certain estates and trusts. Nonresident aliens are not eligible shareholders.

4. One-Class-of-Stock Requirement

A small business corporation may not have more than one class of stock. Differences in rights to profits or assets on liquidation create a second class of stock. Differences in voting rights are disregarded when determining whether a corporation has more than one class of stock. Except in abuse cases, buy-sell and redemption agreements, and stock transfer restrictions also are disregarded. Debt that complies with a "straight debt safe harbor" rule will not be considered a second class of stock.

C. Election, Revocation, and Termination of Subchapter S Status

1. Electing S Corporation Status

The shareholders of a small business corporation must make a unanimous election to be an S corporation. Elections made up to the 15th day of the third month of the taxable year are effective for that taxable year and all succeeding years until terminated.

2. Revocation and Termination of S Corporation Status

An S corporation election may be revoked with the consent of more than 50% of the shares of stock of the corporation. An election is terminated if the corporation ceases to meet the definition of a small business corporation. An election also may be terminated if an S corporation has accumulated E & P (e.g., from when it was a C corporation) and more than 25% of its gross receipts was derived from certain types of passive investment income over a three-year period. Revocations and terminations generally will preclude the corporation from reelecting S corporation status for five years. If a corporation inadvertently terminates its S status, the Treasury has the option to disregard the termination and allow the corporation to continue as an S corporation.

D. Tax Treatment of S Corporation Shareholders

1. Introduction

In general, an S corporation is not a taxable entity. Its income, loss, deductions, and credits are passed through to its shareholders.

2. Corporate Level Determination of Tax Results

a. An S corporation calculates its gross income and taxable income to determine the tax results to be passed through to its shareholders and it may select its own accounting method subject to certain limitations. The taxable year of the S corporation can be either a calendar year or a fiscal year for which it establishes a business purpose. Legislative history, revenue rulings, and revenue procedures have established criteria by which the business purpose standard is evaluated.

b. An S corporation computes its taxable income in the same manner as an individual except that certain deductions unique to individuals are not allowed. Items of income, deductions, losses, and credits which could affect the tax liability of the shareholder if treated separately, such as capital and § 1231 gains and losses, investment interest expense, charitable contributions, and foreign taxes, must be separately reported by the S corporation. Tax elections are made by the S corporation and not its shareholders.

3. Tax Consequences to Shareholders

a. Shareholders of an S corporation must account for their pro rata share (on a per share, per day basis) of the corporation's separately stated items and nonseparately computed income or loss in the taxable year in which the S corporation's taxable year ends.

b. A shareholder's share of an S corporation's losses and deductions is limited to the shareholder's adjusted basis in the stock of the corporation and the bona fide indebtedness of the corporation to the shareholder. Losses and deductions disallowed under this rule may be carried forward and used when the shareholders obtains additional stock or debt basis.

c. S corporation shareholders may not include either their share of the corporation's indebtedness or corporate debt they have guaranteed in their stock or debt basis. If a shareholder is required to make a payment on corporate indebtedness as a result of a guarantee or similar arrangement, the shareholder may increase basis by the amount of the payment.

d. Losses which pass through to a shareholder also may be limited by the § 465 at-risk limitations and the § 469 passive loss limitations.

e. The shareholder's share of the S corporation's income and losses which are passed through to the shareholder will increase and decrease, respectively, the shareholder's basis in the S corporation stock.

f. The regulations apply a partial look-through rule to characterize gain or loss on the sale of S corporation stock. In general, gain or loss on the sale of stock held for more than one year is long-term capital gain. If an S corporation owns appreciated collectibles, some of the shareholder's gain may be treated as collectibles gain taxable at a maximum rate of 28%.

E. Distributions to Shareholders

Since S corporation shareholders are taxed directly on their share of the corporation's taxable income, subsequent distributions of this income by the corporation are generally not taxed to the shareholder.

1. S Corporations Without E & P

If an S corporation has no E & P, a distribution is tax free to the extent of the shareholder's basis in the corporation's stock. Any excess of the distribution over the stockholder's adjusted basis is treated as a gain from the sale or exchange of the stock. The shareholder's adjusted basis is reduced by the amount of any distribution that is not included in the shareholder's taxable income.

2. S Corporations with E & P

If an S corporation has E & P, distributions are first treated as recovery of stock basis and then as stock gain to the extent of corporation's accumulated adjustments account ("AAA"). Any remaining distribution is first treated as a dividend to the extent of the corporation's accumulated E & P and then as recovery of stock basis or gain.

3. Distributions of Property

An S corporation recognizes gain on the distribution of appreciated property. The gain passes through and is taxed to the shareholders in the same manner as other income.

The amount of the property distribution to the shareholder is the fair market value of the property. The shareholder takes a fair market value basis in the property received. The shareholder reduces her adjusted basis in the corporation's stock by the fair market value of the distributed property.

4. Ordering of Basis Adjustments

An S corporation shareholder's stock basis is first increased by her pro rata share of income and gain items for the year before making downward adjustments for distributions. Adjustments for distributions are made before any basis reductions for losses.

5. Distributions Following Termination of S Corporation Status

Shareholders receiving distributions during a "post-termination transition period" (at least one year after the last day of the corporation's last taxable year as an S corporation) can be applied against the shareholder's stock basis to the extent of the AAA.

F. Taxation of the S Corporation

S corporations generally are relieved of paying all corporate-level taxes except for the taxes in § 1374 and § 1375.

1. § 1374 Tax on Built-In Gains

Section 1374 applies to S corporations which were once C corporations. Gain in appreciated assets held by the corporation at the time of its S election may be taxed at the highest corporate rate if the S corporation sells the asset at a gain within five years of making an S election. The amount of built-in gain that may be taxed under this provision is limited to the total net gain inherent in all of the corporation's assets at the time of the election.

2. § 1375 Tax on Excessive Passive Investment Income

An S corporation with E & P from Subchapter C operations is subject to tax (at the highest corporate rate) on its "excess net passive income" if more than 25% of its gross receipts consist of "passive investment income."

G. Coordination of Subchapter S with Subchapter C and Other Tax Provisions

1. Subchapter C

S corporations can engage in the wide range of corporate-shareholder transactions available to C corporations. The provisions of Subchapter C generally apply to an S corporation and its shareholders unless such treatment would be inconsistent with Subchapter S.

2. **Other Tax Provisions**

Tax principles applicable to individuals generally apply to S corporations.

3. **Employment Taxes**

Wages paid to owner-employees of S corporations are subject to federal employment taxes, but neither the distributive share of the corporation's net business income nor distributions to owner-employees are considered self-employment income if reasonable compensation is paid for their services. Attempts to avoid employment taxes by paying no salaries to owner-employees who render significant services, however, generally have not been successful because the courts have reclassified S corporation distributions as "wages" subject to employment tax.

4. **Net Investment Income Tax**

S corporations pass through items subject to the net investment income tax ("NIIT") to their shareholders. Gain from the sale of S corporation stock by shareholders not active in the business is generally subject to the NIIT. Net business income passing through to shareholders who are active in the business and gain on the sale of their stock attributable to assets used in the business are generally not subject to the NIIT.

Perspective

■ ANALYSIS

A.   The Subject in General
B.   Preparing for Examinations
C.   Other Sources
D.   Acknowledgments

A. The Subject in General

This outline has been written for students enrolled in Partnership Tax or combined courses on Taxation of Pass-Through Entities (partnerships, limited liability companies, and S corporations) or Business Enterprise Taxation. It also may be useful for some of the topics covered in more advanced business tax courses.

Partnership tax is regarded as among the most challenging subjects in the law school curriculum. This reputation is well deserved. Quite apart from the intricacies of the Internal Revenue Code, the underlying transactions are complex and the concepts are often unfamiliar even to students with some business or accounting background. The goal of this outline is to make the rules more accessible to students by presenting them in a structured and intelligible format that includes definitions, examples, cross references and practice questions. Although the outline is generally organized to follow the life cycle of a partnership from formation to termination (the so-called "cradle to grave" approach), it should be easily adapted to whatever organization your instructor uses. We reiterate what your instructor no doubt has already preached at the first class—a study aid is no substitute for a careful reading of the primary materials assigned in your course. This outline is intended to support but not replace your armed combat with the Code and regulations.

Students quickly will become aware that the partnership tax course devotes very little time to the determination of the entity's taxable income. Those concepts should have been mastered in the basic income tax class. For students who may have suffered some memory loss, we recommend generally reviewing the concepts of gross income, deductions, timing and characterization, focusing particularly on the issues raised by the *Crane* and *Tufts* cases, the basic workings of a nonrecognition provision (such as § 1031), and some fundamental timing rules (such as installment sale reporting under § 453).

The study of partnership tax revolves, to a large degree, around transactions between the entity and its owners. Particularly challenging topics are the treatment of partnership liabilities, the ability of partners to allocate income and deductions in their partnership agreement, the appropriate tax treatment of partners who provide services to the partnership, and numerous anti-abuse provisions primarily designed to prevent assignment of income among the partners and conversion of ordinary income into capital gain. Your study will be enhanced by an understanding of "the big picture"—the basic models for taxing a business enterprise and how those models influence taxpayer behavior. For some additional perspective, we recommend a careful reading of Chapter I of this outline.

B. Preparing for Examinations

As in any law school course, preparing for an examination requires a student to connect with the instructor's wave length. Some tax teachers emphasize statutory construction and problem solving. Their exams are likely to parallel the coverage during the semester but may require you to understand the relationships of concepts covered at different points in the course.

If your instructor uses the problem method, it is likely that the exam will ask you to analyze the tax consequences of hypothetical fact situations. Other instructors may spend more time on cases, tax policy, and less quantifiable issues, and their essay questions may reflect this approach. Many of these instructors, however, still require students to analyze discrete fact patterns on the exam—in both short answer and essay questions—if only because it is easier to grade a more "objective" exam. In short, it is a safe bet that virtually all partnership tax exams will be rather specific and require a mastery of many statutory details along with the broad concepts and tax policy issues.

As with any law school exam, it is essential that you do not write a mini-treatise on the law in general but relate the applicable rules to the facts presented in the question. Even in tax, there may not be a right answer for the essay questions. Where the law is uncertain, it is best to discuss the possibilities and reach a reasoned conclusion (perhaps one that is consistent with what the instructor may have described in class as "the better view.")

C. Other Sources

So much additional reading is available on the taxation of partnerships and S corporations that students will need to protect themselves against "information overload." Among the leading professional treatises in the area are *Federal Taxation of Partnerships and Partners* by McKee, Nelson and Whitmire; *Partnership Taxation* by Willis, Pennell and Postlewaite (both available in student editions with annual supplements); and *Federal Income Taxation of S Corporations* by Eustice and Kuntz. Although these are all superb texts, keep in mind that they are not written principally for law students and they often prove to be overwhelming in their level of sophistication and detail. It may be best to confine your reading to the assigned materials and a study aid (such as this outline) specifically designed for students.

D. Acknowledgments

Co-authors Schwarz and Lathrope are grateful for the hard work and thoughtful advice of the three student research assistants at Hastings College of the Law who worked on the first edition, Ray Kawasaki, Terri Murray and Mitch Salamon, and to Bruce McGovern and Marc Yassinger for their help on later editions. Special thanks are due to our former colleague, Steve Lind, for his many helpful comments and suggestions on the early editions of this Black Letter, and to Bev Lathrope for her continuing support. With this edition, we also welcome Brant Hellwig as a new co-author and thank him for his contributions and fresh perspective.

Chapter I

Introduction

■ ANALYSIS

A. Forms of Business Organizations
    1. Sole Proprietorship
    2. Corporation
    3. Partnership
    4. Limited Liability Company
    5. Demography
B. Conceptual Taxation Models
    1. Aggregate Concept
    2. Entity Concept
    3. Hybrid Concepts
C. Overview of Taxing Regimes Under the Code
    1. Subchapter C
    2. Subchapter K
    3. Subchapter S
    4. Specialized Tax Regimes
D. Influential Policies
    1. The Double Tax
    2. Rate Structure
    3. Preferential Rates on Capital Gains and Qualified Dividends
    4. Nonrecognition of Gain or Loss
E. Pervasive Judicial Doctrines
    1. Substance over Form
    2. Step Transactions
    3. Business Purpose
    4. Sham Transaction
    5. Economic Substance
    6. Codification of the Economic Substance Doctrine

A. Forms of Business Organizations

The permissible forms for business enterprises in the United States are governed principally by the laws of the various states. The most common forms in which a business may be conducted are sole proprietorships, corporations, partnerships and limited liability companies.

1. Sole Proprietorship

A sole proprietorship is owned and operated by a single individual. Sole proprietors take into account the income and expenses of their businesses on their individual tax returns, filing a Schedule C (sole proprietorships generally), Schedule E (rental real estate and royalties), and Schedule F (farms).

2. Corporation

A corporation is a fictitious legal entity that is the most commonly used form for operating a large, publicly held business. The corporate form is also used by closely held businesses where the owners wish to insulate themselves from personal liability for debts of the enterprise.

3. Partnership

A partnership is a business owned by two or more persons as co-owners.

a. General Partnership

In a general partnership, the partners have unlimited liability and generally are bound by the acts of the other partners. General partners ordinarily are personally liable for partnership debts.

b. Limited Partnership

A limited partnership has a general partner (or partners) who manages the business and limited partners who ordinarily have no role in management. The general partner has unlimited liability, but the limited partners are not personally liable for partnership debts except to the extent of their capital contributions and they generally do not participate in the management of the enterprise.

c. Limited Liability Partnership

Many states authorize limited liability partnerships (LLPs). A partner of an LLP is protected, in varying degrees depending on state law, from vicarious liability for acts of the other partners. Some states authorize limited liability limited partnerships, which extend personal immunity from liability to the general partners.

d. Publicly Traded Partnership

A publicly traded partnership ("PTP") has ownership interests that are traded on an established or secondary securities market. PTPs generally are taxed as C corporations, with a major exception for PTPs having 90% or more of their gross income from certain broadly defined types of investment income. See II.C.3, *infra*, at page 44.

e. Joint Venture

"Joint venture" is a term used to describe an arrangement between two or more parties to share the profits and losses of a particular project. Many tax and nontax rules applicable to partnerships also apply to joint ventures, which typically are organized as partnerships or limited liability companies under state law but also may be governed by a contract between the parties.

4. Limited Liability Company

The limited liability company ("LLC") is a form of noncorporate entity that is now permitted under the laws of every state. All of an LLC's owners, known as "members," have limited liability for the entity's debts and claims. LLCs also may have "managers," who are analogous to general partners. The organizing document of an LLC is known as an "operating agreement." All 50 states and the District of Columbia permit single-member LLCs. For income tax purposes, LLCs with more than one member are treated as partnerships and single-member LLCs are treated as disregarded entities unless the LLC elects corporate status. See II.C.2., at page 43, *infra.*

5. Demography

In 2012, there were approximately 23.5 million sole proprietorships, 1.6 million C corporations, 4.2 million S corporations, 1.2 million partnerships, 2.2 million limited liability companies, and 1.8 million farms.

B. Conceptual Taxation Models

The appropriate tax treatment of a business enterprise initially depends on a policy decision as to the nature of the organization. The two principal views are the "aggregate" and "entity" concepts.

1. Aggregate Concept

Under the aggregate concept, a business organization is viewed as an aggregation of its owners, each of whom holds a direct undivided interest in the assets and operations of the enterprise. The organization itself is not treated as a separate taxable entity under this theory. Rather, each of the owners takes into account his or her respective share of income and expenses. Contributions to or distributions from the entity generally are ignored for tax purposes, and sales of an owner's interest are treated as sales of undivided interests in each of the organization's assets.

2. Entity Concept

Under the entity concept, a business organization is viewed as an entity that is separate and distinct from its owners. As such, the entity is subject to tax on its taxable income, and transactions between the owners and the entity are taxable events. This is sometimes referred to as "a double tax regime."

3. Hybrid Concepts

Partnerships and S corporations are taxed under a hybrid model that treats an organization as a separate entity for some purposes (e.g., determination of income, filing of tax returns) and as an aggregate for other purposes (e.g., by passing through income and expenses to the owners and by treating a sale of an interest in the organization as a sale of the owner's proportionate share of each asset).

C. Overview of Taxing Regimes Under the Code

The Internal Revenue Code ("the Code") has adopted three principal taxing models for business organizations. These three "regimes" are found in Subchapters C, S and K.

1. Subchapter C

All corporations other than "S" corporations (see I.C.3., *infra*) are "C" corporations. § 1361(a)(2). Subchapter C (§§ 301–385) adopts an entity concept by treating C corporations as separate taxpaying entities. The taxable income of a C corporation is subject to tax at the graduated rates in § 11. Subchapter C governs the following categories of transactions between corporations and their shareholders:

a. Nonliquidating distributions of cash, property or stock (§§ 301–317).

b. Complete liquidations (§§ 331–346).

c. Corporate organizations (including formations) and reorganizations (e.g., mergers, recapitalizations, insolvencies), and carryover of tax attributes following a corporate acquisition (§§ 351–384).

d. Classification of corporate interests as stock or debt (§ 385).

The taxation of C corporations is covered in Schwarz & Lathrope, Black Letter on Corporate Taxation (West 2016).

2. Subchapter K

Under Subchapter K (§§ 701–777), partnerships and limited liability companies are not treated as separate taxpaying entities. Partnership income and deductions pass through to the individual partners and are taxed at the partner level. A partnership, however, is treated as an accounting entity for purposes of determining its income, and it must file an informational tax return showing how all the partnership's tax items have been allocated among the partners. A partnership and its partners also are taxed under an entity or modified-entity approach in several substantive contexts, such as formation and termination, transactions between partners and partnerships, and sales of partnership interests. The rules in Subchapter K fall into four principal categories:

a. Determination of tax liability resulting from partnership operations (§§ 701–709).

b. Contributions of property to the partnership (§§ 721–724).

c. Partnership distributions (§§ 731–736).

d. Transfers of partnership interests (§§ 741–743).

The remaining provisions of Subchapter K (§§ 751 et seq.) include rules common to all the previous subparts (e.g., § 752, which relates to the treatment of partnership liabilities), and definitions.

The taxation of partnerships is covered in Chapters III–XIV.

3. Subchapter S

Subchapter S (§§ 1361–1379) is a hybrid model that governs the tax treatment of "S corporations" and their shareholders. It was enacted to minimize the influence of taxes on the choice of form for smaller, closely held businesses. Like partnerships, S corporations are treated as pass-through entities that generally are not subject to tax. S corporation status is limited to eligible corporations that make an election. In general, S corporations can have only one class of stock and no more than 100 shareholders, all of whom must be individual U.S. citizens or residents, or certain qualified trusts and tax-exempt organizations.

S corporations are covered in Chapter XV.

4. Specialized Tax Regimes

The Code also includes taxing regimes tailored for particular industries. Examples include Subchapter F (tax-exempt organizations and cooperatives), Subchapter H (banks), Subchapter L (insurance companies), and Subchapter M (mutual funds and real estate investment trusts). Because these specialized regimes are rarely covered in law school corporate and partnership tax courses, they are not discussed in this Black Letter.

D. Influential Policies

Our system of taxing business organizations has been influenced by at least four broad tax policy decisions. The relationship of these policies impacts taxpayer behavior, both as to the choice of form in which to conduct a business and the tax saving opportunities within each form. Tax legislation enacted over the past several decades has radically altered some of these policies and introduced a measure of instability into the system. As a result, many cases and Code sections that traditionally were studied in business enterprise tax courses (and still are included in some casebooks) are obsolete or less significant, but they could become important again with future changes in the law. The following discussion is a greatly simplified overview of the most influential policies and their past and present impact on taxation of business organizations.

1. The Double Tax

Earnings of C corporations are taxed once at the corporate level when earned and again when distributed as dividends to shareholders. In the Tax Reform Act of 1986, Congress significantly strengthened the double tax by providing that a C corporation generally recognizes gain on all distributions of appreciated property to its shareholders. Under a prior rule known as "the *General Utilities* doctrine," such distributions often were nontaxable events. Partnerships and S corporations, as pass-through entities, are generally not subject to an entity-level tax on either operating income or asset appreciation. These developments, along with changes in the rate structure discussed below, increased the costs of operating as a C corporation and provided an incentive for taxpayers to use partnerships, S corporations or limited liability companies to conduct many closely held business and investment activities.

2. Rate Structure

For most of our tax history, the maximum individual tax rates were much higher than the top corporate rate. Despite the double tax, this rate differential motivated taxpayers to operate profitable businesses as C corporations. The typical strategy was to distribute profits to owner-employees in the form of tax-deductible compensation or interest and accumulate what was left in the corporation. Accumulated profits would compound at a lower rate of tax and often were later withdrawn at highly preferential capital gains rates when the business was sold, or tax-free after an owner died. Congress enacted several anti-avoidance provisions, such as the accumulated earnings and personal holding company taxes, to curtail these strategies.

For a brief time between 1987 and 1992, the maximum corporate rate (then 34%) exceeded the highest marginal individual rate. The pendulum shifted back slightly in 1993, when individual rates were increased to 39.6% and then changed again in 2003, when the top individual rate on ordinary income dropped to 35% (the same as the maximum corporate income tax rate). In 2013, the highest marginal individual rate on ordinary income rose back to 39.6% and a new 3.8% tax on net investment income for high-income taxpayers became effective. The interrelationship of corporate and individual rates may influence the choice of legal form for a closely held business or investment entity. See II.D.2. at page 45, *infra*.

3. Preferential Rates on Capital Gains and Qualified Dividends

Historically, the policy decision to tax long-term capital gains at substantially lower rates than ordinary income motivated C corporations and their shareholders to structure transactions designed to "bail out" earnings at preferential capital gains rates instead of paying dividends taxable at the higher ordinary income rates. Many of the Code sections in Subchapter C were enacted to curtail these conversion devices. Similar attempts by partnerships to convert ordinary income into capital gain have contributed to much of the development and complexity of Subchapter K.

After a brief period during which there was little or no capital gains preference, Congress shifted back to the historical policy by providing a significant rate reduction for long-term capital gains of individual taxpayers. In addition, it reduced the rate on most dividends received by noncorporate shareholders. Since 2003 these "qualified dividends" have been taxed at the same preferential rate as long-term capital gains. As long as dividends and long-term capital gains are taxed at the same rate, the C corporation bailout strategies described above are much less significant. But there is still an incentive to use (and abuse) partnerships to convert ordinary income into tax-preferred capital gain.

4. Nonrecognition of Gain or Loss

The nonrecognition concept has always played an important role in the taxation of corporations and partnerships. In general, all realized gains or losses must be recognized unless the Code provides otherwise. § 1001(c). Transactions typically qualify for "nonrecognition" treatment if they are mere changes in form which result in a continuity of investment. To ensure that realized gain or loss is only deferred, a nonrecognition provision is coupled with transferred and exchanged basis rules that preserve the gain or loss for recognition at a later time. Many corporate and partnership transactions, ranging from simple formations to complex liquidation and acquisitions, will qualify for nonrecognition treatment.

E. Pervasive Judicial Doctrines

Partnership tax issues usually can be resolved by a careful application of the statute and regulations to the transaction in question. To protect the integrity of the system, however, the courts have gone beyond the literal statutory language and formulated "common law" doctrines that may affect the tax treatment of a transaction that literally complies with the Code but is incompatible with its purpose. The Service has successfully invoked these judicial doctrines to attack abusive tax shelter transactions using partnerships and corporations. Despite years of litigation, the judicial doctrines are imprecise and often are applied interchangeably. The purpose of this summary is to introduce some of the most familiar terminology.

1. Substance over Form

In one of the earliest articulations of the "substance over form" doctrine, the Supreme Court stated that "[t]he incidence of taxation depends upon the substance of a transaction. . . . To permit the true nature of a transaction to be disguised by mere formalisms, which exist solely to alter tax liabilities, would seriously impair the effective administration of the tax policies of Congress." *Comm'r v. Court Holding Co.,* 324 U.S. 331, 65 S.Ct. 707 (1945). It is difficult to generalize as to when and how the doctrine is applied.

Despite the substance over form doctrine, the parties to a transaction often can dictate a tax result by utilizing a particular form, but the Service has issued regulations to curb certain perceived abuses of the partnership form. See Reg. § 1.701–2, discussed in XIV.B., at page 192, *infra.*

2. Step Transactions

The substance of a transaction is often determined by application of the step transaction doctrine, under which the separate "steps" of formally distinct transactions are combined into a single integrated transaction for tax purposes. The courts disagree on when and how to apply the step transaction doctrine. Three principal formulations have emerged.

a. The Binding Commitment Test

A series of transactions is combined if, when the first step was taken, there was a binding commitment to undertake the later steps. This is the narrowest formulation of the doctrine and usually is the most favorable to taxpayers, who often can demonstrate that the parties were not legally obligated to engage in the later steps.

b. The End Result Test

Separate steps are combined if it is determined that they were prearranged components of a single transaction in which the parties intended from the outset to reach a particular end result. This is the broadest and least precise articulation of the doctrine because it requires a determination of the "intent" of the parties.

c. The Interdependence Test

This is a variation of the end result test which looks to whether the separate steps are so interdependent that the legal relations created by one transaction would have been fruitless without completion of the later steps. The court must determine whether the steps had independent legal significance or were merely part of the larger transaction.

d. Application by Courts and IRS

Courts have resisted applying the step transaction doctrine when the Service does not simply combine steps but invents new ones that never took place in order to reach a particular result adverse to the taxpayer. See, e.g., *Esmark, Inc. v. Comm'r,* 90 T.C. 171 (1988). In addition, the Service has shown a greater willingness in recent years to "turn off" the step transaction doctrine where it otherwise might apply in deference to statutory policies that require the form of a transaction to be respected.

3. Business Purpose

The business purpose doctrine is sometimes applied to deny tax benefits (e.g., nonrecognition of gain on a corporate acquisition) when a transaction lacks a corporate business purpose. The doctrine is most frequently applied in connection with tax-free corporate divisions, and it has been extended through a regulation to patrol certain abusive partnership transactions. See XIV., at page 191 *infra*.

4. Sham Transaction

A "sham" transaction will not be respected for tax purposes. This is often another way of saying that the transaction is devoid of economic substance because no reasonable possibility of profit exists, or was not motivated by a bona fide business purpose other than obtaining tax benefits. See, e.g., *Rice's Toyota World v. Comm'r*, 752 F.2d 89 (4th Cir. 1985). The term "sham" may include a transaction that never in fact occurred and, in that context, it connotes fraudulent conduct.

5. Economic Substance

Under the common law economic substance doctrine, tax benefits are denied for transactions that actually occur but do not result in a meaningful change in a taxpayer's economic position apart from a reduction in federal income taxes. The courts disagree over the precise formulation of this doctrine. Some apply a conjunctive test requiring a taxpayer to establish the presence of both economic substance and a business purpose. Others apply a disjunctive test under which either a business purpose or economic substance is sufficient. A third approach regards economic substance and business purpose as simply "more precise factors to consider." The courts have disagreed about the type of non-tax economic benefit a taxpayer must establish for a transaction to have economic substance. Some deny tax benefits because a transaction lacks profit potential; others focus on the degree of economic risk or require an objective inquiry of whether a "reasonable possibility of profit" exists apart from tax benefits.

6. Codification of the Economic Substance Doctrine

Congress has codified the economic substance doctrine and enacted a strict liability penalty for transactions lacking economic substance. §§ 7701(*o*); 6662(a), (b)(6) & (i).

Chapter II

Classification

■ ANALYSIS

A. Introduction
   1. Impact of Classification
   2. The Role of State Law
   3. Principal Classification Issues
B. Existence of a Separate Entity
   1. In General
   2. Joint Profit Motive
   3. Separate Entity vs. Co-ownership of Property
   4. Separate Entity vs. Expense Sharing, Employment, Loan, and Other Relationships
C. Classification of Business Entities
   1. Introduction
   2. The "Check-the-Box" Classification Regulations
   3. Publicly Traded Partnerships
   4. Trusts
D. Choice of Entity Considerations
   1. Publicly Traded Businesses
   2. Closely Held Businesses
E. Review Questions

A. Introduction

1. Impact of Classification

The classification of a business relationship may have profound tax consequences. Entities classified as "corporations" are subject to the double tax regime of Subchapter C while income realized by a "partnership," a term that for tax purposes includes limited liability companies, is taxed directly to the partners under the pass-through taxing scheme of Subchapter K. If a business arrangement is classified as a "partnership," a partnership tax return must be filed and tax elections generally must be made at the partnership level. §§ 703(b), 6031. The timing and character of the income realized by the owners also may be affected if a business activity is classified as a partnership. §§ 702(b), 706(a).

The operation of many Code sections also varies depending on whether the taxpayer is an individual, a partnership, a corporation or some other type of entity. For example, under § 179 a taxpayer may elect to currently deduct a certain amount of the cost of "§ 179 property" each year. In the case of a partnership, the dollar limit is applied at both the partnership and partner levels. § 179(d)(8). Thus, if two individuals enter into a business relationship which is not classified as a partnership, each taxpayer will be eligible to expense up to the § 179 cost limit, but if the activity is classified as a partnership the benefits of § 179 will be restricted to one limit for the partnership.

The stakes in the classification area have changed in response to provisions in the Internal Revenue Code that, at different times, have offered incentives to classify entities as partnerships or corporations. See II.C.1. at page 42, *infra.* Under current law, however, the taxpayer's classification of the vast majority of business entities is respected.

2. The Role of State Law

The classification of entities for federal tax purposes is a matter of federal law and depends on standards in the Internal Revenue Code. Reg. § 301.7701–1(a)(1). Thus, the classification or label placed on an organization under state law will not control its classification under the Code.

3. Principal Classification Issues

Tax classification issues generally arise in two settings. In the first, the issue is whether an unincorporated business relationship is an entity separate from its owners, or rather is some other form of arrangement, such as co-ownership of property, employer-employee, principal-agent, debtor-creditor, etc. On this end of the spectrum, the question is whether the business relationship among the parties is such that a separate entity is recognized for tax purposes. If a separate entity is recognized, it generally will be classified as a partnership for federal tax purposes.

In the other setting, the question is whether or not an entity should be classified as a corporation for federal tax purposes. On this end of the spectrum, the issue generally narrows to whether a limited partnership, limited liability company or trust will be classified as a corporation under the Code.

B. Existence of a Separate Entity

1. In General

The regulations provide that a joint venture or other contractual arrangement may create a separate entity for federal tax purposes if the participants carry on a trade, business, financial operation, or venture and divide the profits therefrom. Reg. 301.7701–1(a)(2). If a separate entity is created, its classification for federal tax purposes will be determined under the regulations. Generally, the separate entity will be classified as a partnership. See II.C.2.b. at page 43, *infra*. The determination of whether an organization is an entity separate from its owners for federal tax purposes is a matter of federal law and does not depend on whether the organization is recognized as an entity under local law. Reg. § 301.7701–1(a).

The regulations definition of a separate entity for federal tax purposes is derived from § 761(a) and cases that distinguished partnerships from less formal relationships. In *Comm'r v. Culbertson*, 337 U.S. 733, 742, 69 S.Ct. 1210, 1214 (1949), the Supreme Court held that a critical factor in determining whether a partnership exists is whether "the parties in good faith and acting with a business purpose intended to join together in the present conduct of the enterprise." When determining the intent of the parties, the courts typically have listed a number of elements which must be considered. A critical factor is whether the parties have a *joint* profit motive, that is, whether they are acting as co-owners or co-proprietors seeking a joint profit from the enterprise. This aspect of the case law is incorporated and emphasized in the regulations, which require that the participants "carry on a trade, business, financial operation, or venture" for a separate entity to exist.

2. Joint Profit Motive

The existence of a joint profit motive may be difficult to determine in certain circumstances. In *Allison v. Comm'r,* 35 T.C.M. 1069 (1976), Acceptance, a financing corporation, agreed to arrange for a loan to aid in the purchase and subdivision of real property. In exchange for those services, Acceptance received 75 of the subdivided lots, which it sold in a subsequent year. The arrangement between Acceptance and the developer was labeled a "joint venture" and Acceptance took the position that its receipt of the lots was a tax-free partnership distribution. See § 731(a)(1). The Service argued that no partnership existed and that receipt of the lots was ordinary income as compensation for the services provided by Acceptance. In holding that no partnership existed, the court relied largely on the fact that there were no joint sales of lots. Since each party received its share of the subdivided lots and disposed of them separately, there was no joint profit motive. The court also noted that partnership books were not kept and partnership tax returns were not filed.

In *Madison Gas & Electric Co. v. Comm'r,* 72 T.C. 521 (1979), *aff'd,* 633 F.2d 512 (7th Cir.1980), three electric companies agreed to jointly construct a nuclear power facility, own the facility as tenants-in-common, and share the electricity produced at the facility. Each company paid a share of the facility's expenses and resold its share of the electricity produced at the plant. Madison Gas & Electric argued that its expenses in the venture were currently deductible under § 162 as expenses of its existing business. The Service took the position that the expenses were nondeductible start-up costs of a new venture rather than currently deductible expenses of the taxpayer's preexisting business. The court found that the nuclear power facility constituted a partnership and that the joint profit motive requirement was satisfied by the partnership's distribution of its profits (the electricity produced at the plant) in kind. The court reasoned that partners need not realize a cash profit for a partnership to exist. A possible (but questionable) distinction between *Madison Gas & Electric* and *Allison* is the continuing nature of the business arrangement in *Madison Gas & Electric*.

3. Separate Entity vs. Co-ownership of Property

a. In General

The regulations provide that "mere co-ownership" of property which is maintained, kept in repair, and rented or leased does not constitute a separate entity for federal tax purposes. Reg. § 301.7701–1(a)(2).

> ***Example:*** If two individuals jointly purchase a parcel of real property to hold as an investment, no separate entity is formed. But if they purchase the parcel to subdivide and develop the parcel with the intention of selling lots, a separate entity does exist because they are actively carrying on a trade or business and dividing a joint profit.

In the area of property rental, a separate entity exists if co-owners lease space and in addition provide services to the tenants either directly or through an agent. Id. In Rev. Rul. 75–374, 1975–2 C.B. 261, the Service held that providing "customary tenant services" (heat, air conditioning, hot and cold water, unattended parking, normal repairs, trash removal and cleaning of public area) did not transform a co-ownership relationship into a partnership. The ruling states that providing "additional services" to tenants (such as attendant parking, cabanas, gas and electric or other utilities) will render a co-ownership a partnership if furnished by the owners or their agent, but not if the additional services are rendered by an independent contractor.

b. Fractional Interests in Rental Real Property

The IRS has specified the conditions under which it will rule that an undivided fractional interest in rental real property is not an interest in a business entity so that the arrangement is not treated as a partnership for tax purposes. Rev. Proc. 2002–1 C.B. 733. The determination may be significant on a disposition intended to qualify as a § 1031 like-kind exchange because otherwise eligible property held by tenants-in-common qualifies for like-kind exchange treatment while exchanges of partnership interests do not. Rev. Proc. 2002–22 lists numerous conditions that must be satisfied in order to obtain a favorable ruling.

c. Section 761(a) Election

Section 761(a) permits an unincorporated organization to elect to be excluded from Subchapter K if it is availed of (1) for investment purposes only and not for the active conduct of a business, (2) for the joint production, extraction, or use of property, but not for the purpose of selling services or property produced or extracted, or (3) by dealers in securities for the purposes of underwriting, selling, or distributing a particular issue of securities. In all cases, the participants must be able to determine their income adequately without computing partnership taxable income. A § 761(a) election may be used to assure that the organization is not subject to Subchapter K. The election also permits the members to make inconsistent tax elections (e.g., different accounting elections). See § 703(b). Note that a § 761(a) election only excludes the organization from the application of Subchapter K. The organization still may be considered a partnership for purposes of other Code provisions.

d. Section 761(f): Husband-Wife Qualified Joint Venture

Under Section 761(f), a married couple conducting a "qualified joint venture" may elect not to be treated as a partnership for federal tax purposes. If the election is made, all items of income, gain, loss, and deduction from the venture are divided between the spouses in accordance with their respective interests and the respective shares of the spouses are treated as if they were attributable to a trade or business conducted by the spouse as a sole proprietor. A qualified joint venture involves the conduct of a trade or business where both spouses materially participate under § 469(h), based solely on each spouse's activities (i.e., with no attribution under § 469(h)(5)). The Section 761(f) election permits the co-owner spouses to avoid filing a partnership tax return and receive separate credit for their respective shares of self-employment income for social security and Medicare purposes.

4. Separate Entity vs. Expense Sharing, Employment, Loan, and Other Relationships

Because the existence of a separate entity depends on a joint profit motive, the regulations provide that an expense sharing arrangement does not constitute a partnership. Reg. § 301.7701–1(a)(2).

Example: If Doctor A and Doctor B agree to share office and support expenses but each will retain her own clients, a separate entity is not created because there is no joint profit being produced. If the doctors agree to combine practices and divide profits from their joint activity, a separate entity does exist.

In situations where one person supplies services or capital to a business venture, the determination of whether a separate entity exists generally depends on whether the parties are sharing a joint profit as co-owners or co-proprietors. Thus, if a person supplies services or capital for a share of profits, the classification issue will be affected by the authority of that person over business affairs.

The cases in this area turn on their particular facts. For example, in *Wheeler v. Comm'r,* 37 T.C.M. 883 (1978), Wheeler and Perrault entered into an agreement to acquire and develop real estate. Perrault supplied the money needed for the purchase and Wheeler the "know how." Perrault bore all losses from the venture and was to recoup those losses plus 6% interest. Any additional profits were to be divided 75% to Perrault and 25% to Wheeler. The properties were developed and Wheeler reported his gains as capital gains. The Service took the position that the arrangement was an employer-employee relationship and Wheeler realized ordinary income. In concluding that the arrangement between Wheeler and Perrault was a partnership, the court emphasized Wheeler's authority over day-to-day operations of the venture. The business was also operated under joint names, separate books were kept for the partnership and the parties reported their tax results as if it were a partnership. Factors against a finding of a partnership were that title to the real property was kept in Perrault's name, and Wheeler did not have authority to borrow or lend money.

The court concluded, that these restrictions were designed to protect Perrault and noted that Perrault was restricted in his authority to deal with the venture's assets.

C. Classification of Business Entities

1. Introduction

The Code defines a corporation as including "associations, joint-stock companies, and insurance companies". § 7701(a)(3). Thus, certain unincorporated entities— "associations"—potentially are treated as corporations for federal tax purposes, as are corporations routinely organized under state law.

"Associations" historically were defined in terms of their corporate characteristics. In *Morrissey v. Comm'r*, 296 U.S. 344, 56 S.Ct. 289 (1935), the Supreme Court upheld the Service's classification of a business trust as an association taxable as a corporation. The Court identified four characteristics common to corporations: (1) continuity of life, (2) centralization of management, (3) limited liability of investors, and (4) free transferability of interests. These corporate characteristics, along with two more (associates and an objective to carry on a business and divide the profits) were incorporated in regulations which also took into account other relevant factors. Reg. § 301.7701–2(a)(1) (pre-1997).

At one time, the regulations based on the *Morrissey* resemblance test had an anti-association bias. They were adopted when professionals (doctors, lawyers, accountants, etc.) were prohibited by state law from incorporating but wished to achieve corporate status in order to obtain tax benefits from qualified retirement plans and other employee fringe benefits. Although incorporation was no longer necessary to obtain most of these benefits, the regulations continued to reflect a bias against achieving corporate status.

Beginning in the 1960s, investors in tax shelters sought partnership rather than corporate status. Limited partnerships became the preferred vehicle for tax shelters because they permitted losses to pass through to investors and provided protection for the limited partners against personal liability for debts of the enterprise. The Service argued that limited partnerships should be classified as associations despite its regulations, which then had a bias in favor of partnership status. These efforts to recharacterize limited partnerships as associations were unsuccessful. See *Larson v. Comm'r*, 66 T.C. 159 (1976). The restrictions on deducting losses from tax shelter investments that were enacted in the Tax Reform Act of 1986 reduced but did not eliminate the importance of the association versus limited partnership classification issue.

After 1986, many corporate classification battles were motivated by attempts to avoid the double tax imposed on profits of C corporations. The Treasury eventually concluded that state law developments, such as the popularity of limited liability companies, had largely blurred the classic distinctions between corporations and unincorporated entities. In response, new regulations were proposed to make classification for tax purposes essentially elective for unincorporated entities. Those "check-the-box" regulations were finalized and became effective in 1997. Under the regulations, new unincorporated entities generally are automatically classified as partnerships unless they elect to be taxed as C corporations. These regulations have been upheld as a valid exercise of the IRS's authority. *Littriello v. United States*, 484 F.3d 372 (6th Cir. 2007), *cert. denied*, 128 S.Ct.1290 (2008).

2. The "Check-the-Box" Classification Regulations

a. Introduction

Under the current regulations, if a separate entity is not a trust, it is a "business entity." Reg. § 301.7701–2(a). See II.C.4 at page 44, *infra*, regarding classification of trusts. Certain business entities are automatically classified as corporations for federal tax purposes. These include a business entity organized under a federal or state statute if the statute describes or refers to the entity as "incorporated or as a corporation, body corporate, or body politic." Reg. § 301.7701–2(b)(1). Thus, corporations routinely organized under state corporation statutes are automatically considered corporations for federal tax purposes. A business entity that is taxable as a corporation under some other provision of the Code, such as a publicly traded partnership, also is classified as a corporation for federal tax purposes. Reg. § 301.7701–2(b)(7).

b. Entities with Two or More Members

A business entity with two or more members that is not automatically classified as a corporation is classified as a partnership for federal tax purposes, unless an election is made for the entity to be classified as a corporation. Reg. §§ 301.7701–2(c)(1), –3(a), –3(b)(1)(i). Consequently, an unincorporated entity, such as a limited liability company or limited partnership, with two or more members will automatically be classified as a partnership unless such an election is made.

c. Business Entities with One Owner

A business entity with only one owner that is not automatically classified as a corporation is disregarded for federal tax purposes, unless an election is made for the entity to be classified as a corporation. Thus, if such an election is not made for the entity, it will be treated like a sole proprietorship, branch, or division of the owner. Reg. §§ 301.7701–2(a), –2(c)(2), –3(a), –3(b)(1)(ii).

d. Series LLCs

In some states, an LLC may create one or more "series" within itself ("series LLC"). Each series can be set up to be like a separate LLC, with its own managers, members, assets, business purpose, debts, etc. Debts of a particular series are enforceable only against that series and a series is not liable for the debts of the LLC generally. One advantage of a series LLC is that it is one entity for state law purposes and costs may be reduced because each series does not have to separately comply with state law. For classification purposes, proposed regulations provide that a series generally is considered to be an entity formed under local law. Prop. Reg. § 301.7701–1(a)(5)(i). That makes it so the general classification regulations, including the check-the-box rules, apply to determine whether each series is an entity separate from its owners and its ultimate classification for federal tax purposes.

Example: Properties LLC is a series LLC, with two series each of which owns rental real estate. Series 1 has two owners, and Series 2 has one owner. Under the default check-the-box rules, Series 1 is taxed as a partnership and Series 2 is a disregarded entity, but either series could elect to be taxed as a corporation.

e. Entity Owned as Community Property

An entity that is solely owned by a husband and wife as community property may be treated by the owners as either a disregarded entity or a partnership unless it elects to be taxed as a corporation. Rev. Rul. 2002–69, 2002–2 C.B. 831.

f. Foreign Entities

The regulations list certain entities formed under foreign laws that will be automatically classified as a corporation (e.g., an Aktiengesellschaft formed in Germany). Reg. § 301.7701–2(b)(8). Unless a contrary election is made, a foreign entity that is not a corporation is classified as (1) a partnership if it has two or more members and at least one member does not have limited liability, (2) a corporation if all members have limited liability, or (3) disregarded as an entity if it has a single owner that does not have limited liability. Reg. § 301.7701–3(b)(2)(i).

g. Election

An entity which wishes to change its classification under the regulations must file an election. The election may be effective up to 75 days before or twelve months after it is filed. Reg. § 301.7701–3(c)(1)(iii). An election must be signed by (1) each member of the entity, including prior members affected by a retroactive election, or (2) an officer, manager, or member authorized to make the election. Reg. § 301.7701–3(c)(2). If an entity makes a classification election, it may not make another election to change its classification for 60 months unless the Service permits the change and 50% of the entity's ownership interests are owned by persons who did not own any interests when the first election was made. Reg. § 301.7701–3(c)(1)(iv).

h. Existing Entities

In the absence of an election, an entity in existence before 1997 generally retains the same classification that it had under the prior association regulations. An exception is made for an entity with a single owner that claimed to be a partnership. Such an entity will be disregarded as an entity separate from its owner. Reg. § 301.7701–3(b)(3)(i).

3. Publicly Traded Partnerships

"Publicly traded partnerships" are generally classified as corporations. § 7704(a). A "publicly traded partnership" is a partnership whose interests are traded on an established securities market or are readily tradable on a secondary market (or the substantial equivalent thereof). § 7704(b). Section 7704(c) provides an exception for publicly traded partnerships in which 90% or more of the gross income consists of various types of passive investment income.

4. Trusts

The regulations distinguish between "ordinary trusts"—arrangements created by will or inter vivos declaration under which trustees take title to property in order to protect and conserve it for beneficiaries—and "business trusts." Business trusts are formed to carry on a profit-making business rather than for the protection and conservation of property. Reg. § 301.7701–4(a), (b). The fact that a business is cast in trust form will not prevent it from being classified as a business entity. Reg.

§ 301.7701–4(b). The critical question in determining whether a trust will be classified as a business entity is whether a business objective is present or the trust was established merely to protect and conserve trust property. If a trust is a business entity, it will be classified as a partnership if it has two or more owners or members, unless an election is made for it to be classified as a corporation.

D. Choice of Entity Considerations

1. Publicly Traded Businesses

Publicly traded businesses, whether or not they are incorporated, almost always are taxed as C corporations, except for publicly traded partnerships that qualify for the passive investment income exception (see II.C.3. at page 44, *supra*) or in other very specialized situations (e.g., certain real estate investment trusts).

2. Closely Held Businesses

a. In General

A closely held business must choose whether to be taxed as a C corporation or a pass-through entity, such as an S corporation, partnership, or limited liability company. When, as under current law, the highest marginal individual income tax rate is the same as or only slightly higher than the top corporate rate, there is a greater incentive to operate as a pass-through entity to avoid two levels of taxation. Choice of entity decisions also are heavily influenced by the type of business, the composition of and relationships among the investors, and the exit strategy (e.g., whether an initial public offering or sale is contemplated).

b. C Corporations

C corporations are often used by: (1) businesses able to take advantage of the lower corporate income tax rates by limiting their taxable income to $75,000 or less (e.g., by paying out most of the earnings as tax-deductible salary, interest or rent); and (2) companies intending to reinvest their earnings for the reasonable needs of the business rather than paying dividends. In these situations, a C corporation may be attractive because of: (1) the ability to minimize any corporate-level tax or defer the shareholder-level tax for a considerable time; or (2) avoid it completely upon the major shareholders' deaths. Start-up businesses seeking venture capital financing often are formed as C corporations because they are able to have different types of ownership interests (e.g., convertible preferred stock) and issue small business stock that qualifies for tax benefits on sale. C corporations also can be acquired in a tax-free reorganization or be better positioned than partnerships or LLCs to sell equity in an initial public offering.

c. S Corporations

An S corporation's income is only subject to one level of tax and S corporations have a simpler and more familiar governance structure than LLCs or partnerships. They can have traditional stock option plans; participate in tax-free corporate reorganizations; and more easily convert to C corporation status in anticipation of an initial public offering. S corporation shareholders who are active in the business also may enjoy employment tax advantages as compared to partners and LLC members. S corporations are less flexible, however, because of strict eligibility restrictions (e.g., no more than 100 shareholders; only one class of stock; inability to make special allocations; no shareholder basis credit for entity debt).

d. Limited Liability Companies

Limited liability companies also avoid entity-level tax and, unlike partnerships, provide limited liability to all their owners. LLCs have the flexibility to: (1) issue different classes of ownership interests (unlike S corporations); (2) pass through losses to owners who are active in the business; and (3) enjoy other tax benefits of the Subchapter K tax regime (e.g., special allocations, tax-free distributions of appreciated property, and inclusion of entity-level debt in the basis of LLC members' ownership interests).

e. Limited Partnerships

Limited partnerships enjoy most of the same tax benefits as LLCs but general partners do not have limited liability under state law (although a general partner organized as a corporation or LLC can limit its liability exposure). Some advisors continue to recommend limited partnerships because partnership agreements and governing law are more familiar to them and their clients, as compared to LLCs.

f. Converting from Corporation to Pass-Through Entity

For business ventures already operating as a C corporation, an S corporation election may be a good alternative for moving to a single-tax regime without immediate recognition of gain at either the corporate or shareholder level. Subchapter S, however, has rules that prevent the easy avoidance of the double tax on built-in gains attributable to the period when the business operated as a C corporation. See XV.F.1. at page 218, *infra*. Converting a C corporation to a partnership or LLC requires a complete liquidation, which is a taxable transaction to the corporation and its shareholders.

g. State Tax Considerations

The choice among a limited partnership, LLC or S corporation may be influenced by state and local tax considerations, including whether the entity's resident state provides pass-through tax treatment. Other considerations are whether the state imposes an entity-level tax; the tax treatment of nonresident owners; and overall complexity, such as the need for investors to file nonresident returns in many different states.

E. Review Questions

1. X and Y agree to build an irrigation system to drain surface water from their properties. Are X and Y partners?

2. If A and B form a limited liability company or limited partnership to conduct their business venture, how will the entity be classified for federal tax purposes? What if A alone forms a limited liability company to operate a business?

Chapter III

Formation of a Partnership

■ ANALYSIS

A. Introduction
B. Contributions of Property
   1. General Rules
   2. Related Issues
   3. Basis and Holding Period
C. Treatment of Liabilities
   1. Impact on Partner's Outside Basis
   2. Contributions of Property Encumbered by Recourse Liabilities
D. Organization and Syndication Expenses
   1. General Rule
   2. Deduction and Amortization of Organization Expenses
   3. Syndication Expenses
E. Review Questions

A. Introduction

If a taxpayer contributes property to a newly formed partnership in exchange for an interest in the partnership, the exchange arguably should be taxable to both the new partner and the partnership. The new partner might be required to recognize gain or loss equal to the difference between the fair market value of the partnership interest and the adjusted basis of the contributed property. Likewise, the partnership might have to recognize gain or loss on its receipt of the contributed property. § 1001(a), (c). Section 721 eliminates these theoretical concerns by providing that gain or loss is not recognized by either a partnership or its partners on a contribution of property to the partnership in exchange for a partnership interest. The policy is that the contribution of property to a partnership is a mere change in the form of the taxpayer's investment and not an appropriate taxable event. Consistent with its nonrecognition policy, § 721 is accompanied by Code sections which preserve the unrecognized gain or loss in the new partner's basis in the partnership interest (§ 722) and the partnership's basis in the contributed property (§ 723).

B. Contributions of Property

1. General Rules

The nonrecognition rule in § 721 applies to contributions of property to both newly formed and existing partnerships. Reg. § 1.721–1(a). The principal requirement is that the partner must receive the partnership interest in exchange for "property." "Property" is not defined in the Code, but the courts have been guided by the interpretation of the term under § 351, the counterpart of § 721 in the corporate area. "Property" includes cash, inventory, accounts receivable, patents, installment obligations, and other intangibles such as goodwill and industrial know how. "Property" does not include the performance of services for the partnership, and a partner who receives a partnership interest in exchange for services normally recognizes ordinary income under §§ 61 and 83. Reg. § 1.721–1(b)(1). See VIII.B., at page 121, *infra* for the tax treatment of a partner receiving a partnership interest in exchange for services.

Section 721 does not apply to transactions between a partnership and a partner not acting in the capacity of a partner. Reg. § 1.721–1(a). For example, if a partner sells or leases property to the partnership, the transaction is not governed by § 721. See IX.D., at page 132, *infra*.

2. Related Issues

a. Recapture Provisions

Section 721 overrides the depreciation recapture provisions. See §§ 1245(b)(3); 1250(d)(3). The potential recapture income is preserved in the partnership's basis in the asset.

b. Installment Obligations

A partner does not recognize § 453B gain when an installment obligation is contributed to a partnership in exchange for a partnership interest. Reg. §§ 1.453–9(c)(2) and 1.721–1(a); see also Prop. Reg. 1.453B–1(c).

c. Investment Partnerships

Under § 721(b), transfers of property to a partnership which would be an investment company if incorporated do not qualify for nonrecognition. This rule prevents taxpayers from diversifying their investment portfolios tax free. See § 351(e)(1) and Reg. § 1.351–1(c).

d. Noncompensatory Options

1) In General

Partners may contribute capital directly to a partnership for a partnership interest. Alternatively, a partnership may acquire its necessary capital in more complex financing arrangements, including options or contingent rights to acquire a partnership interest. The regulations set forth the tax consequences of "noncompensatory" options to acquire a partnership interest.

2) Noncompensatory Option Defined

A noncompensatory option is an option that is not issued in connection with performance of services for the partnership. Reg. § 1.721–2(f). A noncompensatory option includes a call option, or warrant to acquire a partnership interest, the conversion feature in a partnership debt instrument, and the conversion feature in a preferred equity interest in a partnership. Reg. § 1.721–2(g)(1).

3) Applicability of Section 721 to Noncompensatory Options

Section 721 does not apply to the transfer of property to a partnership in exchange for a noncompensatory option but it does apply when the option is exercised. Reg. § 1.721–2(a), (b). Thus, if a taxpayer transfers appreciated property to a partnership in exchange for a noncompensatory option to acquire a partnership interest, the taxpayer recognizes gain on the transaction. However, a later exchange by the taxpayer of appreciated property to exercise the option is protected by § 721 and is not taxable. See Prop. Reg. § 1.721–2(h) Example. Section 721 does not apply to the lapse of a noncompensatory option. Reg. § 1.721–2(c).

e. Debt-for-Equity Exchanges

If a creditor of a partnership contributes the partnership's indebtedness in exchange for a capital or profits interest in the partnership, § 721 generally applies to the exchange. Reg. § 1.721–1(d)(1). However, § 721 generally does not apply if the discharged debt is for unpaid rent, royalties, or interest on indebtedness. Reg. § 1.721–1(d)(2). In determining whether there is discharge of indebtedness income, the partnership is treated as satisfying the debt with an amount of money equal to the fair market value of the partnership interest. Reg. § 1.108–8(a). "Fair market value" for this purpose generally is deemed to be the liquidation value of the partnership interest. Reg. § 1.108–8(b).

3. Basis and Holding Period

a. "Outside" and "Inside" Bases

A partner's basis in her partnership interest is referred to as the "outside" basis. A partnership's basis in its assets is referred to as the "inside" basis. These terms will be used to distinguish between the partner's and the partnership's bases.

On a contribution of property in exchange for a partnership interest, a partner's outside basis under § 722 is equal to the sum of the money and the adjusted bases of property contributed to the partnership. Under § 723, the partnership's inside basis is equal to the basis the contributing partner had in the property. Both the contributing partner and the partnership obtain a basis increase if gain is recognized under the investment partnership rule in § 721(b). These basis provisions are designed to preserve the gain or loss that went unrecognized under § 721 on the contribution of the property.

In certain situations, § 724 preserves the character of the gain or loss that the property would have had in the hands of the contributing partner. Section 704(c) also requires the precontribution gain or loss in a partnership asset to be allocated to the contributing partner when the partnership disposes of the asset. See VI.A., at page 90, *infra.*

b. Holding Period

A partner's holding period for her partnership interest includes the period that the partner held any contributed property that was a capital or § 1231 asset. § 1223(1). The holding period for a partnership interest received for other property (cash or ordinary income assets) begins on the date of the exchange. If a partnership interest is received for a mixture of capital, § 1231 and ordinary income assets, it takes a split holding period based on the fair market values of the contributed assets until it is sufficiently "aged" so that it has been held long-term. See Reg. § 1.1223–3(b)(1). For this purpose, recapture gain (e.g., under § 1245) is treated as a separate asset which is not a capital or Section 1231 asset. Reg. § 1.1223–3(e). A partner's holding period in contributed property carries over to the partnership. § 1223(2).

Example: Partner A contributes the following assets to the newly formed ABC partnership in exchange for a one-third interest in the partnership:

Asset	A.B.	F.M.V.
Accounts Receivable for Services Performed in A's Business	$ 0	$ 10,000
Capital Asset	$70,000	$ 60,000
Equipment (all § 1245 gain)	$10,000	$ 30,000
Total	$80,000	$100,000

Under § 721, neither A nor ABC recognizes gain or loss since A transfers property in exchange for the partnership interest. Accounts receivable for services have been held to be property under § 351. *Hempt Brothers, Inc. v. United States*, 490 F.2d 1172 (3d Cir.1974), *cert. denied*, 419 U.S. 826, 95 S.Ct. 44 (1974). The gain on the equipment normally would be recaptured as ordinary income under § 1245(a). Section 1245(b)(3), however, creates an exception to the general recapture rule for certain otherwise tax-free transactions, including § 721 exchanges, when the proper takes a transferred basis. The recapture potential remains in t equipment and will be recognized if the equipment is sold by t... partnership. See § 1245(a)(2).

A's outside basis under § 722 will be $80,000. This is the sum of the bases of the accounts receivable, capital asset and equipment. A will be allowed a tacked holding period on 70% of the partnership interest that is attributable to the fair market value of the capital asset and the basis of the equipment. This only matters until A actually has a long-term holding period for the partnership interest. ABC will take a transferred basis in each of the assets contributed by A and may tack holding periods for all of the properties received. §§ 723; 1223(2).

C. Treatment of Liabilities

1. Impact on Partner's Outside Basis

a. Introduction

Because a partnership is treated as an aggregate of its individual partners for purposes of taxing its income, Subchapter K adopts aggregate principles to determine the impact of partnership liabilities on the partners and their outside bases. Under the *Crane* case, a taxpayer who acquires property subject to a debt includes the amount of the debt in the basis of the property on the assumption that the debt will be repaid. A taxpayer who sells property subject to a debt must include the debt relief in the amount realized on the theory that relief of debt is the same as receipt of an equivalent amount of cash.

For partners, these basic principles are incorporated in § 752, which applies to a wide array of transactions, including contributions of property. Under § 752, an obligation is a "liability" if, when, and to the extent that incurring the obligation (1) increases the basis of an obligor's assets (including cash), (2) gives rise to an immediate deduction, or (3) gives rise to an expense that is not deductible in computing taxable income and is not chargeable to capital. § 1.752–1(a)(4). Obligations that would be deductible when paid (e.g., accounts payable of a cash basis partnership) are not "liabilities" under that definition. See Rev. Rul. 88–77, 1988–2 C.B. 128. Under § 752(a), an increase in a partner's share of partnership liabilities is considered a contribution of money which increases the partner's outside basis under § 722. A decrease in a partner's share of partnership liabilities is considered under § 752(b) to be a distribution of money to the partner which decreases the partner's outside basis (but not below zero) under §§ 705(a) and 733. If a decrease in a partner's share of partnership liabilities exceeds the partner's outside basis, the partner must recognize the excess as capital gain from the sale or exchange of the partnership interest. §§ 731(a)(1); 741.

b. Classification of Liabilities and Partners' Shares of Partnership Liabilities

The § 752 regulations use the concept of "economic risk of loss" both to classify partnership liabilities as recourse or nonrecourse and to determine the partners' shares of recourse liabilities. A partnership liability is classified as "recourse" only to the extent that a partner bears the economic risk of loss for the liability. Reg. § 1.752–1(a)(1). A partner's share of the recourse liabilities of a partnership equals the portion of the recourse liabilities for which the partner bears the economic risk of loss. Reg. § 1.752–2(a). A liability is "nonrecourse" to the extent that no partner bears the economic risk of loss for the liability. Reg. § 1.752–1(a)(2). The partners generally share nonrecourse liabilities in proportion to their share of partnership profits. Reg. § 1.752–3(a).

Example: A, B and C each contribute $20,000 cash to form the ABC partnership and agree to share all partnership profits and losses equally. ABC purchases a parcel of investment real estate for $150,000, paying $60,000 cash and giving the seller a $90,000 purchase money note secured by the real estate. No partner is personally liable for the note. The purchase money obligation is a nonrecourse liability which will be shared equally by the partners because they have equal interests in partnership profits. A, B and C each will be treated as if they contributed $30,000 to ABC under § 752(a) to reflect the increase in their share of partnership liabilities (from zero to $30,000). As a result, each partner's outside basis will be $50,000 under § 722.

A more detailed study of the tax treatment of nonrecourse liabilities requires an examination of the Code provisions for determining the partners' shares of partnership income and profits in more complex situations. The tax treatment of liabilities, both recourse and nonrecourse, will be revisited after those topics are covered. See VII., at page 105, *infra*. The remainder of this chapter introduces the concept of economic risk of loss and the tax treatment of contributions of property encumbered by a liability.

c. Economic Risk of Loss

A partner bears the economic risk of loss for a partnership liability to the extent that the partner would bear the economic burden of discharging the obligation represented by the liability if the partnership were unable to do so. The regulations employ a "doomsday" liquidation analysis to determine whether a partner bears the economic risk of loss for a liability. Basically, the regulations assume that all of the partnership assets are worthless, all of the partnership liabilities are due and payable and the partnership disposes of all its assets in a fully taxable transaction for no consideration. They then ask whether any partner or partners would be obligated to make a payment to a creditor or contribution to the partnership in order to pay the liability. § 1.752–2(b)(1). If a partner or partners are so obligated, the liability is a recourse liability and is shared by the partners who bear the economic risk of loss. For this purpose, guarantees, indemnifications, and other reimbursement arrangements are taken into account. Reg. § 1.752–2(b)(3)(i)–(iii), –2(b)(5). A payment obligation is disregarded if it is: (1) subject to contingencies unlikely to occur, or (2) arises at a future time after an event that is not determinable with reasonable accuracy. Reg. § 1.752–2(b)(4). It generally is assumed that a partner will actually discharge an obligation even if the partner's net worth is less than the amount of the obligation. Reg. § 1.752–2(b)(6).

Example: Equal partners in a general partnership ordinarily will share the economic risk of loss for any partnership recourse liability equally because they share the economic burden of that debt equally. Similarly, limited partners ordinarily do not bear the economic risk of loss for any partnership liability because they generally have no obligation to contribute additional capital to the partnership.

2. Contributions of Property Encumbered by Recourse Liabilities

If property is contributed by a partner to a partnership and the property is subject to a liability, the partnership is considered to have assumed the liability to the extent it does not exceed the fair market value of the property at the time of the contribution. § 752(c); Reg. § 1.752–1(e). For a recourse liability, the partners' shares of the liability will be determined under economic risk of loss analysis. Reg. § 1.752–2(a).

Example (1): A contributes property with a $10,000 adjusted basis to a general partnership for a 25% interest in the partnership. The property is subject to a $2,000 recourse liability and has a fair market value greater than $2,000. The partnership is considered to have assumed the liability and A's individual liabilities are considered to have decreased by $2,000. Under economic risk of loss analysis, A remains personally liable to the creditor for the debt and none of the other partners bears the economic risk of loss for the liability. This assumes that neither state law nor an agreement among the partners makes any partner other than A bear the risk of loss for the liability. Therefore, A's share of partnership liabilities increases by $2,000. Under Reg. § 1.752–1(f), if both an increase and a decrease in a partner's share of partnership liabilities (or individual liabilities) occurs in a single transaction, only the net increase or decrease is taken into account. Since there is no net change in the sum of A's individual liabilities and his share of the partnership liabilities, A's outside basis will be $10,000 (A's basis for the contributed property). See Reg. § 1.752–1(g) Example 1.

Example (2): Assume the same facts as Example (1), above, except that the other partners agree to indemnify A for up to $1,500 of the liability. In that case, A bears the risk of loss for $500 of the $2,000 liability and A's share of partnership liabilities increases by $500. Since the net change in A's individual and partnership liabilities is a decrease of $1,500 ($2,000 decrease in personal liabilities and $500 increase in partnership liabilities), A's outside basis will be $8,500 ($10,000 basis in contributed property less $1,500).

Example (3): Assume the same facts as Example (2), above, except that A's basis in the contributed property is $1,200. Since the net change in A's individual and partnership liabilities is a decrease of $1,500, A's outside basis will be reduced to zero and A will recognize $300 of capital gain.

D. Organization and Syndication Expenses

1. General Rule

Neither a partnership nor any partner may currently deduct amounts paid or incurred to organize a partnership or to promote the sale (or to sell) partnership interests. § 709(a).

2. Deduction and Amortization of Organization Expenses

Under § 709(b), a partnership may elect to deduct up to $5,000 of organizational expenses for the taxable year in which it begins business. The $5,000 amount is reduced by the amount of such expenses that exceed $50,000. § 709(b)(1)(A). Organizational expenses that are not deducted may be ratably amortized over the 180-month period beginning with the month in which the partnership begins business. § 709(b)(1)(B). If the partnership liquidates before the end of the amortization period, any deferred expenses may qualify for a loss deduction under § 165. § 709(b)(2). To qualify for deduction or amortization, an organizational expense must be: (1) incident to the creation of the partnership; (2) chargeable to capital account; and (3) of a character which would be amortizable over the life of a partnership having an ascertainable life. § 709(b)(3). Examples of qualifying expenses are: legal fees for negotiation and preparation of the partnership agreement, accounting services incident to organizing the partnership, and filing fees. Reg. § 1.709–2(a). Expenses incurred in connection with the acquisition of partnership assets are not organizational expenses and must be capitalized and added to the basis of the asset.

3. Syndication Expenses

"Syndication expenses"—i.e., expenses connected with issuing and marketing partnership interests—may not be deducted or amortized under § 709 or deducted once the syndication effort is abandoned. Rev. Rul. 89–11, 1989–1 C.B. 179. Syndication expenses include brokerage fees, registration fees, legal fees for securities advice and tax disclosure, accounting fees for representations in offering materials, printing costs, and other selling and promotional material. Reg. § 1.709–2(b). The Service has ruled that fees paid for the tax opinion in a partnership prospectus is a syndication expense. Rev. Rul. 88–4, 1988–1 C.B. 264. Capitalized syndication expenses may be deductible as a capital loss on the liquidation of the partnership. Cf. Rev. Rul. 87–111, 1987–2 C.B. 160.

E. Review Questions

1. A contributes the following property in exchange for a 50% interest in the AB partnership:

	A.B.	F.M.V.
Cash	$ 5,000	$ 5,000
Installment Obligations	15,000	20,000
Equipment (§ 1245 gain)	20,000	40,000
Land	30,000	10,000
	$70,000	$75,000

(a) What amount of gain or loss is recognized by A and AB when A transfers his property in exchange for the partnership interest?

(b) What is A's outside basis in his partnership interest?

(c) What is AB's inside basis in the contributed property?

2. G, the general partner, and L, the limited partner, each contribute $20,000 and form the GL limited partnership. G and L agree to allocate partnership profits and losses 80% to G and 20% to L. GL purchases land for $40,000 cash and a $60,000 recourse purchase money note.

(a) Who bears the economic risk of loss for the liability?

(b) What is G's outside basis?

(c) What is L's outside basis?

3. Which of the following expenses qualify as organizational expenses under § 709:

(a) Legal fees for the negotiation of the partnership agreement?

(b) Registration fees connected with issuing partnership interests?

(c) Accounting fees for representations in offering materials?

(d) Filing fees?

(e) Accounting fees for services incident to organizing the partnership?

(f) Printing costs of offering materials?

(g) Fees for tax opinion in the partnership prospectus?

Chapter IV

Partnership Operations: General Rules

■ ANALYSIS

A. Aggregate and Entity Theories of Partnership Taxation
B. Taxing Partnership Operations
    1. Partnership Level Determination of Tax Results
    2. Tax Consequences to the Partners
    3. Limitations on Partnership Losses
C. Review Questions

A. Aggregate and Entity Theories of Partnership Taxation

A recurring issue throughout Subchapter K is whether a partnership is treated for tax purposes as an aggregate of its individual partners or an entity separate and apart from its partners. The Code does not exclusively use either approach. Partnerships are treated as entities for some tax purposes and aggregates for others. For example, partnership income is taxed directly to its partners under an aggregate theory. § 701. At other times, the Code blends the two theories and adopts a modified aggregate or entity approach to determine the tax results to the partners. As you study partnership operations, it is important to focus upon the particular approach that the Code employs.

B. Taxing Partnership Operations

1. Partnership Level Determination of Tax Results

Even though a partnership is not a taxable entity, it must calculate its gross income and taxable income to determine the tax results to its partners. §§ 702(c); 703(a). A partnership also must file its own informational tax return by the 15th day of the third month following the end of its taxable year and is subject to audit and examination by the Internal Revenue Service. §§ 6031; 6072(b); 6221–35.

a. Partnership Accounting Method

A partnership generally is free to elect its own accounting method, which may be different from that of its partners. § 703(b). Under § 448, however, a partnership which has a C corporation (other than "a qualified personal service corporation") as a partner or which is a "tax shelter" may not use the cash method of accounting. § 448(a), (b)(2). Partnerships in the farming business or with average annual gross receipts of less than $5 million for the prior three years are not subject to the C corporation-as-shareholder limitation. § 448(b)(1), (b)(3), (c).

b. Partnership Taxable Year

1) Mechanical Rules

A partnership has its own taxable year. § 706(b)(1)(A). In computing taxable income, a partner includes in income his distributive share of partnership items in the taxable year in which the partnership taxable year ends. § 706(a). Under § 706, a partnership generally determines its taxable year according to mechanical rules. First, a partnership is required to use the taxable year of its partners having more than a 50% interest in partnership profits and capital. § 706(b)(1)(B)(i), (4)(A). If partners owning more than a 50% interest do not have the same taxable year, the partnership must use the taxable year of all the principal partners (i.e., partners with a 5% or more interest in profits or capital) of the partnership. § 706(b)(1)(B)(ii), (3). If neither of these rules applies, the regulations require the partnership to use the taxable year that results in the least aggregate deferral of income to the partners. § 706(b)(1)(B)(iii); Reg. § 1.706–1(b)(2)(C).

Example (1):   In the ABC equal partnership, A and B are calendar year taxpayers and C uses a November 30 fiscal year. ABC must use a calendar year because partners owning more than 50% of its profits and capital (A and B) use a calendar year.

Example (2): The Acme Limited Partnership is owned by G, the general partner, who owns 10% of the partnership and uses a June 30 fiscal year, and 90 limited partners, each of whom owns 1% of the partnership. Forty of the limited partners use a calendar year, 40 use a November 30 fiscal year, and 10 use an October 31 fiscal year. Acme must use a June 30 fiscal year. No group of partners with a single taxable year owns more than 50% of Acme's profits and capital so it must use the taxable year of G, its only principal partner. If Acme had another 10% general partner who uses a September 30 fiscal year, it would have to use the taxable year which provides the least aggregate deferral of income to the partners. That calculation is based on the months of deferral for each partner and each partner's interest in profits. Reg. § 1.706–1(b)(3)(i).

2) Business Purpose

A partnership may avoid the mechanical rules of § 706 if it can establish to the satisfaction of the Service a business purpose for adopting a different year. § 706(b)(1)(C). Deferral of income to the partners is not treated as a business purpose. The Service, however, has ruled that the business purpose standard is satisfied if the taxable year of the partnership coincides with its "natural business year." A partnership has a "natural business year" if in each of the prior three years its gross receipts for the last two months of the requested taxable year equaled or exceeded 25% of the gross receipts for the requested year. Rev. Proc. 2006–46, 2006–2 C.B. 859. A partnership unable to satisfy this standard may demonstrate that a particular taxable year satisfies the business purpose test under an all the facts and circumstances test. One of the facts the Service considers is the tax consequences (i.e., tax deferral) of the year selected. Rev. Rul. 87–57, 1987–2 C.B. 117.

3) Fiscal Year Election

Section 444 permits a partnership to adopt a taxable year other than one required by the § 706(b) mechanical rules, provided the year selected results in no more than three months of tax deferral. As a cost for this relief, the partnership must make "required payments" under § 7519 which are designed to offset the financial benefits of the tax deferral provided by § 444. A § 444 election and § 7519 payments, however, are not required if a partnership establishes a business purpose for the taxable year it selects. § 444(e).

c. Partnership Taxable Income

1) In General

A partnership computes its taxable income in the same manner as an individual except it is not permitted certain deductions, such as personal exemptions, medical expenses, alimony and expenses for the production or collection of income under § 212. § 703(a)(2)(A), (E). A partnership is not permitted a net operating loss deduction because a partnership's losses pass through to its partners. § 703(a)(2)(D).

2) Separately Stated Items

The characterization of tax items is determined at the partnership level. § 702(b); see Rev. Rul. 68–79, 1968–1 C.B. 310 (holding period for long-term capital gain is based on the partnership's holding period for the asset). The partnership must separately state certain items to preserve their unique character as they pass through to the partners. This enables the partners to combine the passed through items with their nonpartnership tax items when computing tax liability. The tax items required to be separately stated are listed in § 702(a): short-term capital gains and losses, long-term capital gains and losses, § 1231 gains and losses, charitable contributions, dividends taxed as net capital gain or eligible for the dividends received deduction, and foreign taxes. § 702(a) (1)–(6). This list is expanded by the regulations to include any other tax item (e.g., § 1202 capital gain on qualified small business stock or capital gain on a collectible taxed at a 28% rate) which if separately taken into account by any partner could affect the tax liability of that partner or any other person. § 702(a)(7); Reg. § 1.702–1(a)(8)(i), (ii). Tax items specially allocated under § 704(b) or 704(c) also must be separately stated. Reg. § 1.702–1(a)(8)(i); see V.A.2, at page 70, and VI.A. at page 90, *infra*. Once all of the separately stated items have been identified, the remaining partnership items are combined in a net taxable income or loss calculation. § 702(a)(8). This amount is sometimes referred to as "nonseparately computed" or "bottom line" income or loss.

d. Tax Elections

Elections affecting the determination of partnership taxable income generally are made by the partnership. § 703(b); see *Demirjian v. Comm'r,* 457 F.2d 1 (3d Cir.1972) (§ 1033 election to avoid recognition of gain on an involuntary conversion is made by the partnership).

Example: An election out of the installment method under § 453(d) would be made by the partnership, not on a partner-by-partner basis. An election to deduct or amortize organizational expenses under § 709 also would be made by the partnership.

2. Tax Consequences to the Partners

a. Timing and Character of Pass-Through Items

Partners are required to take into account their distributive shares of the partnership's separately stated items and nonseparately computed income or loss in the taxable year in which the partnership's taxable year ends. §§ 702(a);

706(a). The separately stated items retain their character when reported by the partners. § 702(b). Partners generally must report partnership tax items in a manner consistent with the way that the partnership reported the item. See § 6222.

Example: Assume the ABC cash method partnership has an October 31 fiscal year and during its current year has the following income and expenses:

Operating income	$90,000
Salary expense	30,000
Rental expense	20,000
Auto expense	5,000
§ 179 expense	9,000
Charitable contribution	3,000
§ 1245 gain	10,000
§ 1231 gain	15,000
LTCG from stock sale	20,000
LTCL from stock sale	8,000
STCG from stock sale	6,000

Of these items, the § 179 expense, the charitable contribution, the § 1231 gain, and the capital gains and losses are separately stated items because their separate treatment could affect the tax liability of a particular partner depending on the partner's personal tax results during the year. For example, the § 179 expense and the charitable contribution are separately stated so that the dollar and percentage limitations in those sections can apply at the partner level. See §§ 170(b); 179(b), (d)(8). The regulations permit the separate netting of long- and short-term capital gain transactions. Reg. § 1.702–1(a)(1), (2). Thus, ABC's separately stated items will be: § 179 expense—$9,000; charitable contribution—$3,000; § 1231 gain—$15,000; LTCG—$12,000; and STCG—$6,000. These items will retain their character when they are reported by the partners. ABC's nonseparately stated income will be $45,000 ($90,000 operating income plus $10,000 § 1245 gain less $55,000 of deductions (salary expense, rental expense and auto expense)). Because the § 1245 gain is ordinary income, its tax treatment cannot vary among the partners and thus it is not a separately stated item. Each partner in ABC must include his or her distributive share of the § 179 expense, charitable contribution, § 1231 gain, LTCG, STCG and nonseparately computed income in the taxable year in which ABC's October 31 taxable year ends. Calendar year partners would report their distributive shares of these items on their tax return for the following year.

b. Basis Adjustments

Under § 702, a partner is taxed directly on his distributive share of the partnership's separately stated items and nonseparately computed income or loss. Section 705 adjusts the partner's outside basis to reflect these results. In general, a partner must increase his outside basis by his distributive share of partnership taxable income and tax-exempt income and decrease it (but not below zero) by partnership distributions, as provided in § 733, and his distributive share of partnership losses and expenditures by the partnership which are neither deductible nor chargeable to a capital account. § 705(a).

Example: Partner A has a $10,000 outside basis in her partnership interest and her distributive share of partnership items for the year is:

Long-term capital gain	$3,000
Tax-exempt interest	$2,000
Charitable contribution	$1,000
Nonseparately computed income	$5,000

Each of the items passes through to A and is reported on her personal tax return. A's share of partnership taxable income as computed under § 703(a) is $8,000 (long-term capital gain plus nonseparately computed income). Under § 705(a), her outside basis will be adjusted as follows:

+ $8,000	§ 705(a)(1)(A)
+ $2,000	§ 705(a)(1)(B)
− $1,000	§ 705(a)(2)(B)
+ $9,000	

Thus, A's outside basis will be $19,000 ($10,000 plus $9,000) beginning the next year. The charitable contribution is an expenditure which the partnership is not allowed to deduct under § 703(a)(2)(C) and it is not capitalized. If the partnership distributed $5,000 of cash to A at the end of the year, her outside basis would be reduced to $14,000 by the distribution. §§ 705(a)(2); 733.

3.   Limitations on Partnership Losses

a.   Basis Limitation

Under § 704(d), a partner's distributive share of partnership loss (including capital loss) is limited to the partner's outside basis at the end of the partnership year in which the loss occurred. See *Kingbay v. Comm'r,* 46 T.C. 147 (1966) (limited partners share of partnership losses restricted by § 704(d); corporate general partner liable for partnership liabilities was not disregarded). Losses or deductions disallowed under this rule carry over indefinitely and may be used when the partner obtains sufficient outside basis to use the suspended loss.

Example: A is a partner in the ABC partnership and has a $4,000 outside basis. If A's distributive share of nonseparately computed loss for the year is $6,000, she will be limited to a $4,000 deduction and will have $2,000 of suspended loss which will carry over until she obtains additional outside basis.

If the basis limitation is exceeded by a combination of different types of losses, the regulations provide that the currently allowable losses consist of a proportionate amount of each type of loss. Reg. § 1.704–1(d)(2).

Example: D is a partner in the DEF partnership and has a $6,000 outside basis. D's distributive share of partnership long-term capital loss is $4,000 and his distributive share of nonseparately computed loss is

$8,000. Under § 704(d), D will be allowed a $6,000 loss for the year which will be characterized as follows:

$$\frac{\$\ 4,000}{\$12,000} \times \$6,000 = \$2,000 \text{ LTCL}$$

$$\frac{\$\ 8,000}{\$12,000} \times \$6,000 = \$4,000 \text{ Ordinary Loss}$$

D would have a $2,000 long-term capital loss carryover and a $4,000 nonseparately computed loss carryover at the beginning of the next year.

b. At-Risk Limitation

1) Introduction

Under § 465, a partner's share of partnership losses and deductions is limited to his amount "at risk." The at-risk limitation is applied on a partner-by-partner and activity-by-activity basis. § 465(a)(1), (c)(2)(A). Aggregation rules, however, may apply to combine activities. § 465(c)(2)(B), (3)(B).

2) At-Risk Amount: In General

A partner initially is considered at risk to the extent of (1) cash contributions to the partnership, (2) the adjusted basis of property contributed to the partnership, and (3) amounts borrowed for use in the activity for which the partner is personally liable or has pledged property (other than property used in the partnership) as security to the extent of the property's fair market value. § 465(b)(1), (2). Amounts borrowed from persons with an interest (other than as a creditor) in the activity or related persons generally are not considered at risk. § 465(b)(3). Recourse borrowings are not considered at risk if the taxpayer is protected against loss through guarantees, stop loss agreements, or similar arrangements. § 465(b)(4).

3) Qualified Nonrecourse Financing

In the case of partnerships involved in the holding of real property, a partner's amount at risk also includes "qualified nonrecourse financing." Qualified nonrecourse financing is nonconvertible debt which is (1) borrowed from or guaranteed by a governmental body, or (2) borrowed from a person actively engaged in the business of lending money. § 465(b)(6)(B)(ii), (iv). Qualified nonrecourse financing cannot be borrowed from the seller of property or a person who receives a fee with respect to taxpayer's investment (i.e., promoters). §§ 49(a)(1)(D)(iv); 465(b)(6)(D)(i). Financing borrowed from a "related person" is qualified nonrecourse financing only if it is commercially reasonable and on substantially the same terms as a loan to unrelated persons. § 465(b)(6)(D)(ii).

4)   Other Nonrecourse Debt

Except for qualified nonrecourse financing, a partner is not considered at risk for nonrecourse borrowings of the partnership. As a result, nonrecourse debt of the partnership may produce outside basis for a partner sufficient to avoid the § 704(d) limitation, but the partner still may be denied a deduction for partnership losses and deductions because he is not sufficiently at risk in the venture. In that situation the partner's outside basis is nonetheless reduced by the distributive share of partnership loss passed through from the partnership.

Example: A and B form the AB general partnership with each contributing $50,000. The partnership will engage in mining, which is not a "real estate" activity for purposes of the qualified nonrecourse financing exception. § 465(b)(6)(E)(ii). The AB partnership borrows $200,000 on a nonrecourse basis to finance its operations. A and B will each have a $150,000 outside basis ($50,000 contribution plus $100,000 share of nonrecourse loan) but will be considered at risk only to the extent of their $50,000 contributions.

5)   Limited Partner Guarantees and Other Partner Obligations

Although a limited partner is not considered at risk with respect to partnership liabilities other than qualified nonrecourse financing, several courts have held that a limited partners are at risk to the extent they have an obligation to make additional contributions to the partnership or guarantee a partnership liability. See, e.g., *Gefen v. Comm'r*, 87 T.C. 1471 (1986); *Pritchett v. Comm'r*, 827 F.2d 644 (9th Cir. 1987). The reasoning in these cases is inconsistent with the regulations determining a partner's share of recourse liabilities under § 752. Under those regulations, it generally is assumed that all partners who have obligations to make payments will actually perform them. Reg. § 1.752–2(b)(6). Thus, if a limited partner guarantees a recourse loan, it is assumed that the general partner will pay the liability and the limited partner will not have to satisfy the guarantee. Because the general partner bears the economic risk of loss, the limited partner will not be allocated a share of the liability. See Reg. § 1.752–2(f) Example 3.

In *Hubert Enterprises v. Comm'r*, T.C. Memo 2008–046 (2008), on remand, 230 Fed. Appx. 526 (6th Cir. 2007), the Tax Court held that a deficit capital account restoration provision in a limited liability company operating agreement (requiring a partner to restore a deficit capital account balance after liquidation of the partnership interest) did not make the partner at risk with respect to recourse liabilities of the LLC. The court held that the partner was not the payor of last resort for the recourse liability because the deficit restoration obligation could be avoided by not liquidating the interest. Also, the deficit restoration obligation did not create any additional rights for the lender to proceed against the partner for payment of the liabilities.

6) Adjustments to Amount at Risk and Carryover of Suspended Losses

A partner's at-risk amount is determined annually. If a partner includes a share of the partnership's loss for the year, his at-risk amount is reduced by the amount of the allowable loss. § 465(b)(5). Losses disallowed under § 465 are allowed in subsequent years when the taxpayer is sufficiently at risk. § 465(a)(2).

> **Example:** Assume A is a partner in a partnership and contributed $10,000 to the venture. The partnership borrowed funds on a nonrecourse basis and those borrowings are not included in A's at-risk amount. Thus, A's at-risk amount is $10,000. In the first year of partnership operations, A's distributive share of partnership loss is $2,000. A will be allowed to deduct the loss and his at-risk amount will be $8,000 at the beginning of the partnership's second year. If A's distributive share of partnership loss is $12,000 in the second year, he will be allowed to deduct $8,000 (his remaining at-risk amount) and the $4,000 of disallowed loss will carry over and be allowed in later years when A has additional amounts at risk in the partnership.

c. Passive Activity Loss Limitation

1) Introduction

Under § 469(a), a taxpayer's passive activity loss and credit for the year are disallowed. The purpose of § 469 is to prevent taxpayers from using losses from passive activities to offset salary and investment income. The limitation is applied on a partner-by-partner basis, not at the partnership level. § 469(a)(2)(A). A taxpayer's "passive activity loss" is the amount by which her aggregate losses from all passive activities exceed her aggregate income from such activities. § 469(d)(1). A passive activity is defined as an activity which involves the conduct of a trade or business in which the taxpayer does not materially participate. § 469(c)(1). All rental activity is defined as being passive, with limited exceptions for individual taxpayers who (1) "actively participate" in rental real estate activities and have adjusted gross income below certain specified levels, or (2) perform more than half their personal services in real estate trades or businesses in which they materially participate and devote more than 750 hours per year to those pursuits. §§ 469(i), (c)(7). To prevent easy avoidance of the loss limitation, traditional forms of "portfolio" investment income (interest, dividends, annuities and royalties) and compensation for personal services are not considered passive activity income. § 469(e)(1), (3). A partner's share of partnership portfolio income is nonpassive even if the partner does not materially participate in the partnership's activities. The Service also is granted authority to recharacterize income or gain from a limited partnership as not passive to prevent avoidance of the limitation. § 469(*l*)(3).

2) Material Participation

"Material participation" is defined as involvement in the activity on a regular, continuous, and substantial basis. § 469(h)(1). The regulations set out several specific tests for ascertaining whether a taxpayer materially participates in an activity. The material participation requirement is designed to distinguish passive investors in traditional tax shelters from taxpayers actively engaged in business and the regulation tests are consistent with that purpose. For example, an individual is considered to be materially participating in an activity if she participates for more than 500 hours, her participation constitutes substantially all of the participation for the year, or she devotes more than 100 hours to the activity during the year and no other individual participates more. Temp. Reg. § 1.469–5T(a)(1)–(3). Under these standards, a general partner who manages the partnership or devotes substantial time to its business should be able to satisfy the material participation tests.

Except as provided in regulations, limited partnership interests are considered interests in which the taxpayer does not materially participate. § 469(h)(2). For this purpose, a limited partnership interest is defined as an interest in an entity if (1) the entity is classified as a partnership for federal income tax purposes, and (2) the holder of the interest does not have rights to manage the entity at all times during the entity's taxable year under the law of the jurisdiction in which the entity is organized and under the governing agreement. Prop. Reg. § 1.469–5(e)(3). Under this definition, a member of an LLC would not be a limited partner because LLC members have the right to participate in management.

Under the regulations, a limited partner is considered to be materially participating if she participates for more than 500 hours in the activity or satisfies certain tests regarding material participation in prior years. Prop. Reg. § 1.469–5(e)(2). A limited partner who also holds a general partnership interest is not treated as holding a limited partnership interest. Thus, if a partner is treated as materially participating with respect to the general partnership interest, she also is treated as materially participating with respect to the limited partnership interest. Prop. Reg. § 1.469–5(e)(3)(ii).

3) Definition of "Activity"

A single partnership may engage in more than one passive "activity." The identification of separate activities is important in applying the material participation test and in determining when a taxpayer has fully disposed of the activity. Each "undertaking" in which a taxpayer owns an interest is treated as a separate activity. Temp. Reg. § 1.469–4T(a)(4)(i). An "undertaking" generally consists of all business or rental activities conducted at the same location and owned by the same person. Temp. Reg. § 1.469–4T(a)(3)(ii). The regulations go into great detail defining the scope of activities for § 469 purposes. See Temp. Reg. § 1.469–4T.

4) Later Use of Suspended Losses

Losses disallowed under § 469 carry over and may be deducted in subsequent years against passive income or may be deducted in full upon a taxable disposition of the entire activity. § 469(b), (g)(1). A partner's outside basis is reduced under § 705 by the amount of an otherwise allowable loss which is disallowed under § 469.

Example: G, the general partner, and L, the limited partner, form the GL limited partnership to manufacture a new product. If GL produces tax losses in its early years of operations, both G and L will have to confront the passive loss limitation in § 469. Assuming G devotes substantial time (more than 500 hours) to managing GL, he will be considered as materially participating in the partnership and it will not be a passive activity as to him. Even if G does not spend 500 hours participating in the partnership, it is likely that he will satisfy one of the other tests for material participation. L, as a limited partner, is ordinarily deemed not to materially participate. Thus, L's interest is a passive activity and her distributive share of GL losses will be subject to § 469. In that case, if GL holds assets which produce "portfolio" income (interest, dividends, etc.), L's distributive share of that income will be separated from her share of partnership business losses and will not be considered passive income. Finally, if L also owned a general partnership interest in GL, her limited partnership interest would be ignored and her participation in the partnership would be tested with respect to her general partnership interest.

C. Review Questions

1. The ABC equal partnership owns a swimming facility which has derived 50% of its income in July and August for the last three years. A and B use a November 30 fiscal year, while C uses a calendar year. What taxable year may the partnership adopt?

2. When computing its taxable income, which of the following items must the ABC partnership separately state? What is ABC's nonseparately computed, or bottom line, income?

Gross Business Revenue	$200,000
Salary Expense	$ 20,000
Depreciation Expense	$ 8,000
Interest Income	$ 15,000
§ 1231 Loss	$ 10,000
Gain from Sale of Machine (§ 1245)	$ 25,000
Charitable Contributions	$ 10,000
Maintenance Expense	$ 14,000

3. Elections impacting the determination of taxable income are made on a partner-by-partner basis. True or False?

4. A and B contribute $20,000 each to form the AB partnership and agree to share profits and losses 80% to A and 20% to B. AB's partnership items for the year are as follows:

Long-term Capital Gain	$20,000
Tax-Exempt Interest	$16,000
Nonseparately Computed Income	$24,000

(a)   What is A's portion of partnership income for the year?

(b)   What is A's outside basis at the beginning of the next year?

5.   A and B form the AB partnership by contributing $10,000 each. A and B agree to share profits and losses 75% to A, 25% to B. In Year 1 of operations, AB had business revenues of $10,000, business expenses of $14,000 and a short-term capital loss of $12,000. What are the tax results to A and B?

Chapter V

Partnership Allocations: § 704(b)

■ ANALYSIS

A.   Partnership Allocations: Substantial Economic Effect
    1.   Introduction
    2.   Special Allocations
B.   Allocations Attributable to Nonrecourse Liabilities
    1.   Introduction
    2.   Partnership Minimum Gain
    3.   Nonrecourse Deductions
    4.   Safe Harbor Test for Respecting Allocations of Nonrecourse Deductions
    5.   Minimum Gain Chargeback Requirement
    6.   Refinancings and Distributions
C.   Review Questions

A. Partnership Allocations: Substantial Economic Effect

1. Introduction

Under § 702(a), each partner is required to take into account his distributive share of separately stated items and nonseparately computed income or loss. Unless otherwise provided in Subchapter K, a partner's "distributive share" of these items is determined by the partnership agreement, including amendments made up to the time for filing the partnership's tax return. §§ 704(a); 761(c). If the partnership agreement is silent on the issue, the partners' distributive shares are determined in accordance with their interests in the partnership. § 704(b)(1). Thus, partners initially are given considerable flexibility to fashion their tax results. The following sections examine § 704(b)(2), the Code's basic restriction on the ability of partners to determine their tax results in the partnership agreement.

2. Special Allocations

a. Introduction

Under § 704(b)(2), the partners' distributive shares will be allocated in accordance with their interests in the partnership if the allocations agreed to in the partnership agreement lack substantial economic effect. The regulations originally used the "substantial economic effect" standard to determine whether the principal purpose of a partnership allocation was to avoid or evade income tax. See *Orrisch v. Comm'r*, 55 T.C. 395 (1970), aff'd per curiam, 1973 WL 154461 (9th Cir.1973). In the Tax Reform Act of 1976, the "substantial economic effect" test became the Code's standard for testing all allocations of partnership items, including allocations of bottom line income or loss.

Under the regulations, there are three ways that an allocation in a partnership agreement will be respected: (1) the allocation has substantial economic effect, (2) the allocation is in accordance with the partner's interest in the partnership, or (3) the allocation is deemed to be in accordance with the partner's interest in the partnership under one of several special rules. Reg. § 1.704–1(b)(1)(i).

The "substantial economic effect" standard is amplified by extensive and detailed regulations. The regulations require that partnership allocations be consistent with the underlying economic arrangement agreed to by the partners. Reg. § 1.704–1(b)(2)(ii)(*a*). To determine whether an allocation has substantial economic effect, the regulations apply a two-part analysis at the end of each partnership taxable year. First, the allocation must have "economic effect." Second, the economic effect must be "substantial." Reg. § 1.704–1(b)(2)(i). Partnership capital accounts are used to test those requirements.

b. Partnership Accounting: The Basics

Because the business or financial relationship among partners, as memorialized in the partnership agreement, may not directly correspond to the tax results you have studied in Subchapter K, principles of financial accounting are used to "keep score" of partnership activities. A partnership must maintain records of its assets, liabilities, and each partner's share of partnership capital. Typically, these matters are reflected in the partnership's balance sheet, with assets on the left side and partnership capital and liabilities on the right side. The main rule of thumb for financial accounting is that an enterprise's assets equal its liabilities plus the owner's equity or capital. A simple example illustrates these principles. Assume A and B agree to form the AB general partnership with A contributing $20,000 of cash and B contributing an asset in which she has a $12,000 adjusted basis and which the partners agree has a $20,000 fair market value. A and B agree to be equal partners and share all partnership income or loss equally. B's outside basis will be $12,000 under § 722, and the partnership's inside basis in the asset contributed by B will be $12,000 under § 723. The partnership's financial balance sheet, however, will look like this:

Assets		Liabilities/Partners' Capital	
	Bk. Value		
Cash	$20,000	Liabilities:	None
Asset	20,000		**Bk. Cap.**
		Capital	
		A	$20,000
		B	20,000
Total	$40,000	Total	$40,000

The AB balance sheet reflects assets at their fair market value at the time of acquisition or contribution. This figure is frequently referred to as "book value." Thus, B's asset is recorded at its agreed $20,000 fair market value. On the right side, A's and B's interests in partnership assets are reflected in their capital accounts (referred to as "book capital") which, in accordance with their agreement to be equal partners, are credited with their $20,000 contributions.

The results of operations also will be reflected in the partnership's financial records. Assume that in its first year of operations the AB partnership earns a $10,000 cash profit which is shared equally by A and B. At the end of the year, AB would have $10,000 more of cash and the partnership balance sheet would look like this:

Assets		Liabilities/Partners' Capital	
	Bk. Value		
Cash	$30,000	Liabilities:	None
Asset	20,000		**Bk. Cap.**
		Capital	
		A	$25,000
		B	25,000
Total	$50,000	Total	$50,000

If the $10,000 cash profit were distributed to A and B, the adjustments to the balance sheet would be straightforward. The partnership would have $10,000 less cash and A's and B's capital accounts would be reduced to $20,000 to reflect their reduced interests in partnership assets.

The financial books of the partnership and the partners' capital accounts will be kept in accordance with the partnership agreement and reflect the business arrangement agreed to by the partners. Thus, on the ultimate liquidation of the AB partnership, A and B will have equal capital accounts reflecting the fact that they agreed to share partnership assets equally.

c. Economic Effect

1) Introduction

To have economic effect, an allocation must be consistent with the underlying economic arrangement of the partners. The economic benefit or burden corresponding to an allocation must be borne by the partner receiving the allocation. Reg. § 1.704–1(b)(2)(ii)(a). The regulations use a three-part test to determine whether an allocation is consistent with the underlying economic arrangement of the partners. This basic test is backed up by an alternate test and an economic effect equivalence test which, if satisfied, can validate an allocation.

2) Basic Test: "The Big Three"

The basic test to determine whether an allocation has economic effect is mechanical. Generally, an allocation has economic effect if, throughout the full term of the partnership, the partnership agreement provides:

a)   That the partners' capital accounts will be determined and maintained in accordance with the rules in Reg. § 1.704–1(b)(2)(iv);

b)   That upon the liquidation of the partnership (or a partner's partnership interest) liquidating distributions will be made in accordance with the positive capital account balances of the partners; and

c)   That if a partner has a deficit capital account balance after all adjustments for the year, he is unconditionally obligated to restore the deficit by the end of the partnership taxable year (or, if later, within 90 days of the liquidation) in order to pay partnership creditors or partners with positive capital account balances.

To determine whether these requirements are met, the "partnership agreement" is deemed to include all agreements among the partners or between one or more partners and the partnership. The agreements can be written or oral and need not be embodied in a document the partners call "the partnership agreement." Reg. § 1.704–1(b)(2)(ii)(*h*).

Collectively, the three requirements for economic effect will be referred to as "The Big Three." The first requirement (determination and maintenance of capital accounts) generally is satisfied if each partner's capital account is *increased* by (1) the amount of money contributed by the partner to the partnership; (2) the fair market value of property contributed by the partner to the partnership, net of liabilities secured by the property; and (3) allocations to the partner of partnership income or gain (including tax-exempt income); and *decreased* by (1) the amount of money distributed to the partner; (2) the fair market value of property distributed to the partner net of liabilities secured by the property; (3) allocations to the partner of partnership expenditures which are not deductible and not properly chargeable to capital account; and (4) allocations of partnership loss and deduction of other than those described in (3), above. Reg. § 1.704–1(b)(2)(iv)(*b*). These rules are quite similar to the rules for determining and adjusting a partner's outside basis. The principal difference is that property contributions and distributions of property are accounted for at the property's fair market value, rather than at its basis. When determining capital accounts, the fair market value assigned to property will be accepted if it was agreed to in arm's length negotiations among partners with sufficiently adverse interests. Reg. § 1.704–1(b)(2)(iv)(*h*). The Big Three, by linking allocations to the partners' capital accounts, requiring that the partnership liquidate in accordance with capital account balances, and requiring each partner to restore any deficit in her capital account, assures that the economic benefit or burden of each allocation will correspond to the allocation.

Example (1):   A and B form a general partnership with each contributing $30,000 cash, which it uses to purchase depreciable personal property with a value of $60,000. The partnership agreement provides that A and B will share partnership taxable income and loss (other than cost recovery deductions) and cash flow equally, but all cost recovery deductions will be allocated to A. A and B agree to properly maintain capital accounts but on liquidation partnership assets will be distributed equally (regardless of capital account balances) and no partner has an obligation to restore a deficit balance in her capital account. Assume for simplicity that in its first year AB breaks even (income equals expenses) except it has a $15,000 cost recovery deduction which under the terms of the partnership agreement is all to be allocated to A. The allocation does not have economic effect. To understand the problem with the allocation, assume all the cost recovery deductions are allocated to A. A's and B's initial capital accounts were credited with $30,000. A's would decrease by $15,000 as a result of the allocation, leaving a balance of $15,000, while B's would remain at $30,000. If the depreciable personal property declined in value to $45,000, as the regulations require us to assume, and the partnership were liquidated, it would have $45,000 of assets to distribute. Under the partnership agreement the assets would be distributed $22,500 each to A and B. As structured, B actually bore $7,500 of the economic burden associated with the cost recovery deduction because the partnership agreement did not require liquidation of the partnership in accordance with the partners' capital account balances. That is, B receives $22,500 while her capital account is $30,000. Consequently, the regulations require that the $15,000 of cost recovery deductions be reallocated $7,500 to A and $7,500 to B.

Example (2):   Assume the same facts as Example (1), except that the partners agree to properly maintain capital accounts and to distribute partnership assets on liquidation in accordance with positive capital account balances, but no partner has an obligation to restore a deficit balance in her capital account. On these facts, The Big Three would not be satisfied because there is no unconditional obligation to restore a deficit capital account balance throughout the term of the partnership. The cost recovery deduction will be allocated in accordance with the partners' interests in the partnership. The next section (V.A.2.c.3., at page 74, *infra*) demonstrates that this allocation will be respected under the alternate test for economic effect if the partnership agreement is properly structured.

Example (3):   Assume the same facts as Example (1), except that the partnership agreement includes The Big Three. In each of its first three years AB breaks even (income equals expenses) except that in each year it has a $15,000 cost recovery deduction which under the partnership agreement is all to be allocated to A. Since The Big Three is satisfied, the allocation has economic effect. At the end of the third year, A's and B's capital accounts would be:

A	B
$30,000	$30,000
$45,000 deductions	
− $15,000	

If the depreciable personal property declined in value to $15,000 ($60,000 adjusted basis less $45,000 cost recovery deductions) and the partnership were liquidated, it would have $15,000 of assets to distribute. Under the partnership agreement, the $15,000 of assets must go to B (liquidation in accordance with positive capital account balances). In addition, A must contribute $15,000 to restore her deficit capital account balance. The $15,000 contributed by A would go to B to pay her remaining positive capital account balance. On these facts it is clear that complying with The Big Three ensures that A will bear the economic burden of the cost recovery deductions. Therefore, the allocation of those deductions has economic effect.

3)   Alternate Test for Economic Effect

Limited partners typically are unwilling to be obligated to restore a deficit capital account balance. If the partnership agreement satisfies the first two requirements of The Big Three but fails to include an unconditional deficit restoration obligation, the regulations provide an alternate test to establish that an allocation has economic effect. Reg. § 1.704–1(b)(2)(ii)(*d*). Under that test, an allocation will be respected to the extent it does not cause or increase a deficit in the partner's capital account. For purposes of this rule, certain limited obligations of a partner to restore capital account deficits— promissory notes given to the partnership meeting certain conditions, obligations under the partnership agreement, and obligations under state law—are recognized. Reg. § 1.704–1(b)(2)(ii)(*c*).

When determining whether the allocation causes or increases a capital account deficit, various *reasonably expected* events must be considered. The most important of these are distributions which, at the end of the year, are reasonably expected to be made to the partner. Finally, the partnership agreement must contain a "qualified income offset"—i.e., a provision which requires that if a partner has a deficit capital account balance as a result of one of the listed events occurring *unexpectedly* (e.g., an unexpected distribution) that partner will be allocated items of income or gain in an amount and manner sufficient to eliminate the deficit as quickly as possible. Reg. § 1.704–1(b)(2)(ii)(*d*).

Example (1):
(Basic Example of Alternate Test)

A and B form a general partnership with each contributing $30,000 cash. The partnership uses the $60,000 to purchase depreciable property. The partnership agreement provides that A and B will share partnership taxable income and loss (other than cost recovery deductions) and cash flow equally, but all cost recovery deductions will be allocated to A. A and B agree to properly maintain capital accounts and on liquidation of the partnership (or any partner's interest) partnership assets will be distributed in accordance with capital account balances, but no partner has an obligation to restore a deficit balance in her capital account. The partnership agreement also contains a qualified income offset. Assume that in its first year AB breaks even (income equals expenses) except that it has a $15,000 cost recovery deduction which under the terms of the partnership agreement is all to be allocated to A. Assuming future distributions are not reasonably expected to create a deficit in A's capital account, the allocation will have economic effect under the alternate test for economic effect. At the end of the year, B's capital account will be $30,000 and A's capital account will be:

$$\begin{array}{r} \$30,000 \\ -\ \$15,000 \quad \text{cost recovery deduction} \\ \hline \$15,000 \end{array}$$

Example (2):
(Reallocation to Reflect Economic Burden)

Assume the same facts as Example (1) and assume that in its second year of operation AB again breaks even except that it has a $20,000 cost recovery deduction and future distributions are not reasonably expected to create a deficit in A's capital account. Under the alternate economic effect test, only $15,000 of the allocation would have economic effect because a greater allocation would create a deficit in A's capital account. The remaining $5,000 of cost recovery deductions will be allocated in accordance with the partners' interests in the partnership. Under the partnership agreement, if the property were sold at the end of the partnership's second taxable year for $25,000 (its adjusted basis) the $25,000 would be distributed to B (in accordance with positive capital account balances). Thus, B, who has a positive capital account balance, not A, bears the economic burden of the additional cost recovery deductions and $5,000 of those deductions will be reallocated to B. See Reg. § 1.704–1(b)(5) Example (1)(iv).

Example (3):
(Reasonably Expected Distribution)

Assume the same facts as Example (2) except that in AB's second taxable year a $3,000 cash distribution (from proceeds of a partnership loan secured by the depreciable property) is reasonably expected to be made to A. In that situation the reasonably expected distribution must be considered when determining if the allocation of cost recovery deductions will create a deficit in A's capital account. Thus, if no capital account increases are reasonably expected, only $12,000 of the allocation will have economic effect ($15,000 capital account at the beginning of year two less the $3,000 reasonably expected distribution).

Example (4):
(Partial Deficit Restoration Agreements)

Assume again that A's capital account is $15,000 at the beginning of AB's second taxable year, no distributions are reasonably expected, and AB breaks even in its second year except that it has a $20,000 cost recovery deduction which is allocated to A. If A has a $5,000 partial deficit restoration obligation because either the partnership agreement or state law requires A to restore a $5,000 deficit or A gave a $5,000 promissory note (meeting certain conditions) to the partnership, the full $20,000 allocation would have economic effect under the alternate test. It is important to remember that *partial* deficit restoration obligations are recognized under the alternate test even though they are not recognized under The Big Three.

Example (5):
(Qualified Income Offset)

Assume that at the beginning of AB's third taxable year A's capital account is zero and A has no deficit restoration obligation (unconditional or partial). If a previously unexpected distribution occurs, resulting in a deficit in A's capital account, under the qualified income offset A must be allocated items of income and gain (a pro rata portion of each partnership item, including gross income) in an amount and manner sufficient to eliminate the deficit as quickly as possible.

4)   Economic Effect Equivalence

Allocations which do not have economic effect under The Big Three or the alternate economic effect test will be deemed to have economic effect if at the end of each partnership taxable year a liquidation of the partnership would produce the same economic results to the partners as The Big Three. Reg. § 1.704–1(b)(2)(ii)(*i*).

Example: Assume C and D form a partnership and agree that partnership income, gain, loss and deduction will be allocated 60% to C and 40% to D. The CD partnership agreement fails to require the maintenance of capital accounts, but under a state law right of contribution C and D are ultimately liable for 60% and 40%, respectively, of partnership debts. The partnership allocation will have economic effect under the economic effect equivalence test. See Reg. § 1.704–1(b)(5) Example (4)(ii).

d. Substantiality

1) Introduction

In order to be respected, the economic effect of an allocation must be "substantial," which requires that there be a reasonable possibility that the allocation will affect substantially the dollar amounts to be received by the partners from the partnership, independent of tax consequences. Reg. § 1.704–1(b)(2)(iii)(*a*). The regulations clarify this standard by providing a general rule and more specific rules for "shifting" and "transitory" allocations.

2) General Rule for Substantiality

Under the regulations, the general rule is that the economic effect of an allocation is not substantial if, at the time the allocation becomes part of the partnership agreement: (1) the after-tax economic consequences of at least one partner may, in present value terms, be enhanced compared to such consequences if the allocation were not contained in the partnership agreement, and (2) there is a strong likelihood that the after-tax economic consequences of no partner will, in present value terms, be substantially diminished compared to such consequences if the allocation were not contained in the partnership agreement. In determining the after-tax economic benefit or detriment to a partner, the interaction of the allocation with the partner's nonpartnership tax attributes is considered. *Id.* Thus, for an allocation to have *substantial* economic effect, it must have the potential to actually impact the economic relationship among the partners, apart from the tax results.

Example: A and B are equal partners in the AB partnership. Over the next several years, A expects to be taxed at the highest federal tax rate and B expects to be taxed at the lowest. There is also a strong likelihood that over the next several years AB will realize approximately equal amounts of taxable interest and tax-exempt interest. The AB partnership agreement complies with The Big Three. Assume the partners allocate a disproportionate amount of the tax-exempt interest to A and a disproportionate amount of the taxable interest to B so as to take advantage of their respective tax rates and increase their total after-tax returns from the partnership. Such allocations would have economic effect but the economic effect will not be substantial. At the time the allocation became part of the partnership agreement, the after-tax economic consequences of A are expected to be enhanced and there is a strong likelihood that the after-tax economic consequences of neither A nor B will be substantially diminished. Put more simply, the allocation does not have the potential to actually affect the economic relationship between A and B, apart from tax results, so the taxable interest and tax-exempt interest will have to be reallocated in accordance with the partners' interests in the partnership. See Reg. § 1.704–1(b)(5) Example (5)(i).

3) Shifting and Transitory Allocations

a) Shifting Allocations

The regulations amplify the general rules regarding substantiality by focusing on what are referred to as "shifting" and "transitory" allocations. An allocation is shifting and not substantial if, at the time the allocation becomes part of the partnership agreement, there is a strong likelihood that (1) the net increases and decreases in the partners' capital accounts will not differ substantially from the net increases and decreases if the allocation was not part of the partnership agreement, and (2) the total tax liability of the partners will be reduced as a result of the allocation (taking into account the impact of the partners' nonpartnership tax items). If, at the end of a partnership's taxable year, the net increases and decreases in the partners' capital accounts do not differ substantially from the net increases and decreases if there had been no allocation, and the tax liability of the partners is reduced, it is presumed that there was a strong likelihood that those results would occur at the time the allocation became part of the partnership agreement. Reg. § 1.704–1(b)(2)(iii)(*b*). Again, the test is whether the allocation has the potential to actually change the economic relationship among the partners, disregarding the tax consequences.

Example (1):   C and D are equal partners in the CD partnership. In the partnership agreement, C and D agree to comply with The Big Three. C expects to be taxed at the highest federal tax rate during the current year and D expects to be taxed at the lowest. During the current taxable year, C and D agree to share the first $10,000 of the partnership's tax-exempt income on a 90/10 basis (90% to C, 10% to D), and the first $10,000 of the partnership's dividend income on a 10/90 basis (10% to C, 90% to D). The allocations will have economic effect. If there is a strong likelihood that the partnership will earn more than $10,000 of both tax-exempt income and dividends, the economic effect of the allocations will not be substantial because the net increases and decreases in C's and D's capital accounts will be the same as they would have been if the allocations had not been made and the partner's total tax liability is reduced. Assuming the partnership realizes at least $10,000 of both tax-exempt income and dividends, those items will be reallocated equally between C and D.

Example (2): Assume the same facts as Example (1). If there is not a strong likelihood that the partnership will earn at least $10,000 of both tax-exempt income and dividends, and the amount of tax-exempt income and dividends will be the same, the regulations state that the economic effect of the allocations generally will be substantial. Reg. § 1.704–1(b)(5) Example (7)(iii).

b) Transitory Allocations

Transitory allocations are similar to shifting allocations except that they involve more than one taxable year. Again, the issue is whether there is a strong likelihood at the time the allocations became part of the partnership agreement that: (1) the net increases and decreases in the partners' capital accounts as a result of allocations over more than one year will not differ substantially from the net increases and decreases had the allocations not been made, and (2) the partners' total tax liability is reduced. If these results occur it is presumed that there was a strong likelihood of that result. But if there is a strong likelihood that an offsetting allocation (increase or decrease) will not be made within five years, the original and offsetting allocations will be considered substantial. Reg. § 1.704–1(b)(2)(iii)(*c*).

Example (1): E and F are equal partners in the EF partnership. In the partnership agreement E and F agree to comply with The Big Three. For the next three years the partnership will invest in equal amounts of tax-exempt bonds and corporate stock and over that period of time E expects to be in a higher tax bracket than F. Assume that during the three-year period the partners agree to allocate the tax-exempt interest 90% to E and 10% to F, and the dividends 10% to E and 90% to F. If there is a strong likelihood that the amount of tax-exempt interest and dividends realized will not differ substantially over the three-year period, the economic effect of the allocations will not be substantial because at the end of that period the net increases and decreases to the partners' capital accounts will be the same as they would have been without the allocations and the tax paid by the partners will be reduced. If the tax-exempt interest and dividends are the same over the three-year period, they will be reallocated equally between E and F. See Reg. § 1.704–1(b)(5) Example (7)(i).

Example (2): Assume the same facts as Example (1). Assume further that any gain or loss on the tax-exempt bonds is allocated to E and any gain or loss on the stock is allocated to F. If at the time the allocations became part of the partnership agreement there is not a strong likelihood that the gain or loss on these assets will be substantially equal, the allocations of gain and loss will have substantial economic effect. Id.

4)   The Baseline for Testing Substantiality

The determination whether an allocation fails the general rule regarding substantiality, or runs afoul of the prohibitions on shifting or transitory allocations, is to be made by comparing it to the result if the allocation were not contained in the partnership agreement. Reg. § 1.704–1(b)(2)(iii)(a). The comparison is made to an allocation that would be made if it were determined in accordance with the partners' interests in the partnership, disregarding the allocation that is being tested. Id. If the partners have an overall sharing relationship (e.g., 50/50), that relationship often is the basis for the comparison. But in more complicated arrangements where there are different sharing arrangements for several partnership items, determining the partners' interests in the partnership may be more complex.

5)   Presumption Validating "Gain Chargeback" Provisions

For purposes of determining whether an allocation's economic effect is substantial, the adjusted basis of property is presumed to be its fair market value and cost recovery deductions are presumed to be matched by a corresponding decrease in the property's value. Reg. § 1.704–1(b)(2)(iii)(c). Under this presumption, there cannot be a strong likelihood that the economic effect of an allocation of cost recovery deductions will be largely offset by an allocation of corresponding gain on the disposition of the property. This presumption validates so-called "gain chargeback" provisions.

Example: G and H are equal partners in the GH partnership. In the GH partnership agreement the partners agree to comply with The Big Three and all partnership cost recovery deductions are allocated to G. In addition, the partnership agreement contains a "gain chargeback" provision under which any gain on the sale of partnership depreciable property is allocated to G to the extent of the prior allocations to G of cost recovery deductions, and any additional gain is allocated equally between G and H. Even if it is likely that gain on a sale will be sufficient to offset prior cost recovery deductions, the allocation has substantial economic effect because in testing whether the economic effect of the allocation is substantial, the property is presumed to decrease in value by the amount of the cost recovery deductions.

e.   Partner's Interest in the Partnership

If either the partnership agreement is silent or partnership allocations lack substantial economic effect, a partner's distributive share of partnership items is determined in accordance with the partner's interest in the partnership. § 704(b). Also, the sharing arrangement for an item may or may not correspond to the overall economic arrangement of the partners. A partner's interest in the partnership is determined by the manner in which the partners have agreed to share the economic benefit or burden corresponding to the partnership's tax items. Reg. § 1.704–1(b)(3)(i). This determination is made by taking into account all facts and circumstances, including: (1) the partner's contributions to the partnership, (2) the interests of the partners in economic profits and losses (if different from that in taxable income or loss) and cash flow, (3) the interests of the partners in cash flow and non-liquidating distributions, and (4) the rights of the partners to distributions of capital on liquidation of the partnership. Reg. § 1.704–1(b)(3)(ii).

If an allocation satisfies the first two requirements of The Big Three and is substantial but the partnership agreement does not have an unlimited deficit restoration provision, the regulations provide that a partner's interest in the partnership for purposes of reallocating an item is determined by comparing the manner in which distributions (and contributions) would be made if all partnership property were sold at book value and the partnership were liquidated at the end of taxable year to which the allocation relates with the results of an identical liquidation at the end of the prior taxable year. Reg. § 1.704–1(b)(3)(iii). This test may save simple allocations that failed The Big Three or the alternate test because the partnership agreement did not include all the provisions required by those tests.

Example (1):   Assume A and B form the AB partnership by making equal cash contributions. The AB partnership agreement provides that A and B will have equal shares of taxable income and loss (except any cost recovery deductions) and cash flow and that all cost recovery deductions will be allocated to A. The agreement requires proper maintenance of capital accounts but, upon liquidation of the partnership, distributions will be made equally to A and B and no partner is required to restore a deficit capital account balance. The allocation of cost recovery deductions to A does not have economic effect because the partnership agreement does not comply with The Big Three, and the allocation fails the alternate test because the agreement does not include a qualified income offset provision. As a result, the cost recovery deductions will be reallocated in accordance with the partners' interests in the partnership. Since A and B made equal contributions, share equally in cash flow, and will share liquidation distributions equally, the cost recovery deductions will be reallocated equally between A and B. If the partners' interests in these items had not been equal, the regulations do not give clear guidance as to how they should be balanced to determine the partners' interests in the partnership.

Example (2):   J and K are equal partners in the JK partnership. In the JK partnership agreement the partners agree to comply with The Big Three. During the year the partnership expects to incur § 1231 losses and other ordinary losses. In the partnership agreement, the partners allocate the first $20,000 of § 1231 losses to J, who does not have any § 1231 gains, and the first $20,000 of ordinary loss to K, who does have nonpartnership § 1231 gains. These allocations have economic effect. If there is a strong likelihood that the partnership will have at least $20,000 of both § 1231 and ordinary losses, the economic effect of the allocations is not substantial because there was a strong likelihood at the time the allocations became part of the partnership agreement that the net increases and decreases in the partners' capital accounts would not differ substantially from the net increases and decreases had the allocations not been made and the partners' tax liability will be reduced. The partners' taxes are reduced because K is allocated ordinary losses from the partnership which will not impact the capital gain characterization of his nonpartnership § 1231 gains. If K had been allocated § 1231 losses from the partnership, those losses would reduce the potential tax advantages available to the nonpartnership § 1231 gains.

If in fact the partnership recognizes at least $20,000 of both § 1231 and ordinary loss, those items will be reallocated equally between J and K. If not, the § 1231 losses and ordinary losses will be reallocated in proportion to the net decreases in their capital accounts due to the allocations of those items under the partnership agreement. For example, if the partnership actually ends up recognizing $20,000 of § 1231 losses (which are allocated to J) and $10,000 of ordinary losses (which are allocated to K) for the year, the allocation will not have substantial economic effect if there was a strong likelihood the partnership would have $20,000 of both types of losses when the allocations became part of the partnership agreement. Based on these facts, the losses would be reallocated as follows:

J:	$13,333	§ 1231 loss
	$ 6,666	ordinary loss
K:	$ 6,666	§ 1231 loss
	$ 3,333	ordinary loss

See Reg. § 1.704–1(b)(5) Example (6).

f. Allocations of Depreciation Recapture

Allocations of depreciation recapture cannot have substantial economic effect because classifying part of the gain as recapture merely changes its tax character. The identification of part of the gain taxed to a partner as ordinary or capital gain does not change the economic arrangement among the partners; instead, it simply changes their tax results. Consequently, the regulations attempt to minimize the mismatching of depreciation and recapture allocations. Reg. §§ 1.704–3(a)(11); 1.1245–1(e)(2); 1.1250–1(f). Under the regulations, a partner's share of recapture gain generally is equal to the lesser of (1) the partner's share of the total gain from the disposition of the property, or (2) the total amount of depreciation previously allocated to the partner with respect to the property. Reg. §§ 1.1245–1(e)(2)(i) & (ii); 1.1250–1(f).

g. Allocations of Tax Credits

Allocations of tax credits and credit recapture generally are not reflected in the partners' capital accounts and cannot have economic effect. Thus, tax credits and credit recapture generally must be allocated in accordance with the partners' interests in the partnership. Reg. § 1.704–1(b)(4)(ii).

h. Target Allocations

An emerging trend is for partners to forgo special allocations based on tax items and instead specify how cash proceeds from the partnership's operations will be distributed to the partners. Thus, a partnership agreement could provide that cash is first distributed to particular partners to provide them with a specific preferred return on investment (e.g., 5%), next to the partners to recover their invested capital, and finally to the partners in their agreed sharing relationship (e.g., 50/50). For tax purposes, the partnership agreement then would allocate tax items to arrive at "the correct results"—i.e., tax items would be allocated to result in capital accounts that correspond to the how distributions were made. These "target allocations" can be made after cash and tax results are known. The uncertain question is how this approach fares under the § 704(b) regulations. Some practitioners believe target allocations should be respected under one or more of the tests in the regulations because they are consistent with the partners' interests in the partnership test.

B. Allocations Attributable to Nonrecourse Liabilities

1. Introduction

Even though partners do not bear the economic risk of loss for partnership nonrecourse liabilities, they must bear the corresponding tax burden of including relief from those liabilities in their amount realized upon a disposition of property encumbered by the debt. *Comm'r v. Tufts*, 461 U.S. 300, 103 S.Ct. 1826 (1983), *rehearing denied*, 463 U.S. 1215, 103 S.Ct. 3555 (1983). The regulations provide a four-part test which basically requires that, in order to be respected, allocations attributable to nonrecourse liabilities must correspond to any later gain attributable to that debt. If the test is satisfied, the allocations are deemed to be in accordance with the partners' interests in the partnership. Reg. § 1.704–2(b)(1). The four-part test employs several very detailed definitions. The basics of the definitions are provided in the following sections.

2. Partnership Minimum Gain

Partnership minimum gain with respect to a particular nonrecourse liability is defined as the amount of gain, if any, that would be realized if the partnership disposed of the partnership property subject to the liability in full satisfaction of such liability and no other consideration. Reg. § 1.704–2(d)(1). Under Reg. § 1.704–2(d)(3), partnership minimum gain is determined with reference to the book value of partnership property if book value differs from the property's adjusted tax basis. Partnership minimum gain is the aggregate of the separately computed gains. The increase or decrease in partnership minimum gain is determined by comparing the partnership minimum gain on the last day of the preceding taxable year with the partnership minimum gain on the last day of the current taxable year. Id.

3. Nonrecourse Deductions

A partnership's "nonrecourse deductions" for the year generally equal the net increase in the amount of partnership minimum gain for the year. Reg. § 1.704–2(c). Increases in minimum gain generally would occur as the result of cost recovery deductions which would reduce the bases of assets encumbered by nonrecourse liabilities.

4. Safe Harbor Test for Respecting Allocations of Nonrecourse Deductions

Allocations of nonrecourse deductions are deemed to be in accordance with the partners' interests in the partnership only if they meet the following requirements:

a.   During the life of the partnership the partnership agreement complies with the first two requirements of The Big Three (proper maintenance of capital accounts and liquidation of the partnership in accordance with positive capital account balances); and either: (1) the third requirement of The Big Three (deficit restoration obligation) is satisfied, or (2) the partnership agreement contains a qualified income offset;

b.   Beginning in the first taxable year in which there are nonrecourse deductions, the partnership agreement allocates such deductions in a manner reasonably consistent with allocations, which have substantial economic effect, of some other significant partnership item attributable to the property securing nonrecourse liabilities of the partnership;

c.   Beginning in the first taxable year in which there are nonrecourse deductions or a distribution of the proceeds of a nonrecourse liability that are allocable to an increase in partnership minimum gain, and thereafter, the partnership agreement must contain a provision that complies with the "minimum gain chargeback" requirement; and

d.   All other material allocations and capital account adjustments under the partnership agreement must be recognized under the § 704(b) regulations. Reg. § 1.704–2(e).

5. Minimum Gain Chargeback Requirement

If there is a net decrease in partnership minimum gain for a partnership taxable year, the minimum gain chargeback requirement applies and generally each partner must be allocated items of income and gain for the year equal to that partner's share of the net decrease in partnership minimum gain. Reg. § 1.704–2(f)(1). A partner's share of net decrease in partnership minimum gain is generally based on the nonrecourse deductions allocated to that partner. Reg. § 1.704–2(g)(1) & (2). A partner's share of partnership minimum gain increases the limited dollar amount, if any, of a deficit capital account balance that the partner is obligated to restore under the alternate test for economic effect. Reg. § 1.704–2(g)(1).

In essence, a minimum gain chargeback forces each partner to bear the burden of his share of minimum gain if nonrecourse liabilities produce recognition of gain on the disposition of encumbered property. A net decrease in partnership minimum gain also commonly occurs when the partnership makes principal payments on nonrecourse liabilities. In that situation, partners with deficit capital account balances from nonrecourse deductions must be allocated income and gain sufficient to restore the deficit.

Example: G and L form the GL limited partnership with G, the general partner, contributing $20,000 and L, the limited partner, contributing $180,000. GL purchases a building (on leased land) for $1,000,000 paying $200,000 cash and borrowing $800,000 on a nonrecourse basis. The loan is secured by the building and no principal payments are due for ten years (only interest is payable during that period). The partnership agreement requires proper maintenance of the partners' capital accounts and liquidation of the partnership in accordance with positive capital account balances. Only G is obligated to restore a deficit in her capital account. The partnership agreement also contains a qualified income offset and a minimum gain chargeback. Except as required by the qualified income offset or minimum gain chargeback, all partnership items are allocated 10% to G and 90% to L until the partnership has recognized items of income and gain that exceed the items of loss and deduction it previously has recognized, and thereafter all additional partnership items will be allocated equally between G and L.

The partnership agreement provides that all distributions, other than in liquidation of the partnership or of a partner's interest in the partnership, will be made 90% to L and 10% to G until a total of $200,000 has been distributed and thereafter all distributions will be made equally to L and G.

Assume that in each year of operations the partnership generates $95,000 of rental income, $10,000 of operating expenses (including land lease payments), $80,000 of interest deductions, and a $90,000 depreciation deduction, for a taxable loss of $85,000. The allocations of the first two years of those losses have substantial economic effect:

	L	G
Capital Account at Formation	$ 180,000	$ 20,000
Loss in Years 1 and 2	− 153,000	− 17,000
Capital Account after Year 2	$ 27,000	$ 3,000

In its third taxable year, the partnership again has a loss of $85,000 and makes no distributions. The building's adjusted basis at the end of the third year would be $730,000 ($1 million less $270,000 of depreciation) and if the partnership disposed of the building in full satisfaction of the $800,000 nonrecourse liability at the end of the third year it would realize $70,000 of gain. Because the net increase in partnership minimum gain for the third year is $70,000, there are $70,000 of partnership nonrecourse deductions for that year. The nonrecourse deductions are considered to consist first of the depreciation deductions. Reg. § 1.704–2(c). Under the partnership agreement the $85,000 net taxable loss, including the $70,000 of nonrecourse deductions, is allocated 90% to L and 10% to G.

	L	G
Capital Account at Year 2	$27,000	$3,000
Year 3 Loss Without Nonrecourse Deductions	− 13,500	− 1,500
Year 3 Nonrecourse Deductions	− 63,000	− 7,000
Capital Accounts	− 49,500	− 5,500

The allocation of the $15,000 of taxable loss (excluding nonrecourse deductions) has substantial economic effect under the alternate test because it does not create a deficit in L's capital account. The allocation of the $70,000 of nonrecourse deductions is deemed to be made in accordance with the partners' interests in the partnership because it satisfies the four-part test in the regulations for allocations of nonrecourse deductions. The second requirement of that test is satisfied because the allocation of the nonrecourse deductions is consistent with the allocations having substantial economic effect of other significant items attributable to the building. At the end of the third year L's and G's shares of partnership minimum gain are $63,000 and $7,000, respectively. L therefore is treated as obligated to restore a $63,000 deficit capital account balance under the alternate test for economic effect. Since L's deficit capital account balance is only $49,500, 13,500 of partnership deductions and losses that are not nonrecourse deductions could be allocated to L in the next year.

If the partnership were to dispose of the building in full satisfaction of the nonrecourse liability ($800,000) at the beginning of the fourth year, partnership minimum gain would decrease by $70,000 and the minimum gain chargeback would require that L and G be allocated $63,000 and $7,000, respectively, of the gain from the disposition. See Reg. § 1.704–2(m) Example (1)(i).

The four-part test in the regulations requires that nonrecourse deductions be allocated in a manner reasonably consistent with allocations that have substantial economic effect of some other significant partnership item attributable to the property securing the nonrecourse liability. In this example all deductions (including nonrecourse deductions) were allocated 90% to L and 10% to G, so the requirement was satisfied. The § 704 regulations provide that if: (1) the nonrecourse deductions were allocated in any ratio between 90% to L/10% to G and 50% to L/50% to G, and (2) it is likely that over the partnership's life it will realize amounts of income and gain significantly in excess of amounts of loss and deduction (other than nonrecourse deductions), the reasonable consistency requirement is satisfied. But an allocation of 99% of the nonrecourse deductions to L and 1% to G does not satisfy that requirement. Reg. § 1.704–2(m) Example (1)(ii) & (iii).

6. Refinancings and Distributions

If a partnership incurs additional nonrecourse liabilities through refinancings or additional borrowings, there is an increase in partnership minimum gain and an increase in nonrecourse deductions. The increase in nonrecourse deductions is reduced by distributions during the year of proceeds of a nonrecourse liability that are allocable to an increase in partnership minimum gain. Reg. § 1.704–2(c).

Example (1):   Assume the ABC limited partnership satisfies the requirements in the regulations regarding allocations attributable to nonrecourse liabilities. The partnership owns real property with an adjusted basis of $200,000 which is subject to a $250,000 nonrecourse liability. Thus, there is $50,000 of partnership minimum gain. Assume the partnership obtains an additional nonrecourse loan of $100,000 on the real property, secured by a second mortgage. Partnership minimum gain increases by $100,000 to $150,000. If the proceeds of the loan are not distributed, nonrecourse deductions increase by $100,000. Under the regulations, the first $100,000 of partnership deductions for the year are treated as nonrecourse deductions, and each partner's share of partnership minimum gain is increased by that partner's allocable share of those deductions. Reg. § 1.704–2(m) Example (1)(vi).

If a partnership distributes nonrecourse liability proceeds allocable to an increase in partnership minimum gain, then nonrecourse deductions are not produced by the liability to the extent of the distribution. Reg. § 1.704–2(c). The distribution is allocable to an increase in partnership minimum gain, which means that the partners receiving the distribution can add the additional share of partnership minimum gain to their limited deficit restoration obligation under the alternate test for economic effect. Reg. § 1.704–2(g)(1), (h)(1). See V.A.2.c.3, at page 74, *supra*.

Example (2):   Assume the same facts as in Example (1), except that the partnership distributes the $100,000 of loan proceeds to its partners. No nonrecourse deductions result from the new borrowings. The distributions are allocable to the increase in partnership minimum gain and will increase the deficit restoration obligation of the limited partners under the alternate test for economic effect. The deficit restoration obligation will be made up when partnership minimum gain is reduced, for example, on a disposition of the property or a repayment of the liability.

C. Review Questions

1. A and B form the AB equal general partnership. A contributes $10,000 cash and a depreciable asset with an adjusted basis of $40,000 and a fair market value of $90,000. B contributes $50,000 cash and a parcel of land with an adjusted basis of $70,000 and a fair market value of $50,000.

    (a) What are A and B's outside bases?

    (b) What is the balance in A's and B's capital accounts at formation?

2. A and B form the AB partnership with each contributing $50,000. The partners agree to comply with The Big Three and to share profits and losses equally. At the beginning of Year 1, AB purchases a $50,000 depreciable asset. Assume the property is depreciated over five years under the straight line method. Per the partnership agreement, A is allocated all the cost recovery deductions. Assume AB breaks even each year except for $10,000 of cost recovery. If AB sells the property at the end of Year 3 for $20,000 and immediately liquidates, how must the proceeds be distributed to qualify under The Big Three?

3. Can an allocation that does not have economic effect be cured by state law?

4. A and B form the AB partnership with each contributing $50,000. A and B agree to comply with The Big Three. AB purchases $50,000 of stock and $50,000 of tax-exempt bonds and there is a strong likelihood the stock and bonds will produce approximately equal amounts of dividend income and tax-exempt interest. In Year 1, A expects to be in a higher marginal tax bracket than B. A and B agree that in Year 1 the tax-exempt interest will be allocated 90% to A, 10% to B and the dividend income will be allocated 10% to A and 90% to B.

    (a) Does this allocation have substantial economic effect?

    (b) If AB receives $10,000 of tax-exempt interest and $5,000 of dividends in Year 1, and the allocation does *not* have substantial economic effect, how will the amounts be reallocated to A and B?

Chapter VI

Partnership Allocations: Income-Shifting Safeguards

■ ANALYSIS

A. Allocations with Respect to Contributed Property
    1. § 704(c) Allocations: General Principles
    2. § 704(c) Allocation Methods
    3. Application of § 704(c)(1)(A) Principles to the Entry of a New Partner
    4. Distributions of Contributed Property Within Seven Years of Contribution
    5. Characterization of Gain or Loss upon Partnership's Disposition of Contributed Property
    6. Anti-Abuse Rule for Loss Property
B. Partnership Interests Created by Gift or Acquired by Purchase from Family Member
    1. Purpose of § 704(e)
    2. Definitions of Partnership and Partner
    3. Determination of Distributive Share of Donee
C. Allocations Where Partners' Interests Vary During the Year
    1. Introduction
    2. Determination of Distributive Shares
    3. Distributive Shares of Allocable Cash Basis Items: § 706(d)(2)
    4. Tiered Partnerships
D. Review Questions

A. Allocations with Respect to Contributed Property

1. § 704(c) Allocations: General Principles

Section 704(c)(1)(A) provides that income, gain, loss and deduction items with respect to property contributed by a partner to a partnership shall be shared among the partners so as to take account of the variation between the inside basis of the property and its fair market value at the time of the contribution. The purpose of this rule is to prevent the shifting of precontribution gains and losses among partners. Reg. § 1.704–3(a)(1). Section 704(c)(1)(A) principally applies to sales and exchanges by a partnership of contributed property and depreciation and depletion with respect to contributed property. "Contributed property" (also known as "§ 704(c) property") is property which, at the time it is contributed to a partnership, has a fair market (book) value that differs from the contributing partner's adjusted tax basis (a "book/tax disparity"). Reg. § 1.704–3(a)(3)(i). Because contributed property is recorded on the partnership's books at its fair market value, allocations of precontribution gain or loss are tax allocations that do not have economic effect. For example, if contributed property is sold by the partnership for its book value, there is no book gain and no adjustments to the partners' capital accounts.

Example: A and B form the AB equal partnership with A contributing property with a $30,000 fair market value and $18,000 adjusted basis and B contributing $30,000 cash. A and B agree to share all partnership income or loss and distributions equally and the partnership agreement includes The Big Three. Neither A nor B will recognize gain on their contributions. A's outside basis will be $18,000 and B's will be $30,000. AB's inside basis in the asset contributed by A will be $18,000. Both A and B will have a $30,000 capital account since A's capital account is credited with the fair market value of the property she contributed. After its formation, AB's balance sheet will be as follows:

		Assets		**Liabilities/Partners' Capital**		
	A.B.	**Bk. Value**		Liabilities:	None	
Cash	$30,000	$30,000				
Asset	18,000	30,000		Capital	**A.B.**	**Bk. Cap.**
				A	$18,000	$30,000
				B	30,000	30,000
Total	$48,000	$60,000			$48,000	$60,000

Assume the partnership sells the asset contributed by A for its fair market value of $30,000. AB will have a $12,000 recognized gain which, absent § 704(c)(1)(A), would be allocated under the partnership agreement $6,000 to A and $6,000 to B, thereby increasing their outside bases to $24,000 and $36,000, respectively. If this result is permitted, $6,000 of A's precontribution gain in the asset will be shifted to B. The shift is not permanent since B's outside basis is increased to $36,000, and on a sale or cash liquidation of her partnership interest she will recognize $6,000 of loss. But that event may occur many years later and the character of B's loss may not be the same as the income recognized on the disposition of the asset. To prevent these distortions, § 704(c)(1)(A) requires that the $12,000 of precontribution gain inherent in the asset shall be allocated to A, which will increase her outside basis to $30,000.

2. § 704(c) Allocation Methods

a. In General

Under the regulations, a partnership may use any reasonable method of making § 704(c) allocations that is consistent with the purpose of § 704(c). Reg. § 1.704–3(a)(1). The regulations specifically authorize three methods: the "traditional" method, the "traditional method with curative allocations," and the "remedial method." A partnership may use different allocation methods with respect to different items of contributed property, but the method used for a particular property must be consistently applied by the partnership and the partners from year to year. Reg. § 1.704–3(a)(2). In all events, the overall method or combination of methods used must be reasonable under the facts and circumstances. Id. An allocation method is not reasonable if the contribution of the property and the corresponding § 704(c) allocations with respect to it are made with a view to shifting the tax consequences of built-in gain or loss in a manner that substantially reduces the present value of the partners' aggregate tax liability. Reg. § 1.704–3(a)(10). For example, the partners may not manipulate § 704(c) to shift income over a short period of time from a partner in a high marginal tax bracket to a partner who anticipates no tax liability because of expiring net operating losses. The IRS also reserves the right to recast a contribution of property in order to avoid tax results inconsistent with the intent of Subchapter K. Reg. § 1.704–3(a)(1).

b. The Ceiling Rule

Under the "ceiling rule," the total income, gain, loss or deduction allocated to a partner for a taxable year with respect to any § 704(c) property may not exceed the total partnership income, gain, loss, or deduction with respect to that property for the taxable year. The ceiling rule, which has traditionally been incorporated into the regulations by the Service, has the effect of temporarily shifting precontribution gains or losses among partners or limiting tax depreciation allocated to noncontributing partners. The purpose of a curative or remedial allocation (see below) is to eliminate the distortions resulting from the ceiling rule.

c. Sales and Exchanges of Contributed Property

1) Traditional Method

Under the traditional method, if a partnership sells § 704(c) property and recognizes gain or loss, the built-in gain or loss inherent in the property at the time of its contribution is allocated for tax purposes to the contributing partner. Reg. § 1.704–3(b)(1). Any additional book gain or loss is allocated in accordance with the partnership agreement if the allocation has substantial economic effect. Reg. § 1.704–1(b)(2)(iv)(b), (d), and (g); –1(b)(5) Example (13)(i). A general principal is to allocate tax gain or loss to the noncontributing partners in an amount equal to their shares of book gain or loss. Under the "ceiling rule," however, the total precontribution gain or loss allocated to the contributing partner with respect to § 704(c) property may not exceed the partnership's total tax gain or loss with respect to that property. Reg. § 1.704–3(b)(1).

Example (1): A and B form the AB equal partnership with A contributing an asset (fair market value, $30,000; basis, $18,000) and B contributing $30,000 cash. If AB sells the asset contributed by A for $30,000, its tax gain is $12,000 ($30,000 amount realized less $18,000 adjusted basis) and its book gain is zero ($30,000 amount realized less $30,000 book value). Under the traditional method, the $12,000 difference between the tax and book gains (all of the precontribution or "built-in gain") is allocated to A and there is no additional book gain.

Example (2): Assume that AB in Example (1) sells the asset contributed by A for $38,000. In that situation its tax gain is $20,000 ($38,000 amount realized less $18,000 adjusted basis) and its book gain is $8,000 ($38,000 less $30,000 book value).

Again, under the traditional method the $12,000 difference between the tax and book gain ($20,000 less $8,000) is allocated to A under § 704(c)(1)(A) and the $8,000 book gain is allocated $4,000 to A and $4,000 to B in accordance with the partnership agreement. A's outside basis would be increased by $16,000 to $34,000. Both A's and B's capital accounts would be increased by $4,000, their respective shares of the partnership's book gain.

Example (3): C and D form the CD equal partnership with C contributing property with a $20,000 fair market value and $24,000 adjusted basis and D contributing $20,000 cash. C and D agree to share all partnership income or loss and distributions equally and in the CD partnership agreement they agree to comply with The Big Three. Assume CD sells the asset contributed by C for $18,000. CD's tax loss is $6,000 ($18,000 amount realized less $24,000 adjusted basis) and its book loss is $2,000 ($18,000 amount realized less $20,000 book value). The $4,000 precontribution built-in loss is allocated to C under the traditional method, and the $2,000 book loss is allocated $1,000 to C and $1,000 to D in accordance with the partnership agreement.

Example (4):
(Ceiling Rule) Assume CD in Example (3) sells the asset contributed by C for $22,000. CD's tax loss is $2,000 ($22,000 less $24,000 adjusted basis) and it has a $2,000 book gain ($22,000 amount realized less $20,000 book value). Ideally, one would like to allocate $4,000 of tax loss (the amount of the precontribution loss) to C and $1,000 of gain (one-half of the total book gain) to both C and D. The traditional method, however, contains a "ceiling" rule under which § 704(c) allocations are limited to the recognized tax gain or loss of the partnership. Thus, all of

the $2,000 tax loss is allocated to C. This has the effect of not requiring D to include the $1,000 of book gain, and the disparity between the partnership's tax and capital accounts is not totally eliminated.

2) Traditional Method with Curative Allocations

A partnership using the traditional method may make reasonable "curative allocations" to correct book/tax disparities created by the ceiling rule. A curative allocation is an allocation that differs from the partnership's allocation of the corresponding book item. Reg. § 1.704–3(c)(1). In the case of sales of § 704(c) property, a curative allocation must be made with respect to the gain or loss from the partnership's sale of other property of similar character. A curative allocation may not exceed the amount necessary to offset the effect of the ceiling rule and must be made using a tax item that would have the same effect on the partners as the tax item affected by the ceiling rule. Reg. § 1.704–3(c)(3)(i) & (iii). Curative allocations may be made to offset ceiling rule distortions from a prior taxable year if they are made over a reasonable period of time and were authorized by the partnership agreement in effect for the year of the contribution of the § 704(c) property. Reg. § 1.704–3(c)(3)(ii). Because curative allocations have only tax effect and not economic effect, they are not reflected in the partners' book capital accounts.

Example: A and B form the AB equal partnership with A contributing Oldacre (value $30,000, basis $22,000) and B contributing $30,000 cash. Oldacre is a capital asset. At the end of its first year, AB sells Oldacre for $25,000. Under the traditional method, AB's $3,000 tax gain ($25,000 amount realized less $22,000 tax basis) is all allocated to A, while the $5,000 book loss ($30,000 book value less $25,000 amount realized) is allocated $2,500 each to A and B. The ceiling rule causes a $2,500 disparity between the partners' book and tax accounts, requiring $2,500 more tax gain to be allocated to A and $2,500 of tax loss to be allocated to B to cure the disparity. If the partnership had other capital gains and losses, an allocation of $2,500 of capital gain to A and $2,500 of capital loss to B would be reasonable curative allocations because they would offset the disparity caused by the ceiling rule.

3) Remedial Method

Curative allocations are allocations of tax items actually realized by the partnership. Remedial allocations are tax allocations of income, gain, loss, or deduction created by the partnership that are offset by other tax allocations of income, gain, loss, or deduction created by the partnership. Reg. § 1.704–3(d)(1). Under the remedial method, if the ceiling rule results in a book allocation to a noncontributing partner that differs from the corresponding tax allocation, the partnership makes a remedial allocation to the noncontributing partner equal to the full amount of the disparity and a simultaneous offsetting remedial allocation to the contributing partner. Id. A remedial allocation must have the same effect on each partner's tax liability as the item limited by the ceiling rule—e.g., capital loss must offset capital gain. Reg. § 1.704–3(d)(3). Remedial allocations are solely for tax purposes and have no effect on the partnership's book capital accounts.

Example: I and J form the IJ equal partnership with I contributing Blackacre (value $10,000, basis $4,000) and J contributing Whiteacre (value $10,000, basis $10,000). At the end of IJ's first taxable year, the partnership sells Blackacre for $9,000, recognizing a capital gain of $5,000 ($9,000 amount realized less $4,000 tax basis), and a book loss of $1,000 ($9,000 amount realized less $10,000 book basis). Under the ceiling rule, I would be allocated the entire $5,000 of tax gain, and the $1,000 book loss would be allocated equally to the partners, creating a $500 disparity between each partner's book and tax accounts. Under the remedial method, IJ may make an allocation of $500 capital loss to J and an offsetting remedial allocation of $500 capital gain to I. This has the same effect as allocating to I the entire $6,000 precontribution gain less I's share ($500) of postcontribution loss (for a net gain of $5,500), and of allocating to J her $500 share of postcontribution loss.

d. Depreciation and Depletion

Section 704(c)(1)(A) also governs the allocation of depreciation and depletion with respect to contributed property. Where a partner contributes depreciable property with a built-in gain to a partnership, a general goal of § 704(c) is to allocate that gain to the contributing partner (even before the asset is sold). A related goal is to ensure that noncontributing partners do not suffer when a contributing partner contributes depreciable property with a tax basis that is less than its book value to the partnership. These goals are accomplished by allocating tax depreciation to the *noncontributing* partners in an amount equal to their share of book depreciation, and then allocating any remaining tax depreciation to the contributing partner. As explained below, the ceiling rule may frustrate these policies.

1) Traditional Method

Under the traditional method, tax depreciation is allocated first to the noncontributing partner in an amount equal to his share of book depreciation and the balance of tax depreciation is allocated to the contributing partner. Reg. § 1.704–3(b)(1). Book and tax depreciation must be computed using the same depreciation method and useful life. Reg. § 1.704–1(b)(2)(iv)(*g*)(3). The ceiling rule, however, limits the tax depreciation allocated to the noncontributing partner to the partnership's total tax depreciation with respect to the contributed property.

Example (1):
(Traditional Method)

L and M form the LM equal partnership with L contributing depreciable equipment with a fair market value of $10,000 and an adjusted basis of $6,000 and M contributing $10,000 cash. The LM partnership agreement complies with The Big Three and provides that § 704(c) allocations shall be made under the traditional method. The equipment has a 10-year remaining recovery period and is depreciated using the straight-line method. The partnership's book depreciation is $1,000 per year (10% × $10,000) and tax depreciation is $600 (10% × $6,000). M, the noncontributing partner, is allocated tax depreciation in an amount up to his share of book depreciation, or $500. The remaining $100 of tax depreciation is allocated to E.

Example (2):
(Ceiling Rule)

Assume that in Example (1), the equipment contributed by L has a basis of $4,000. Book depreciation would again be $1,000 per year, but the partnership's tax depreciation would be only $400 per year (10% × $4,000). Noncontributing partner M should be entitled to $500 of tax depreciation (equal to M's book depreciation). But under the ceiling rule, the partnership may only allocate $400 of tax depreciation, and it must be allocated entirely to M. See Reg. § 1.704–3(b)(2) Example 1(ii).

2) Traditional Method with Curative Allocations

If the ceiling rule causes the noncontributing partner to be allocated less tax depreciation than book depreciation with respect to an item of depreciable § 704(c) property, the traditional method with curative allocations permits the partnership to make a curative allocation to the noncontributing partner of tax depreciation from *another item* of partnership property to make up the difference.

Example (3):
(Curative Allocation)

Assume the same facts as in Example (2), except that LM uses the $10,000 cash contributed by M to purchase inventory for resale. The partnership agreement provides that LM will use the traditional method with curative allocations. As in Example (2), the partnership's annual book depreciation is $1,000 and the tax depreciation is $400, and the ceiling rule requires that no more than $400 of tax depreciation is allocated to M.

Finally, assume that LM sells the inventory for $10,700 at the end of its first year, recognizing $700 of ordinary income, allocated $350 each to L and M for book and tax purposes. Because the ceiling rule creates a $100 disparity between the partners' book and tax accounts, LM may make a curative allocation to L (and away from M) of an additional $100 of ordinary income from the sale of the inventory. See Reg. § 1.704–3(c)(4) Example 1.

3) Remedial Method

To eliminate ceiling rule distortions from depreciation of § 704(c) property, the remedial method allocates ordinary income to the contributing partner and additional tax depreciation to the noncontributing partner. For this purpose, the determination of book and tax depreciation differs from the traditional method. Under the remedial method, the portion of the partnership's book basis in § 704(c) property that is equal to the tax basis of the property at the time of contribution is depreciated under the same method used for tax depreciation (generally, over the property's remaining recovery period at the time of contribution). The amount by which the book basis exceeds the tax basis ("the excess book basis") is depreciated using any applicable recovery period and depreciation method available to the partnership for newly acquired property. Reg. § 1.704–3(d)(2).

Example (4):
(Remedial Method)

Assume the same facts as in Example (2) except that the partnership agreement provides that LM will make § 704(c) allocations using the remedial method and that the straight-line method will be used to recover any excess book basis. Assume that the equipment, which has a $4,000 tax basis, has 10 years remaining on its 20-year recovery period when it is contributed to LM. Tax depreciation is thus $400 per year for 10 years. Under the remedial method, LM's book depreciation for each of its first 10 years is $400 ($4,000 tax basis divided by remaining 10 years in recovery period) plus $300 ($6,000 excess of book value over tax basis divided by a new 20-year recovery period), or $700. To simplify the example, book depreciation is determined without regard to any first-year depreciation convention. L and M are each allocated $350 of book depreciation (50% of $700), M is allocated $350 of tax depreciation and L is allocated the remaining $50 of tax depreciation. No remedial allocations are yet necessary because the ceiling rule does not cause a book allocation of depreciation to the noncontributing partner that differs from the tax allocation. For years 11 through 20, however, LM has $300 of book depreciation, allocated $150 each to L and M, but no more tax depreciation. Since M is allocated $150 of book depreciation but no tax depreciation, LM must make a remedial allocation of $150 of tax depreciation to M and an offsetting allocation of $150 of ordinary income to L for each of years 11 through 20. See Reg. § 1.704–3(d)(5) Example 1.

3. Application of § 704(c)(1)(A) Principles to the Entry of a New Partner

a. Allocation of Preexisting Gains and Losses: In General

The entry of a new partner to an ongoing partnership raises a question as to how the preexisting gains and losses in partnership assets should be allocated among the partners. Ideally, those gains and losses should be allocated to the old partners. The new partner should share in gains and losses accruing after entry into the partnership. The regulations apply § 704(c) principles to resolve this question.

Example (1): G and H form the GH equal partnership by each contributing $20,000 cash, and the partnership uses the $40,000 to purchase securities. In the GH partnership agreement, G and H agree to comply with The Big Three. When the securities are worth $60,000, J joins the partnership as a one-third partner for a contribution of $30,000 cash. The $20,000 of preexisting book gain in the securities should be allocated to G and H, and any subsequent appreciation in the securities above $60,000 should be shared equally among the partners. If the gain is not allocated in this fashion, G and H will have transferred one-third of the $20,000 of appreciation ($6,666) to J and that transfer may be a gift or disguised compensation and treated as such for tax purposes.

b. Methods of Allocating Preexisting Gains and Losses

The regulations provide two ways for partners to accomplish the allocation of preexisting gains and losses.

1) Allocation in Partnership Agreement

The first method is to specifically provide in the partnership agreement for the allocation of such gains and losses to the partners previously in the partnership. Such an allocation has substantial economic effect and will be respected. See Reg. § 1.704–1(b)(5) Example (14)(iv).

2) Revaluation and Restatement of Capital Accounts

Alternatively, the regulations permit the partners to restate their capital accounts to reflect the revaluation of partnership property upon the entry of a new partner. Reg. § 1.704–1(b)(2)(iv)(*f*). Upon revaluation and restatement of the capital accounts, the difference between the partnership's tax and book gain or loss is allocated to the prior partners and any book gain or loss is allocated among all the partners (including the new partner). See Reg. § 1.704–1(b)(4)(i), –1(b)(5) Example (14)(i). These "reverse § 704(c) allocations" may be made under any reasonable method that is consistent with the § 704(c) regulations. Reg. § 1.704–3(a)(6).

Example (2): Assume the same facts as in Example (1), above. If the partnership agreement requires revaluation of partnership assets and restatement of capital accounts upon the entry of a new partner, the securities will be revalued at their fair market value of $60,000 when J enters the partnership. G's and H's capital accounts will each be restated at $30,000. If the securities are later sold for $66,000, the difference between the tax gain of $26,000 ($66,000 amount realized less $40,000 basis) and the book gain of $6,000 ($66,000 amount realized less $60,000 restated book value), or $20,000, would be allocated $10,000 each to G and H. The $6,000 book gain would be allocated $2,000 each to G, H, and J.

4. Distributions of Contributed Property Within Seven Years of Contribution

In most situations, distributions of property by a partnership to a partner do not result in gain or loss to either the partner or the partnership. § 731; see XI.A.2.a., at page 154, *infra*. Under § 704(c)(1)(B), however, if property contributed by a partner is distributed to another partner within seven years of its contribution, the contributing partner is treated as recognizing gain or loss from the sale or exchange of the property in an amount equal to the gain or loss which would have been allocated to that partner under § 704(c)(1)(A) if the property had actually been sold for its fair market value. § 704(c)(1)(B)(i). A related anti-abuse rule applies to a partner who contributes appreciated property and receives a distribution of other property. See § 737. Because these transactions are related to the operating distribution rules, they are discussed in Chapter XI. See XI.C., at page 161, *infra*.

5. Characterization of Gain or Loss upon Partnership's Disposition of Contributed Property

Section 704(c) prevents the shifting among partners of built-in gain or loss when a partnership disposes of contributed property and § 724 prevents the conversion of the character of that gain or loss. Normally, the characterization of partnership gains and losses is determined at the partnership level. § 702(b). Section 724, however, provides different rules for three categories of contributed property: "unrealized receivables," "inventory items," and "capital loss property." To prevent easy avoidance, these rules also apply to any substituted basis property (other than corporate stock received in a § 351 exchange) received in a nonrecognition transaction (or series of transactions) for contributed property subject to § 724. § 724(d)(3).

a. Unrealized Receivables

Under § 724(a) any gain or loss recognized on the disposition of a contributed unrealized receivable is characterized as ordinary income or loss. "Unrealized receivables" generally are defined as rights (contractual or otherwise) to payment not previously included in income for services or property which is not a capital asset. §§ 724(d)(1), 751(c).

Example: A contributes accounts receivable which have a $5,000 fair market value and zero basis to the ABCD partnership. If the partnership collects the receivables or sells them for $5,000, A will be taxed on $5,000 of ordinary income under § 704(c)(1)(A) and § 724. The receivables were unrealized receivables in A's hands and under § 724(a) any income on the receivables is characterized as ordinary even if the receivables might have been a capital asset in the hands of the partnership.

b. Inventory Items

Under § 724(b) any gain or loss recognized on the disposition of a contributed inventory item within five years of contribution is characterized as ordinary income or loss. "Inventory items" generally are defined as property described in § 1221(1) (stock in trade, inventory, and property held primarily for sale to customers) and any other property which if sold by the contributing partner would be considered property other than a capital asset or § 1231 property (without regard to holding period). §§ 724(d)(2), 751(d)(2).

Example: B contributes inventory which has a fair market value of $5,000 and a basis of $3,000 to the BC equal partnership. If the partnership sells the inventory within five years of contribution for $7,000, the first $2,000 of gain will be allocated to B under § 704(c)(1)(A).

The $2,000 of book gain ($7,000 amount realized less $5,000 book value) will be allocated $1,000 to B and $1,000 to C in accordance with the partnership agreement. All of the gain would be characterized as ordinary income under § 724(b). If the inventory is sold for $7,000 more than five years after B's contribution, the gain will be allocated in the same manner. The character of the gain, however, will be determined at the partnership level and would be capital gain if the inventory is a capital asset in the hands of the partnership. § 702(b).

c. Capital Loss Property

Under § 724(c) any loss recognized on the disposition of an asset which was a capital asset in the hands of the contributing partner within five years of the contribution is characterized as a capital loss to the extent that the basis of the property exceeded its fair market value at the time of contribution.

Example (1): D contributes a capital asset which has a fair market value of $12,000 and a basis of $16,000 to the DE equal partnership. Assume DE is a dealer in the type of property contributed by D. If DE sells the property contributed by D within five years of contribution for $10,000, the first $4,000 of loss will be allocated to D under § 704(c)(1)(A). The remaining $2,000 of book loss will be allocated $1,000 to D and $1,000 to E in accordance with the partnership agreement. Under § 724(c) the first $4,000 of loss allocated to D will be capital loss and the remaining $2,000 of loss is characterized at the partnership level as ordinary loss. If the property is sold for $10,000 more than five years after D's contribution, the loss will be allocated in the same manner. The character of the loss, however, will be determined at the partnership level and will all be ordinary loss.

Example (2): If DE in Example (1) sold the property contributed by D for $19,000, the $3,000 of gain ($19,000 amount realized less $16,000 adjusted basis) would be allocated $1,500 to both D and E. The gain would be characterized at the partnership level and will all be ordinary income.

d. Depreciation Recapture

If a partner contributes depreciable property which has potential recapture income under § 1245 or § 1250 to a partnership, the character of that income is preserved by the definition of "recomputed basis" in § 1245(a)(2) and "depreciation adjustments" in § 1250(b)(3).

6. Anti-Abuse Rule for Loss Property

If a partner contributes property with a built-in loss (i.e., the property's adjusted basis exceeds its fair market value) to a partnership, the contribution may eventually result in the loss being shifted to other partners. While Section 704(c)(1)(A) is designed to prevent shifts of precontribution gain or loss to other partners, that section does not apply if the contributing partner is no longer a partner in the partnership. To prevent the shift of precontribution losses to other partners, § 704(c)(1)(C) provides that if contributed property has a built-in loss at the time of contribution, then (1) the built-in loss shall be taken into account only in determining the amount of items allocated to the contributing partner, and (2) except as provided in regulations, in determining the amount of items allocated to other partners, the partnership's basis in the contributed property is deemed to be its fair market value at the time of contribution.

B. Partnership Interests Created by Gift or Acquired by Purchase from Family Member

1. Purpose of § 704(e)

Section 704(e) largely codifies the assignment of income principles studied in individual income tax. Its purpose is to prevent the shifting of income among partners who are not dealing at arm's length, such as family members and others who receive partnership interests by gift. Historically, the provisions in § 704(e) were known as "the family partnership rules" even though they also apply to donees who may not be related to the donor.

2. Definitions of Partnership and Partner

Section 704(e)(1) applies only in the context of a partnership. Thus, there may be an initial question of whether an economic relationship constitutes a partnership. In general, the existence of a partnership is established under case law by showing a bona fide intent to conduct an enterprise as partners. *Comm'r v. Culbertson*, 337 U.S. 733, 69 S.Ct. 1210 (1949). A "partner" means a member of a "partnership." § 761(b). In the case of a partnership in which capital is a material income-producing factor, whether a person is a partner with respect to such interest is determined without regard to whether the interest was derived by gift from any other person. Id.

3. Determination of Distributive Share of Donee

Under § 704(e)(1), when a partnership interest is created by gift (from a family member or otherwise), the donee's distributive share that is includible in gross income is determined under the partnership agreement but must be adjusted to the extent that: (1) it is determined without reasonably compensating for services provided by the donor to the partnership, or (2) the portion of the donee's distributive share attributable to donated capital is proportionately greater than the donor's distributive share attributable to the donor's capital. This rule also applies to partnership interests purchased from a family member, and the fair market value of the purchased interest is considered to be donated capital. The "family" of an individual includes only his spouse, ancestors, lineal descendants, and trusts for the primary benefit of such persons. § 704(e)(2).

Example: Mother owns $500,000 of securities which she contributes to a partnership in which she is an equal partner with Daughter, who provides no capital for her one-half interest in the partnership. The income from the partnership is $75,000. Assume that under *Culbertson* Daughter will be recognized as a partner in the partnership because Mother and Daughter had a bona fide intent to join together in the present conduct of an enterprise. Daughter's distributive share must be determined so as to reasonably compensate Mother for all services she has rendered to the partnership. § 704(e)(1). If, for example, Mother provides investment management services to the partnership with a reasonable value of $15,000, an allocation of partnership profits which did not compensate her for those services (e.g., $37,500 of profits to both Mother and Daughter) would not be respected. An allocation which did not compensate Mother for her partnership capital at the same rate as Daughter also would not be respected. The same analysis would apply if Daughter purchased her partnership interest from Mother for $250,000. § 704(e)(2).

C. Allocations Where Partners' Interests Vary During the Year

1. Introduction

The taxable year of a partnership generally does not close as a result of shifts during the year in the partners' interests in the partnership. For example, if a new partner enters the partnership, or a partner disposes of part of her partnership interest through a gift or sale, the partnership's taxable year closes at its normal time and the partners include their distributive share of partnership items at that time. § 706(c)(1), (2)(B). If, however, there are changes during the year in any partner's interest in the partnership (by entry of a new partner, partial liquidation of the partner's interest, gift or otherwise), § 706(d)(1) requires that each partner's distributive share of partnership items be determined by taking into account the partners' varying interests in the partnership during the year. The varying interest rule in § 706(d)(1), however, applies only if there is some shift in the capital interests of the partners. If the capital interests of the partners do not shift during the year, the partners generally are free at year end to amend the partnership agreement and reallocate profits and losses. §§ 704(a); 761(c).

2. Determination of Distributive Shares

a. Permissible Allocation Methods

When there is a change in a partner's capital interest in the partnership, the regulations generally require the distributive shares of the partners to be determined by either (1) an interim closing of the partnership's books in which the items of income and deduction are allocated to different segments of the year under the partnership's accounting method or (2) by prorating partnership items over the year as if they were earned or incurred ratably throughout the year.

Conventions (i.e., rules of convenience such as calendar day, semi-monthly, and monthly) are also used to determine the timing of variations in the partners' interests. Reg. § 1.706–4(c).

The regulations provide that the interim closing of the books method is the default method unless the partners formally agree to use the proration method. § 1.706–4(a)(3)(iii), (f). The partnership may use different methods (interim closing or proration) for different transactions producing variations in partnership interests occurring during the taxable year, subject to guidance from the IRS Reg. § 1.706–4(a)(3)(iii).

The regulations (and § 706(d)) do not apply to changes in allocations of § 702(a) items among contemporaneous partners for the entire partnership taxable year if (1) the allocations are not attributable to a contribution of money or capital or a distribution that is a return of capital, and (2) the allocations satisfy § 704(b). Reg. § 1.706–4(b)(1).

> ***Example:*** Assume Nupartner joins a partnership as a one-fourth partner on July 1 of the current year. Under § 706(d)(1) all of the partners' distributive shares must be determined by taking into account their varying interests during the year. Under the default interim closing of the books method, Nupartner would be allocated one-fourth of the partnership items properly allocated to the July 1 to December 31 period under the partnership's method of accounting. If the partnership properly elected the proration method, Nupartner would be allocated one-half of his hypothetical one-fourth share of partnership items for the full year.

b. Services Partnerships

A special safe harbor is provided for services partnerships, which are defined as partnerships in which capital is not a material-income producing factor. Services partnership may use any reasonable method to account for the varying interests of the partners provided the allocations are valid under § 704(b). Reg. 1.706–4(b)(2).

c. Allocation of Extraordinary Items

"Extraordinary items" must be allocated by a partnership among the partners in proportion to their interests at the time of day on which the extraordinary item occurred regardless of the method and convention otherwise used by the partnership. Extraordinary events are defined with a "small item" exception and generally include dispositions of assets, and certain "special events," like changes in accounting methods, items from discharge of indebtedness, and settlement of a tort (or similar liability) or payment of a judgment.

3. Distributive Shares of Allocable Cash Basis Items: § 706(d)(2)

a. Determination on Per-Day, Per-Partner Basis

To prevent cash method partnerships from using the interim closing of the books method to shift deductions to partners entering the partnership at or near year end, § 706(d)(2)(A) requires that, if there is a change in any partner's interest in the partnership, each partner's distributive share of any "allocable cash basis item" must be determined on a per-day, per-partner basis. This requirement effectively puts cash method partnerships on the accrual method of accounting for allocable cash basis items, which are defined as interest, taxes, payments for services or the use of property, and any other item identified in regulations by the Service. § 706(d)(2)(B).

Example: Nupartner joins a cash method partnership as a 50% partner on December 31 of the current year. Late in the afternoon of December 31, the partnership pays $100,000 of interest which is the annual payment on a partnership loan. Under the interim closing of the books method of allocation Nupartner could have been allocated one-half of the $100,000 interest deduction. Under § 706(d)(2)(A), however, Nupartner will be allocated one-half of 1/365th of the $100,000 interest deduction.

b. Items Attributable to Periods Not Within Taxable Year

If an allocable cash basis item is attributable to a prior year (e.g., rental paid for property used in the preceding year), it is assigned to the first day of the taxable year in which it is paid. § 706(d)(2)(C)(i). It is then allocated among the partners who were partners in such prior year in proportion to their varying interests in the partnership for that period. Amounts which are allocable under this rule to persons who are no longer partners must be capitalized as part of the bases of partnership assets. § 706(d)(2)(D). If an allocable cash basis item is attributable to a period after the close of the taxable year (e.g., prepaid rent for the next year), it is assigned to the last day of the taxable year in which it is paid and allocated to the partners in accordance with their proportionate interests on that date. § 706(d)(2)(C)(ii).

Example: Assume the ABCD equal partnership fails to pay $40,000 of rental expense in year one. On December 31 of year one, A sells her 25% interest in the partnership to B so that beginning in year two B owns 50% of the partnership and C and D each own 25%. If the partnership pays the $40,000 of rental expense in year two, B, C and D will each be allocated $10,000 of the deduction (corresponding to their 25% interests in year one). A cannot be allocated a share of the year two expenditure since she is no longer a partner. Her $10,000 share of the rental expense will be capitalized and added to the bases of partnership assets under the rules in § 755. See X.C.2.b.2., at page 146, *infra*.

4. Tiered Partnerships

The potential exists for these rules to be avoided by using tiers of partnerships. For example, a business could be operated in a partnership (the "lower-tier" partnership) which has other partnerships ("upper-tier" partnerships) as its partners. Changes in ownership of upper-tier partnerships would not alter ownership of the lower-tier partnerships and would not be subject to § 706(d). In order to prevent easy avoidance of the varying interest and allocable cash basis item rules in § 706(d), if there is a change in any partner's interest in an upper-tier partnership then the distributive shares of the partners in the upper-tier partnership attributable to a lower-tier partnership must be determined on a per-day, per-partner basis. § 706(d)(3).

D. Review Questions

1. A and B form the AB equal general partnership. A contributes $50,000 cash and a parcel of land with a fair market value of $50,000 and an adjusted basis of $20,000, while B contributes $100,000 cash. A and B agree to comply with The Big Three, to share all profits and losses equally, and to use the traditional method in making § 704(c) allocations.

    (a) If AB sells the parcel of land for $70,000, what are the tax consequences to A and B?

    (b) If AB sells the parcel of land for $40,000, what are the tax consequences to A and B?

2. A and B form the AB equal general partnership. A contributes $50,000 cash and a depreciable asset with a fair market value of $50,000 and an adjusted basis of $20,000. Assume the property is depreciable by the partnership over five years under the straight line method. B contributes $100,000 cash. A and B agree to comply with The Big Three, to share all profits and losses equally, and to use the traditional method in making § 704(c) allocations.

    (a) What is the amount of depreciation in Year 1 for book purposes and for tax purposes?

    (b) How is the depreciation allocated between A and B?

    (c) What are A's and B's outside bases in their partnership interests at the end of Year 1? Assume that AB breaks even except for cost recovery deductions.

    (d) What are the balances in A's and B's capital accounts at the end of Year 1? Assume that AB breaks even except for cost recovery deductions.

3. If A contributes accounts receivable with a fair market value of $50,000 and zero adjusted basis to a partnership, what are the tax consequences to A in the following circumstances?

    (a) The partnership sells the receivables in Year 1 for $50,000?

    (b) The partnership sells the receivables in Year 6 for $50,000?

4. If A, a car dealer, contributes cars with a fair market value of $100,000 and an adjusted basis of $60,000 to the ABC partnership, what are the tax consequences to A under the following circumstances:

    (a) If ABC (not in the car business) sells the cars for $100,000 in Year 1?

    (b) If ABC (not in the car business) sells the cars for $100,000 in Year 6?

5. D joins the ABC partnership as a one-quarter partner on July 1. If the partnership has income of $36,000 for the year and the partners properly elect to use the proration method of allocation, how will the income be allocated to A, B, C and D?

Chapter VII

Partnership Liabilities

■ **ANALYSIS**

A. Introduction
B. Economic Risk of Loss
    1. General Rules
    2. The Relationship Between Economic Risk of Loss and Economic Effect
    3. Proposed Regulations
C. Nonrecourse Liabilities
    1. General Rules
    2. Proposed Regulations
D. Special Rules
    1. Part Recourse and Part Nonrecourse Liabilities
    2. Tiered Partnerships
E. Review Questions

A. Introduction

The basis of a partnership interest has important tax consequences for the partner owning that interest. Under § 704(d), a partner's ability to currently deduct his share of partnership losses is limited to the amount of the partner's outside basis. Outside basis also is the limit on the amount of cash which may be distributed to the partner without recognition of gain. And, of course, outside basis will be a determinant of the amount of the partner's gain or loss if the partnership interest is sold.

The effect of partnership liabilities on outside basis was introduced in Chapter 2, when formation of a partnership was discussed. This chapter provides greater detail on allocation of partnership liabilities among partners. First, recall the basics. Under § 752(a), an increase in a partner's share of partnership liabilities is considered a contribution of money which increases the partner's outside basis under § 722. A decrease in a partner's share of partnership liabilities is considered under § 752(b) to be a distribution of money to the partner which decreases the partner's outside basis (but not below zero) under §§ 705(a) and 733. If a decrease in a partner's share of partnership liabilities exceeds the partner's outside basis, the partner must recognize the excess as capital gain from the sale or exchange of the partnership interest. §§ 731(a)(1); 741.

Liabilities are classified as recourse or nonrecourse using the concept of "economic risk of loss." A partnership liability is classified as "recourse" only to the extent that a partner bears the economic risk of loss for the liability. Reg. § 1.752–1(a)(1). A partner's share of the recourse liabilities of a partnership also equals the portion of the recourse liabilities for which the partner bears the economic risk of loss. Reg. § 1.752–2(a). A liability is "nonrecourse" to the extent that no partner bears the economic risk of loss for the liability. Reg. § 1.752–1(a)(2). The partners generally share nonrecourse liabilities in proportion to their share of partnership profits. Reg. § 1.752–3(a).

The remainder of the chapter closely examines the concept of economic risk of loss and the detailed rules for allocating nonrecourse liabilities.

B. Economic Risk of Loss

1. General Rules

A partner bears the economic risk of loss for a partnership liability to the extent that the partner would bear the economic burden of discharging the obligation represented by the liability if the partnership were unable to do so. The regulations employ a "doomsday" liquidation analysis to determine whether a partner bears the economic risk of loss for a liability. Basically, the regulations assume that all of the partnership assets are worthless, all of the partnership liabilities are due and payable and the partnership disposes of all its assets in a fully taxable transaction for no consideration. They then ask whether any partner or partners would be obligated to make a payment to a creditor or contribution to the partnership in order to pay the liability. § 1.752–2(b)(1). If a partner or partners are so obligated, the liability is a recourse liability and is shared by the partners who bear the economic risk of loss. For this purpose, guarantees, indemnifications, and other reimbursement arrangements are taken into account. Reg. § 1.752–2(b)(3)(i)–(iii), –2(b)(5). A payment obligation is disregarded if it is: (1) subject to contingencies unlikely to occur, or (2) arises at a future time after an event that is not determinable with reasonable accuracy. Reg. § 1.752–2(b)(4). It generally is assumed that a partner will actually discharge an obligation even if the partner's net worth is less than the amount of the obligation. Reg. § 1.752–2(b)(6).

Example (1):   Equal partners in a general partnership ordinarily will share the economic risk of loss for any partnership recourse liability equally because they share the economic burden of that debt equally. Similarly, limited partners ordinarily do not bear the economic risk of loss for any partnership liability because they generally have no obligation to contribute additional capital to the partnership.

Example (2):   C and D each contribute $500 in cash to the new CD general partnership. CD purchases property from an unrelated seller for $10,000, paying $1,000 cash and borrowing $9,000. The debt is evidenced by a note that is a general obligation of the partnership— i.e., no partner is relieved from personal liability. Under the partnership agreement, C and D agree to share partnership profits and losses 40% to C and 60% to D. The partners' shares of the $9,000 note depend on how they would bear the economic risk of loss for the liability in a constructive liquidation of the partnership. That depends on the effect of their allocation of profits and losses on their capital accounts and obligations to the partnership. Reg. § 1.752–2(f) Examples 1 and 2. That topic is covered below. See VII.B.2., at page 108, *infra,* for a discussion of this issue and an example.

Example (3):   G, the general partner, and L, the limited partner, form the GL limited partnership with each contributing $10,000 cash. G and L agree to share partnership profits and losses equally. GL purchases a parcel of rental real estate for $20,000 cash and $80,000 of nonrecourse financing which is secured by the property. Under the terms of the loan the lender may only look to the rental real estate if GL defaults on the loan. In addition, G personally guarantees the loan. Under the guarantee, if GL defaults on the loan, G will pay the lender the difference between the balance of the loan and the property's value. Under the doomsday liquidation analysis, if the property becomes worthless and the loan becomes due, G will be obligated to pay the lender under the guarantee. Accordingly, G bears the economic risk of loss for the full liability and it is a "recourse" liability. See Reg. § 1.752–2(f) Example 5.

Example (4):   Assume the same facts as Example (3), except that in connection with G's guarantee, G and L enter into an indemnification agreement under which L agrees to reimburse G for 50% of any payment that G is required to make under the guarantee. Under these facts, G and L each bear the economic risk of loss for 50% of GL's liability under the guarantee and indemnification agreement. The liability is a recourse liability which will be shared equally by G and L. See Rev. Rul. 83–151, 1983–2 C.B. 105.

Example (5):   G, the general partner, and L, the limited partner, form the GL limited partnership with each contributing $20,000. G and L agree to share partnership profits and losses equally. GL purchases investment real property for $40,000 cash and a recourse purchase money note for $60,000. Under the regulations, G bears the economic risk of loss for the liability because she would be legally obligated to make a contribution to GL to pay the liability in a doomsday liquidation.

Example (6): Assume the same facts as Example (5), except that L, the limited partner, guarantees GL's liability. Under the guarantee, if GL defaults on the liability, L is obligated to pay the outstanding balance of the debt. In addition, L is subrogated to the lender's rights against GL under the loan for any payments made pursuant to the guarantee. Under the regulations, G still bears the economic risk of loss for the liability. While L may have to pay the liability under the guarantee, he is entitled to reimbursement by GL for any payments made under the guarantee pursuant to his right to subrogation. G, as general partner, is obligated to make a contribution to GL in order to pay the balance of the loan to L, as subrogee. See Reg. § 1.752–2(f) Examples 3 & 4.

2. The Relationship Between Economic Risk of Loss and Economic Effect

Under the § 752 regulations, a partnership liability is classified as "recourse" to the extent that one or more partners bear the economic risk of loss for the liability. Reg. § 1.752–1(a)(1). A partner's share of a recourse partnership liability equals the portion of the liability for which the partner bears the economic risk of loss. Reg. § 1.752–2(a). A partner is considered to bear the economic risk of loss for a partnership liability to the extent that, if the partnership constructively liquidated, the partner would be obligated to make a payment because that liability became due and payable. Reg. § 1.752–2(b)(1). All statutory and contractual obligations are taken into account in determining whether a partner has such an obligation, including the obligation to make a capital contribution to restore a deficit capital account on liquidation of the partnership. Reg. § 1.752–2(b)(3)(ii). See V.A.2.c., at page 72, *supra*. Thus, the economic risk of loss analysis used to allocate partnership liabilities under § 752 and the § 704(b) economic effect test are conceptually linked and often correspond to one another. Because of this relationship, capital account analysis frequently assists in determining which partners bear the economic risk of loss for a partnership liability in more complicated situations.

Example: A and B form a general partnership with each contributing $20,000 cash. A and B agree to share all partnership profits equally but partnership net taxable loss will be allocated 90% to A and 10% to B. A and B also agree to comply with The Big Three. The partnership purchases depreciable personal property for $40,000 in cash and a recourse purchase money note of $60,000. Under the doomsday liquidation analysis employed by the § 752 regulations, all partnership assets are deemed worthless and all partnership liabilities are deemed due and payable. If the partnership immediately liquidated after incurring the purchase money obligation, it would recognize a $100,000 tax loss on the disposition of its depreciable personal property for no consideration. Under the partnership agreement, A would be allocated $90,000 of the loss and B $10,000. Their capital accounts would be adjusted as follows:

	A	**B**
Capital Account	$20,000	$20,000
Less Loss	− $90,000	− $10,000
	$70,000	$10,000

If the partnership were liquidated, A would be required to contribute $70,000 to restore her deficit capital account balance. The $70,000 would be used to repay the $60,000 purchase money obligation and distribute $10,000 to B. Thus, even though the lender could attempt to recover the balance on the note from either general partner, A and B have agreed, as between them, that A will bear the economic risk of loss for the loan. Therefore, the liability is allocated entirely to A. See Reg. § 1.752–2(f) Example 1.

3. Proposed Regulations

Regulations have been proposed which, if finalized, would fundamentally change the allocation of recourse liabilities under § 752. The proposed regulations would end the "doomsday" liquidation analysis. The new test would basically attempts a more realistic examination of whether the partner will be called upon to honor a financial commitment on behalf of the partnership. Under the proposed regulations, an obligation will be respected for § 752 purposes *only if* the partner satisfies a number of conditions: (1) the partner must maintain a reasonable net worth throughout the term of the payment obligation or is subject to commercially reasonable contractual restrictions on the transfer of assets for inadequate consideration; (2) the partner is required to periodically provide commercially reasonable documentation regarding the partner's financial condition; (3) the term of the payment obligation does not end prior to the term of the partnership liability; (4) the payment obligation does not require that the primary obligor or any other obligor hold money or other liquid assets in an amount that exceeds the reasonable needs of such obligor; (5) the partner received reasonable arm's length consideration for assuming the payment obligation; (6) in the case of a guarantee or similar arrangement, the partner is or would be liable for the full amount of the partner's payment obligation if and to the extent any amount of the partnership liability is not otherwise satisfied; and (7) in the case of an indemnity, reimbursement agreement, or similar arrangement, the partner is or would be liable for the full amount of such partner's payment obligation if and to the extent any amount of the indemnitee's or benefitted party's payment obligation is satisfied. See Prop. Reg. § 1.752–2(b)(3)(ii).

C. Nonrecourse Liabilities

1. General Rules

A partner's share of partnership nonrecourse liabilities is equal to the sum of: (1) the partner's share of "partnership minimum gain" and (2) the amount of any taxable gain that would be allocated to the partner under § 704(c) if the partnership disposed of its property subject to nonrecourse liabilities for relief of such liabilities and no other consideration. Reg. § 1.752–3(a)(1) & (2). Any remaining partnership nonrecourse liabilities are shared by the partners in accordance with their shares in partnership profits. Reg. § 1.752–3(a)(3). The partners' interests in partnership profits are determined by taking into account all facts and circumstances relating to the economic arrangements of the partners. The regulations also permit the partners to specify their interests in partnership profits for purposes of determining their shares of nonrecourse liabilities as long as the interests are reasonably consistent with allocations of some significant items of partnership income or gain among the partners.

Alternatively, the partners may agree to allocate any remaining nonrecourse liabilities in the manner in which it is reasonably expected that the deductions attributable to those nonrecourse liabilities will be allocated. Additionally, in the case of contributed property subject to a nonrecourse liability, the partnership may first allocate an excess nonrecourse liability to the contributing partner to the extent that Section 704(c) gain on the property is greater than the gain resulting from the liability exceeding the property's basis. The method used to allocate nonrecourse liabilities remaining after considering partnership minimum gain and § 704(c) gain may vary from year to year.

Example (1):
(Allocation per Specified Interests in Profits and Minimum Gain)

G and L form the GL limited partnership with G, the general partner, contributing $20,000 and L, the limited partner, contributing $180,000. The partnership purchases a building (on leased land) for $1,000,000, paying $200,000 cash and borrowing $800,000 on a nonrecourse basis. The loan is secured by the building and no principal payments are due for ten years (only interest is payable during that period). The partnership agreement requires proper maintenance of the partners' capital accounts and liquidation of the partnership in accordance with positive capital account balances. Only G is obligated to restore a deficit in her capital account. The partnership agreement also contains a qualified income offset and a minimum gain chargeback.

Except as required by the qualified income offset or minimum gain chargeback, all partnership items are allocated 10% to G and 90% to L until the partnership has recognized items of income and gain that exceed the items of loss and deduction it previously has recognized, and thereafter all additional partnership items will be allocated equally between G and L. Finally, the partnership agreement specifies that G and L have equal interests in partnership profits for purposes of determining their share of partnership nonrecourse liabilities and at the time the partnership agreement is entered into there is a reasonable likelihood that over its life GL will recognize income and gain significantly in excess of the amount of loss and deduction it recognizes. Assume for simplicity that each year GL's business operations break even (cash income equals cash expense), except that it also has $50,000 of cost recovery deductions.

The $800,000 partnership liability is a nonrecourse liability because no partner bears the economic risk of loss. At the end of each of GL's first four years, the nonrecourse liability will be allocated equally between G and L ($400,000 to each) because the partnership agreement provision so directing is reasonably consistent with the equal division of partnership income and gain that is required once cumulative income and gain exceeds cumulative loss and deduction. See Reg. § 1.704–2(m) Example (1)(ii) & (iii).

At the end of GL's fifth year there is $50,000 of partnership minimum gain ($800,000 nonrecourse liability less property's $750,000 adjusted basis) and G's and L's shares will be $5,000 and $45,000, respectively. The $800,000 nonrecourse liability will be allocated to the partners first according to their shares of minimum gain and any excess will be allocated equally according to the provision in the partnership agreement. Thus, at the end of year five, G's and L's shares of nonrecourse liabilities are $380,000 ($5,000 share of partnership minimum gain plus $375,000 share of the excess) and $420,000 ($45,000 share of minimum gain plus $375,000 share of excess), respectively. See generally, Reg. § 1.752–3(b) Example (1).

Example (2):
(Allocation upon Contribution of Property Encumbered by Nonrecourse Liability)

B and C form a general partnership to operate residential rental property. B contributes $500,000 cash to the partnership and C contributes an apartment building with a fair market value of $1,200,000 and a $520,000 adjusted basis. The apartment building contributed by C is subject to a $700,000 nonrecourse loan. It is expected that B will actively manage the partnership and B and C agree to share all partnership profits and losses equally.

The liability encumbering the apartment building will be a nonrecourse liability of the partnership because no partner bears the economic risk of loss for the liability. Under § 752(c) the partnership is considered to have assumed the liability upon C's contribution of the building to the partnership. As a result of this assumption, C's individual liabilities decrease by $700,000.

The partners' shares of nonrecourse liabilities will be determined under the three-tiered regime of Reg. § 1.752–3.

Tier 1 Allocation. First, partnership minimum gain is computed using the apartment building's book value rather than its tax basis. Reg. § 1.704–2(d)(3). Thus, because the book value ($1,200,000) exceeds the amount of the nonrecourse liability ($700,000), there is no partnership minimum gain.

Tier 2 Allocation. Under Reg. § 1.752–3(a)(2), a partner's share of the nonrecourse liabilities next includes the amount of taxable gain that would be allocated to the contributing partner under § 704(c) if the partnership, in a taxable transaction, disposed of the contributed property in full satisfaction of the nonrecourse liability and for no other consideration. If BC sold the apartment building in full satisfaction of the liability and for no other consideration it would recognize a $180,000 taxable gain ($700,000 amount of the nonrecourse liability over $520,000 adjusted basis). The hypothetical sale would also result in a $500,000 book loss to BC (excess of $1,200,000 book value over $700,000 amount of nonrecourse liability). Under the partnership agreement, the book loss would be allocated equally between B and C. Because B receives a $250,000 book loss and no corresponding tax loss, the hypothetical sale would result in a $250,000 disparity between B's book and tax allocations.

If BC used the traditional method of making § 704(c) allocations, C would be allocated a total of $180,000 of taxable gain from the hypothetical sale of the contributed property. Therefore, C would be allocated $180,000 of nonrecourse liabilities under the regulations. If BC adopted the remedial allocation method of making § 704(c) allocations, it would make a remedial allocation of $250,000 of loss to B to eliminate the $250,000 disparity between B's book and tax allocations. BC would also be required to make an offsetting remedial allocation of tax gain to C of $250,000. Thus, C would be allocated a total of $430,000 of tax gain ($180,000 of actual gain to C plus $250,000 allocation of remedial gain) from the hypothetical sale. Therefore, if BC adopts the remedial allocation method, C would be allocated $430,000 of nonrecourse liabilities immediately after the contribution. If BC uses the traditional method with curative allocations to reduce or eliminate the difference between B's book and tax allocations, the IRS takes the position that curative allocations to C are not taken into account in allocating nonrecourse liabilities because such allocations cannot be determined solely from the hypothetical sale of the apartment building. Rev. Rul. 95–41, 1995–1 C.B. 132. Thus, under the traditional method with curative allocations, C would be allocated $180,000 of nonrecourse liabilities immediately after the contribution.

Tier 3 Allocation. Finally, under the regulations, the remaining nonrecourse liabilities ($520,000 under the traditional method and the traditional method with curative allocations; $270,000 under the remedial method) are allocated between B and C in accordance with their shares in partnership profits. The partner's interests in partnership profits is determined by taking into account all facts and circumstances relating to the economic arrangement of the partners. The partnership agreement also may specify the partner's interests in profits for purposes of determining their shares of nonrecourse liabilities as long as the interests are reasonably consistent with allocations of some other significant item of partnership income or gain. Alternatively, the partners may agree to allocate the remaining nonrecourse liabilities in the manner in which it is reasonably expected that the deductions attributable to the excess nonrecourse liabilities will be allocated. Additionally, the partnership could allocate the remaining nonrecourse liabilities to C, up to the amount of built-in gain that is allocable to C in excess of the gain resulting from the liability exceeding the property's basis.

In this example, the partnership agreement provides that each partner will be allocated 50% of all partnership items. Assuming that those allocations have substantial economic effect, BC could choose to allocate the additional nonrecourse liabilities 50% to each partner. Alternatively, if the partners agreed to allocate the additional nonrecourse liabilities in the manner in which it is reasonably expected that the deductions attributable to those liabilities will be allocated, all the remaining liabilities would be allocated to B. As 50 percent partners, B and C would each be allocated $600,000 of book depreciation over the life of the apartment building. However, because the apartment building only has a $520,000 adjusted basis, the entire $520,000 of tax depreciation over the life of the property must be allocated to B. Therefore, BC must allocate all of the excess liabilities to B if it chooses to allocate the excess nonrecourse liabilities in accordance with the manner that the deductions attributable to the excess nonrecourse liabilities will be allocated. See Rev. Rul. 95–41, 1995–1 C.B. 132. The partnership also could allocate the remaining nonrecourse liabilities to C, up to the amount of built-in gain that is allocable to C in excess of the gain resulting from the liability exceeding the property's basis. There is $680,000 of total § 704(c) gain allocable to C [$680,000 tax gain ($1,200,000 amount realized less $520,000 adjusted basis) and zero book gain ($1,200,000 amount realized less $1,200,000 book value)]. Thus, there is $500,000 of total § 704(c) gain in excess of the gain resulting from the liability exceeding the property's basis ($680,000 of total § 704(c) gain less $180,000 of gain under the traditional method from the liability exceeding the property's basis). Up to $500,000 of the remaining nonrecourse liability could be allocated to C. Under the remedial allocation method there would be $250,000 of total § 704(c) gain in excess of the gain resulting from the liability exceeding the property's basis ($680,000 of total § 704(c) gain less $430,000 of gain allocated under the remedial method). Up to $250,000 of the remaining nonrecourse liability could be allocated to C.

C's individual liabilities decrease by $700,000. Once C's increase in partnership liabilities is determined, the net decrease is taken into account under § 752. Reg. § 1.752–1(f). The net decrease will be treated as a distribution of money which reduces C's outside basis. See §§ 731; 733.

2. Proposed Regulations

Proposed regulations have been issued which, if finalized, would alter the allocation of nonrecourse liabilities among partners. The proposed regulations would alter the manner in which excess nonrecourse liabilities (Tier 3) are allocated. Under the proposed regulations such liabilities would be allocated based on the percentages of the amounts the partners would be entitled to receive if the partnership sold all of its property and each partner received his or her share of the proceeds. See Prop. Reg. § 1.752–3(a)(3).

D. Special Rules

1. Part Recourse and Part Nonrecourse Liabilities

The regulations provide that if a partner or partners bear the economic risk of loss for only a portion of a liability, the liability is bifurcated and treated as part recourse and part nonrecourse. Reg. § 1.752–1(i). For example, if a partner personally guarantees 50% of a nonrecourse liability, the partner bears the economic risk of loss for 50% of that liability and the liability is treated as recourse to that extent. See Rev. Rul. 84–118, 1984–2 C.B. 120.

2. Tiered Partnerships

If a partnership (the "upper-tier partnership") is a partner in another partnership (the "subsidiary partnership"), the upper-tier partnership's share of the subsidiary partnership's liabilities (other than liabilities owed to the upper-tier partnership) are treated as liabilities of the upper-tier partnership for purposes of applying § 752 to the partners of the upper-tier partnership. Reg. § 1.752–4(a); see Rev. Rul. 77–309, 1977–2 C.B. 216.

Example: The AB equal general partnership is a 30% general partner in another general partnership which has a $20,000 recourse liability outstanding. As a 30% general partner, AB's share of the $20,000 liability is $6,000 which will be treated as a liability of the AB partnership for purposes of applying the § 752 regulations to A and B. If the $6,000 were AB's only liability, it would be shared equally by its general partners, $3,000 to A and $3,000 to B.

E. Review Questions

1. A and B form the AB equal general partnership. A contributes $100,000 of cash and B contributes property with a $160,000 fair market value, $20,000 adjusted basis and subject to a $60,000 nonrecourse loan. The AB partnership agreement complies with The Big Three, provides that the partners share profits and losses equally, and uses the traditional method to make § 704(c) allocations. What are A and B's outside bases in their partnership interests?

2. L, a limited partner in the HL Partnership, guarantees a partnership liability which is a general liability of the partnership. Under state law, L will be subrogated to the rights of the lender. Does L bear the economic risk of loss for the liability?

Chapter VIII

Compensating the Service Partner

■ ANALYSIS

A. Payments for Services: General Rules
    1. Services Rendered in a Nonpartner Capacity: § 707(a)(1)
    2. Disguised Payments for Services: § 707(a)(2)(A)
    3. Guaranteed Payments for Services: § 707(c)
B. Partnership Equity Issued in Exchange for Services
    1. Introduction
    2. Capital Interest vs. Profits Interest
    3. Receipt of a Capital Interest for Services
    4. Receipt of a Profits Interest for Services
    5. Proposed Regulations
C. Policy Issues: Carried Interests
    1. Tax Advantages of Carried Interests
    2. Criticisms of Current Tax Treatment
D. Review Questions

A. Payments for Services: General Rules

1. Services Rendered in a Nonpartner Capacity: § 707(a)(1)

a. General Rules

A partner and a partnership may engage in a wide variety of transactions. Section 707(a)(1) generally adopts an entity theory for determining the tax consequences of these transactions by providing that if a partner engages in a transaction with a partnership "other than in his capacity as a member of such partnership," the transaction is to be taxed as if it occurred between the partnership and a nonpartner unless § 707 provides otherwise. The key question under § 707(a)(1) is whether the partner is engaging in the transaction in an independent, nonpartner capacity.

b. Tax Stakes

Classifying a payment for services as being between the partnership and a nonpartner may affect the character and timing of income and deductions arising from the transaction.

Example: The ABC partnership has $150,000 of bottom line income and $50,000 of long-term capital gain for the year. If A receives $50,000 for performing services for the partnership, plus one-third of any remaining partnership income, the classification of A's services will affect the tax results to A and the remaining partners. If the $50,000 is an allocation of partnership income, A will be taxed on $100,000 of partnership income ($50,000 plus one-third of the remaining $150,000 of partnership income), consisting of $75,000 of ordinary income and $25,000 of long-term capital gain, in the year in which the partnership's taxable year ends. § 706(a). The distributive shares of the remaining partners, B and C, would be proportionately reduced to $50,000 each, consisting of $37,500 of ordinary income and $12,500 of long-term capital gain. If the $50,000 paid to A is a § 707(a) payment because the services were performed in a nonpartner capacity, A would have $50,000 of ordinary income under § 61 upon receipt of the payment, assuming A is a cash method taxpayer. Assuming the partnership uses the cash method and the payment for A's services is currently deductible, A, B, and C would be taxed on their one-third distributive shares of the partnership's remaining $100,000 of net income ($150,000 less the $50,000 deduction for A's services) and $50,000 of long-term capital gain. Thus, each would include $33,333 of ordinary income and $16,666 of long-term capital gain. If the payment to A had to be capitalized by the partnership, A, B, and C would be taxed on their one-third distributive shares of $150,000 of net income and $50,000 of long-term capital gain. If the partnership uses the accrual method of accounting and A is a cash method taxpayer, no deduction would be allowed to the partnership for the services until it pays the $50,000 to A. § 267(a), (e).

c. Determination of Partner or Nonpartner Status

The regulations offer little guidance concerning how to determine whether services are being provided in a partner or nonpartner capacity, stating only that "the substance of the transaction will govern rather than its form." Reg. § 1.707–1(a). In the area of services, the courts have held that when partners perform "basic duties" or "services within the normal scope of their duties as general partners" pursuant to the partnership agreement, they are acting in their capacity as partners. *Pratt v. Comm'r*, 64 T.C. 203 (1975), *aff'd in part*, 550 F.2d 1023 (5th Cir.1977); but see *Armstrong v. Phinney*, 394 F.2d 661 (5th Cir.1968) (holding that a partner providing services may qualify as an "employee" for purposes of the § 119 exclusion for meals and lodging provided by an employer); contra Rev. Rul. 69–184, 1969–1 C.B. 256 (bona fide members of a partnership are not employees of the entity). Thus, nonpartner status is more likely to be found if the partner performs limited consultant-type services as an independent contractor, such as acting as the partnership's lawyer or accountant.

2. Disguised Payments for Services: § 707(a)(2)(A)

a. Tax Planning Agenda

If a § 707(a)(1) payment made by a partnership to a partner is capital in nature (e.g., a payment to a partner for drafting the partnership agreement and other organizational documents), the partnership must treat the payment in the same manner as a capital expenditure made to a nonpartner. The expense must be capitalized and, if permitted, deducted or amortized over the applicable recovery period. A distributive share allocated to a partner, on the other hand, has the same impact as an immediate deduction on the distributive shares of the other partners. This difference in tax treatment provides an incentive for a partnership to compensate a partner who provides services which are capital in nature with a special allocation of partnership income rather than a § 707(a)(1) payment.

> ***Example:*** Partner A is a lawyer. In connection with the creation of the new ABC syndicated partnership, Partner A performs services which are organizational and syndication fees under § 709. Partner A would normally charge $15,000 for the services. If the partnership pays A $15,000 for the services, it will have to capitalize the expenditure and determine its tax consequences under § 709. Syndication fees will be nondeductible and organization fees may be amortized under the rules in that section. Alternatively, if the partnership could give a $15,000 special allocation of gross income in the first year to partner A, that allocation would have the same effect as an immediate $15,000 deduction in that it would reduce the distributive shares of the other partners.

b. Recharacterization Under § 707(a)(2)(A)

Section 707(a)(2)(A) curtails this strategy by providing that a direct or indirect allocation and distribution received by a partner for services or property will be treated as a § 707(a)(1) payment if the performance of services and the allocation and distribution, when viewed together, are properly characterized as a transaction between the partnership and a nonpartner. An allocation recharacterized under § 707(a)(2)(A) as a § 707(a)(1) payment is then analyzed to make certain that the partnership is entitled to an immediate deduction.

The legislative history makes it clear that, in enacting § 707(a)(2)(A), Congress did not intend to reverse the general rule that a partner may receive an allocation for an extended period to reflect his services to the partnership. Section 707(a)(2)(A) is targeted at a more limited category of transactions and the legislative history lists factors which help to determine whether a partner is receiving an allocation and distribution as a partner.

c. § 707(a)(2)(A) Factors

The factors listed in the legislative history for analyzing services transactions are: (1) risk as to amount of the payment to the partner; (2) transitory status of the partner; (3) closeness in time between the allocation and distribution and the performance of services; (4) whether the recipient of the allocation and distribution became a partner primarily to obtain tax benefits which would not have been available if he had acted in a nonpartner capacity; and (5) whether the value of the partner's continuing profits interest is small in comparison to the allocation being tested (a substantial continuing interest, however, does not suggest that the allocation should be recognized). The legislative history also invited the Treasury to describe other relevant factors.

Example: Partnership wishes to acquire an office building to use in its business. Attorney will do the legal work on the acquisition for the partnership and normally charges $15,000 for such services. Attorney contributes cash for a 10% interest in the partnership and receives both a 10% distributive share of net income for the life of the partnership and an allocation of the first $15,000 of the partnership's gross income in its first year of operation. The partnership expects to have sufficient cash in its first year to distribute $15,000 to Attorney.

It is likely that the $15,000 allocation and distribution will be recharacterized under § 707(a)(2)(A) as a § 707(a)(1) payment. When recharacterized the payment will be capitalized as part of the cost of the building. Key factors in recharacterizing the allocation and distribution are: (1) the allocation is fixed in amount and it is likely the partnership will have the gross income and cash to pay Attorney, and (2) the distribution is close in time to Attorney's performance of services.

If Attorney were a partner for only one year or had a very small partnership interest (e.g., 1%), those would be additional factors indicating that the allocation and distribution were not made to Attorney in a partner capacity.

d. Proposed Regulations

1) Focus on Entrepreneurial Risk

The IRS has issued proposed regulations under § 707(a)(2)(A) dealing with whether certain partnership arrangements should be treated as disguised payments for services rather than distributive shares. The regulations, applying a "facts and circumstances" test, adopt the general approach of the legislative history by focusing on whether the transaction is structured so that it lacks significant entrepreneurial risk to the service provider relative to the overall risk of the partnership at the time the arrangement is made. For example, if the facts and circumstances demonstrate that the service provider will receive an allocation of income regardless of the overall success of the partnership's business, the arrangement will be presumed to lack significant entrepreneurial risk. Many of the other factors set out in the legislative history also are taken into account by the proposed regulations.

2) Application to Management Fee Waivers

The proposed regulations are aimed at arrangements where managers of private equity partnerships seek to convert ordinary compensation income into long-term capital gain by waiving all or part of the management fees to which they are entitled under the partnership agreement in exchange for an additional and relatively risk-free interest in the future profits of the partnership.

3) Breadth of Proposed Regulations

Although primarily targeted at management fee waivers, the proposed regulations could be interpreted to extend to other arrangements used by managers of investment partnerships to convert ordinary income into capital gain. For the conceptually related problem of taxing "carried interests," see VIII.C., at page 126, *infra*.

3. Guaranteed Payments for Services: § 707(c)

a. Guaranteed Payment Defined

Fixed payments to partners for services performed in their capacity as a partner are guaranteed payments taxable under § 707(c).

Example: Partner A provides ongoing management services to the ABC limited partnership. The ABC partnership agreement provides that A will be paid $40,000 each year for these services. The $40,000 payments to A are § 707(c) guaranteed payments. These amounts are not § 707(a)(1) payments because A's services are performed as a partner. The payments also are not distributive shares because they are "guaranteed," that is, not contingent on partnership profits.

b. Tax Consequences to the Service Partner

A guaranteed payment for services produces § 61 ordinary income and is includible by a partner in the taxable year in which the partnership's taxable year ends. §§ 706(a); 707(c). Because a partner must include a guaranteed payment in income even if it has not been received, the partner should receive an upward adjustment in the outside basis of his partnership interest when the guaranteed payment is included and a downward adjustment when it is paid. *Gaines v. Comm'r*, 45 T.C.M. 363 (1982).

c. Tax Consequences to the Partnership

On the partnership side, a guaranteed payment is potentially deductible under § 162, subject to the capitalization requirement of § 263. Thus, a guaranteed payment to a partner which is capital in nature will produce ordinary income to the partner and either no deduction or deferred deductions (such as depreciation or amortization) to the partnership.

d. Treatment Under Other Code Provisions

A guaranteed payment generally is treated as a distributive share for purposes of other Code provisions. For example, as noted above, guaranteed payments must be included in the service partner's gross income whether or not they are actually received. The regulations, however, provide that a guaranteed payment is not considered to be an interest in partnership profits for purposes of § 706(b)(3) (partner's interests for selecting a taxable year), § 707(b) (disallowing losses and recharacterizing gains on sales of property), and § 708(b) (termination of partnership by sale or exchange of partnership interests). Reg. § 1.707–1(c). If a partnership transfers property in satisfaction of a guaranteed payment under § 707(c), the transfer is a sale or exchange of the property under § 1001 and not a distribution under § 731. Rev. Rul. 2007–40, 2007–1 C.B. 1426.

e. Calculation of Guaranteed Payments

1) Current Approach of IRS

Some partnership agreements provide that a partner who performs services will receive a guaranteed minimum amount together with a percentage of partnership income. These and similar arrangements require the amount of the guaranteed payment to be distinguished from the partner's distributive share. The IRS's longstanding approach for calculating guaranteed payments in these situations is best illustrated by the examples below.

Example (1): Partner A in the AB partnership is to receive $30,000 for deductible services, plus 50% of any partnership income or loss. After deducting the $30,000 payment to A the partnership has a $20,000 loss. A will report $30,000 of ordinary income plus her $10,000 distributive share of partnership loss. If the partnership also had a $6,000 long-term capital gain, that item would be separately stated and A also would include a $3,000 distributive share of the gain.

Example (2): Partner C in the CD partnership is to receive 40% of partnership income but not less than $25,000. If partnership income is $100,000, C will receive a $40,000 distributive share (40% of $100,000), none of which is a guaranteed payment. If partnership income were $50,000 instead of $100,000, C's distributive share would be $20,000 (40% of $50,000) and the remaining $5,000 payable to C would be a guaranteed payment.

Example (3): Partner E in the EF partnership is to receive 40% of partnership income but not less than $90,000. For the taxable year the partnership's income before taking into account any guaranteed amount is $150,000, consisting of $110,000 of ordinary income and $40,000 of long-term capital gain. E's guaranteed payment is $30,000 ($90,000 guaranteed amount less $60,000 distributive share (40% of $150,000 of partnership income)). After taking into account E's guaranteed payment, the taxable income of the partnership is $120,000: $80,000 of ordinary income ($110,000 less the $30,000 guaranteed payment) and $40,000 of long-term capital gain. E's distributive share of that income under the partnership agreement is $60,000 and F's is also $60,000. Hence, the effective profit sharing ratio is 50/50 for the year and both E and F will have distributive shares of $40,000 of partnership ordinary income and $20,000 of long-term capital gain. In addition, E will have $30,000 of ordinary income as a result of the guaranteed payment.

2) Proposed Regulations

Proposed regulations would alter the manner in which the guaranteed payment is calculated in Example (3), above. See Prop. Reg. § 1.707–1(c) Example 2. Under the revised method, the guaranteed payment to E is the full minimum amount ($90,000) not just the excess of the minimum over the partner's income allocation. Thus, E's guaranteed payment and ordinary income would be $90,000, leaving the partnership with $20,000 of ordinary income ($110,000 less the $90,000 guaranteed payment) and $40,000 of long-term capital gain. All of the partnership's remaining income would be allocated to F.

B. Partnership Equity Issued in Exchange for Services

1. Introduction

Section 721 does not provide nonrecognition for contributions of services. A partner who receives a partnership interest for services, either in connection with the formation of a partnership or at a later time, is being compensated for those services and is taxable under §§ 61, with the timing determined under § 83.

2. Capital Interest vs. Profits Interest

A service partner may receive either a "capital" or "profits" interest in a partnership in exchange for services. A capital interest generally is an interest in both the partnership's assets and its future profits. At any given point in time, a holder of a capital interest is entitled to a share of the proceeds if the partnership sold its assets and fair market value and distributed the proceeds in a complete liquidation. A profits interest only entitles a partner to share in future partnership profits (usually including asset appreciation). A holder of a profits interest is not entitled to share in partnership assets if the partnership liquidates at the time the interest is granted or the partner withdraws from the partnership before any profits have been earned. Rev. Proc. 93–27, 1993–2 C.B. 343; see Reg. § 1.704–1(e)(1)(v).

3. Receipt of a Capital Interest for Services

a. Tax Consequences to the Service Partner

A partner who receives a capital interest in a partnership in exchange for services has gross income under § 61 and § 83(a) when the interest is either transferable or no longer subject to a substantial risk of forfeiture. A capital interest is subject to a substantial risk of forfeiture if the service provider's right to full enjoyment is conditioned upon the performance of substantial future services. § 83(c). If the service provider makes an election under § 83(b) within 30 days of the receipt of an unvested interest, the value of the interest is included in gross income at the time it is received. The amount of income is equal to the fair market value of the capital interest when it is included in income less any amount paid by the partner. See § 83; Reg. § 1.721–1(b)(1).

Example: The AB general partnership has $90,000 of assets. A and B wish C to join the partnership because C is familiar with the partnership's business and is regarded as an excellent manager. To entice C to join the firm, A and B have offered C a one-third capital interest. If C leaves the partnership within three years, C, or any transferee of C, must forfeit the partnership interest. C accepts the offer, and at the end of Year 3 the partnership's assets are worth $150,000. C's partnership interest is subject to a substantial risk of forfeiture for three years because her rights to full enjoyment are conditioned on the performance of substantial future services. § 83(c). The interest is also not transferable because a transferee of C is subject to a substantial risk of forfeiture. Under § 83(a), C has $50,000 of gross income (fair market value of the interest when the restrictions lapse) at the end of Year 3 and C's outside basis is $50,000. Alternatively, under § 83(b), C could elect to include $30,000 of gross income (the fair market value of the interest when it is received) in the year of transfer when the partnership interest is still restricted. Subsequent appreciation generally will be taxed as capital gain when the partner disposes of the interest. A disadvantage of a § 83(b) election is that no deduction is allowed if the partnership interest is subsequently forfeited because C fails to work for the partnership for three years. § 83(b)(1).

b. Tax Consequences to the Partnership

1) Business Expense Deduction to the Partnership

If a capital interest is transferred in exchange for services, the partnership may take a § 162 business expense deduction for the amount of ordinary income that is includible in the service partner's income in the taxable year that the income is recognized unless the nature of the services requires the partnership to amortize (e.g., nondeductible organizational expenses) or capitalize (e.g., services related to the acquisition or construction of an asset) the expense. § 83(h). See Reg. §§ 1.83–6(a)(4); 1.721–1(b)(2); 1.707–1(c). Any allowable deduction logically should be allocated to the existing partners, not the new service partner, and the partners may assure this result by a special allocation under § 704(b).

2) Taxable Event to Partnership

Under the longstanding majority view, a partnership that transfers a capital interest for services is treated as transferring an undivided interest in each of its assets to the service partner in a taxable transaction and must recognize any gain or loss inherent in the transferred portion of each asset. Reg. § 1.83–6(b); cf. *McDougal v. Comm'r,* 62 T.C. 720 (1974). The service partner is then treated as retransferring the assets back to partnership in a tax-free § 721 transaction. Some commentators took the position that the transfer of a capital interest for services should not be a taxable event to the partnership, noting by analogy that a corporation does not recognize gain when it issues stock as compensation for services. Cf. § 1032(a). This position is supported by proposed regulations, which provide that a partnership does not recognize gain or loss upon the transfer or vesting of a capital interest to a service partner. Prop. Reg. § 1.721–1(b)(1). See VIII.B.5., at page 126, *infra.*

Example: Assume the AB partnership in the preceding example has $90,000 of assets, consisting solely of land used in AB's business which has a $60,000 adjusted basis. Assume C accepts the offer of a one-third partnership interest, does not make a § 83(b) election, and works three years for AB. At the end of the third year, the AB assets are worth $150,000 and consist of the land which is now worth $120,000 and $30,000 of cash. When the restrictions lapse, AB will be entitled to a $50,000 deduction, assuming C's services qualify as ordinary and necessary business expenses. Under the majority view, AB will be viewed as having transferred one-third of its land ($40,000 fair market value, $20,000 adjusted basis) and cash ($10,000) to C for services and must recognize $20,000 of gain on the land. The one-third interest in the land and cash is then deemed to be transferred back to AB by C, who takes a $50,000 outside basis in her partnership interest. The land would now have an $80,000 inside basis ($40,000 in the two-thirds interest which remained in the partnership plus $40,000 in the one-third interest deemed transferred by C).

The $20,000 gain and $50,000 deduction logically should be allocated to partners A and B because the appreciation in the land took place before C became a partner and A and B paid for C's services with their partnership capital. The remaining $40,000 of gain in the land should be taxable to A and B when the land is sold since that gain represents appreciation prior to C's entry into the partnership. The partners can assure these results by including "special allocations" for these tax items in their partnership agreement and complying with the requirements of § 704(b). See V.A.2., at page 70, *supra.*

The proposed regulations would simplify the analysis by providing that the partnership does not recognize gain or loss upon the transfer of a capital interest for services.

4. Receipt of a Profits Interest for Services

a. Tax Consequences to the Service Partner

1) Historical Approach

Prior to the *Diamond* case (see below), it was generally believed that the receipt of a profits interest in exchange for services was not a taxable event to the service partner. That position largely was based on Reg. § 1.721–1(b)(1), which provides:

> To the extent that any of the partners gives up any part of his right to be repaid his contributions (as distinguished from a share in partnership profits) in favor of another partner as compensation for services * * *, section 721 does not apply.

It was argued that the purpose of the parenthetical in the regulation was to ensure that the receipt of an interest in future partnership profits was not a currently taxable event. Dictum in one Tax Court opinion supported this position. See *Hale v. Comm'r,* 24 T.C.M. 1497, 1502 n. 3 (1965).

2) The *Diamond* Case

In *Diamond v. Comm'r,* 492 F.2d 286 (7th Cir.1974), the Seventh Circuit affirmed the Tax Court's ruling that Sol Diamond was taxable on the receipt of a profits interest in a real estate partnership. In return for his services as a mortgage broker, Diamond received a 60% interest in future partnership profits after the other partner recovered his investment. Three weeks later, Diamond sold his interest for $40,000, claiming a short-term capital gain. This treatment was preferable to ordinary income because Diamond could offset the gain with capital losses from other transactions. The court held that Diamond realized $40,000 of ordinary income on the receipt of the profits interest for past services. The value of the interest was established by Diamond's sale. The court distinguished Reg. § 1.721–1(b)(1) as applying only to capital interests and acknowledged that the receipt of a profits interest with a more speculative value might not be taxable.

3) Safe Harbor: Revenue Procedure 93–27

For many years after the decision in *Diamond,* the tax consequences of the receipt of a profits interest for services were unsettled. *Diamond* involved taxable years prior to the enactment of § 83, and it was unclear whether a profits interest was "property" for § 83 purposes. Some courts held that receipt of a profits interest was a taxable event under § 83 but concluded, on the facts of the case, that the interest had no value or its value was too speculative and could not be ascertained with reasonable certainty. See, e.g., *Campbell v. Comm'r,* 943 F.2d 815 (8th Cir.1991).

This area was clarified by the issuance of Rev. Proc. 93–27, 1993–2 C.B. 343, under which the Service generally will not treat the receipt of a profits interest as a taxable event when the interest is received for the provision of services to or for the benefit of a partnership by a person acting in a partner capacity or in anticipation of being a partner. See VIII.A.1.c., at page 117, *supra,* regarding when a partner is acting in a partner capacity. A service partner, however, is taxable under Rev. Proc. 93–27 on the receipt of a profits interest when:

a. The profits interest relates to a substantially certain and predictable stream of income from partnership assets, such as income from high-quality debt securities or a high-quality net lease;

b. The partner disposes of the profits interest within two years of its receipt; or

c. The interest is in a publicly traded limited partnership as defined by § 7704(b).

The Service has indicated that it may add a fourth exception to Rev. Proc. 93–27 to include a profits interest issued in conjunction with a partner forgoing payment of an amount payable for the performance of services that is substantially fixed (e.g., a management fee based on a percentage of partner capital commitments) and in certain other specialized situations. Preamble to Proposed Regulations, REG-115452-14 (July 23, 2015).

4) Timing Issues: Revenue Procedure 2001–43

Under Rev. Proc. 2001–43, 2001–2 C.B. 191, the determination of whether an interest granted to a service provider is a profits interest for purposes of the safe harbor discussed above is tested at the time the interest is granted even if the interest is not substantially vested under § 83. The Service will not treat the grant of a nontaxable profits interest, or the event that causes the interest to be substantially vested under § 83, as a taxable event. These rules apply if: (1) the partnership and the service provider treat the service provider as the owner of the interest from the date of its grant and the service provider takes into account all items associated with the interest for as long as the service provider has the interest, (2) neither the partnership not the partner deducts any amount for the fair market value of the interest either upon the grant of the interest or when it becomes substantially vested, and (3) all the other requirements of Rev. Proc. 93–27 (see above) are satisfied. Rev. Proc. 2001–43 states that a § 83(b) election is not required if the partnership profits interest is not substantially vested when it is received, but many cautious tax advisors still recommend filing a § 83(b) election because it is easy to do, there is no downside, and it will protect the service provider if the IRS later finds that the requirements of the Rev. Proc. 93–27 safe harbor were not satisfied.

b. Tax Consequences to the Partnership

In the rare situation where a service partner is taxable on receipt of a profits interest, the partnership logically should be allowed a § 162 deduction (or, at worst, an amortizable or capital expenditure) for the amount included in the service partner's income. § 83(h). In addition, the partnership may be considered as having transferred a portion of its future profits in exchange for the services performed by the partner. The disposition will be taxable to the partnership and the profits share then should be treated as if it were transferred back to the partnership, resulting in a tax cost outside basis for the service partner and a fair market value inside basis in the profits share for the partnership. The partnership's basis in the profits share should be amortized over some period of time to offset the future partnership profits it represents. The benefit of those deductions should be allocated to the service partner to prevent double taxation of the same profits. See V.A.2., at page 70, *supra*.

5. Proposed Regulations

The IRS has issued proposed regulations and a proposed revenue procedure that would change the approach to taxing a transfer of a partnership interest in connection with the performance of services. IRS Notice 2005–43, 2005–1 C.B. 1221; Prop. Reg. § 1.83–1(*l*). The proposed regulations define "property" under § 83 to include a partnership interest and provide a safe harbor election for valuation of a transferred partnership interest (whether capital or profits) and nonrecognition for the partnership. Reg. § 1.83–1(e). Under this safe harbor election, the fair market value of a partnership interest transferred in connection with the performance of services is its liquidation value—i.e., the cash the partner would receive if immediately after the transfer the partnership sold all of its assets for cash and liquidated. The liquidation value for a profits interest at the time it is received normally will be zero because the partner would not receive any cash on an immediate liquidation of the partnership. The safe harbor election is subject to a number of conditions and applies only to a "safe harbor partnership interest," which essentially is an interest that could have been received tax-free under Rev. Proc 93–27. As a result, the partner may be taxed on receipt of a partnership interest for services when the partnership interest (1) relates to a substantially certain and predictable stream of income from partnership assets, (2) is transferred in anticipation of a subsequent disposition (a sale or disposition within two years creates a presumption the transfer was in anticipation of a disposition), or (3) is an interest in a publicly traded partnership. The partnership generally does not recognize gain or loss on the transfer of the partnership interest to a services partner except in the case of transfers that result in the creation of a partnership. Special rules deal with the service partner's capital account, the partnership's deduction, subsequent recognition of gain or loss in the partnership's assets, and forfeiture of the partnership interest.

C. Policy Issues: Carried Interests

1. Tax Advantages of Carried Interests

The managers of many investment partnerships usually are compensated with a flat fee ranging from 1 to 2% of the assets under management, and also are allocated a percentage (often 20%) of the fund's profits. The profits allocation has become known as a "carried interest." The tax treatment of carried interests benefits from many of the rules outlined in this chapter. Because it is a profits interest outside the exceptions in Rev. Proc. 93–27, a carried interest may be received tax-free by the managers. And because it is received for managing the venture in the service provider's capacity as a partner, is not fixed in amount, and is usually subject to significant entrepreneurial risk, the carried interest is treated for tax purposes as a distributive share. The profits of many investment partnerships, such as private equity and venture capital funds, largely consist of qualified dividends and long-term capital gains, all taxed at preferential rates. Thus, a significant portion of the manager's income will be tax deferred (receipt of the interest was not taxed) and taxed as profits are earned at preferential capital gains rates.

2. Criticisms of Current Tax Treatment

Carried interests have received considerable media and political attention. Critics of the current tax treatment, led by academic commentators, have noted that billions of dollars of what is essentially compensation have been paid to fund managers through carried interests, converting what should be taxed as ordinary income into tax-deferred capital gains.

For many years, legislation has been introduced in Congress to change the tax treatment of carried interests but, despite some bipartisan support, these proposals have failed to gain traction. Basically, these proposals would tax a fund manager's share of partnership income as ordinary income and impose an employment tax obligation on the manager. The details, however, are extremely complex, and concerns have been expressed as to whether the legislation would (or should) extend to other industries, such as real estate development, where service partners active in the business often receive a larger profit share than the limited partner investors.

As noted earlier in this chapter (see VIII.A.2.d., at page 118, *supra)*, the IRS also has issued proposed regulations under § 707(a)(2)(A) to attack similar strategies used by investment fund managers to defer income and convert ordinary income into capital gain in situations where the manager lacks significant entrepreneurial risk and the overall arrangement is a disguised payment for services.

These developments demonstrate that pressure is building to reform the tax treatment of carried interest and related deferral and conversion strategies, but the ultimate outcome is far from certain and highly dependent on political factors, including the likely influence of lobbyists for affected industries.

D. Review Questions

1. Partner A intends to perform $10,000 worth of services in Year 1 for her partnership. Disregarding A's services, the partnership has $80,000 of ordinary income and $20,000 of long-term capital gain during Year 1. Both A and the partnership are calendar year taxpayer's, A uses the cash-method of tax accounting, and the partnership uses the accrual method. Determine the tax consequences to A and the partnership assuming:

   (a) For the services, A receives a special allocation of the partnership's first $10,000 of income, which is part of her distributive share.

   (b) For the services, A receives a $10,000 payment in Year 2. § 707(a)(1) applies to the payment because A did not perform the services as a partner.

   (c) For the services, the partnership's $10,000 obligation is characterized as a § 707(c) guaranteed payment. The partnership pays $10,000 to A in Year 2.

2. The ABC partnership transfers to D a 25% capital interest in ABC on the condition that D must continue to work for the partnership for five years. If D should cease to perform services within the five years, he forfeits the partnership interest. When ABC transfers the partnership interest to D, ABC's assets have a fair market value of $100,000 and an adjusted basis of $40,000. At the end of five years, ABC's assets have a fair market value of $400,000.

   (a) If D does not make a § 83(b) election, when does he recognize income and how much income will he have?

   (b) How much gain or loss does ABC recognize in (a), above?

(c)   If D makes a § 83(b) election, when does he recognize income and how much will he have?

(d)   If D makes a § 83(b) election and leaves the partnership after three years, what are D's tax consequences? Assume ABC's assets have a fair market value of $200,000 at the end of year three.

(e)   What is D's outside basis in the one-quarter partnership interest in (a) and (c) above?

Chapter IX

Property Transactions Between Partnerships and Partners

■ ANALYSIS

A. Introduction
B. § 707(a)(1) Property Transactions
    1. In General
    2. Disguised Payments for the Use of Property: § 707(a)(2)(A)
C. Guaranteed Payments: § 707(c)
D. Sales and Exchanges of Property Between Partners and Partnerships: General Rules
E. Disguised Sales Between Partners and Partnerships: § 707(a)(2)(B)
    1. Key Factors
    2. Debt-Financed Distributions
F. Review Questions

A. Introduction

A partner and a partnership may engage in a wide variety of property transactions, such as sales, leases and loans. In Chapter VIII, partner-partnership services arrangements were covered. Similar tax issues arise with property transactions between a partner and a partnership, which may be characterized as: (1) a transaction between the partnership and an unrelated person under § 707(a)(1); (2) a guaranteed payment under § 707(c); or (3) a distributive share. Thus, many of the rules already discussed in Chapter VIII also may apply to various property transactions. This chapter begins with a brief overview of those principles and then turns to material specifically directed at sales and exchanges of property.

B. § 707(a)(1) Property Transactions

1. In General

Section 707(a)(1) generally adopts an entity theory for determining the tax consequences of transactions between a partner and a partnership. See VIII.A.1., at page 116, *supra*. It provides that if a partner engages in a transaction with a partnership "other than in his capacity as a member of such partnership," the transaction is to be taxed as if it occurred between the partnership and a nonpartner unless § 707 provides otherwise. Under the regulations, § 707(a)(1) transactions include loans of money, leases of property, and sales and purchase of property, but the regulations also reaffirm that § 721 contributions of property and partnership distributions are not within the jurisdiction of § 707(a)(1). In sorting out the application of § 707(a)(1), the regulations caution that "the substance of the transaction will govern rather than its form." Reg. § 1.707–1.

2. Disguised Payments for the Use of Property: § 707(a)(2)(A)

a. Tax Planning Agenda

As with services, partners may have an incentive to use distributive shares in transactions involving the use of property in order to avoid the Code's capitalization requirements.

Example: Partner A plans to lease equipment to the ABC partnership for five years at an annual $10,000 rental fee. If the partnership pays A the full $50,000 five-year rental fee in the first year, A will have $50,000 of income and the partnership will have to capitalize the $50,000 expenditure and deduct it at the rate of $10,000 per year. Alternatively, if the partnership could give a $50,000 special allocation of gross income in the first year, that allocation would have the same effect as an immediate $50,000 deduction in that it would reduce the distributive shares of the other partners.

b. Recharacterization Under § 707(a)(2)(A)

Section 707(a)(2)(A) again deters this strategy by providing that a direct or indirect allocation and distribution received by a partner for a transfer of property will be treated as a § 707(a)(1) payment if the transfer of property and the allocation and distribution, when viewed together, are properly characterized as a transaction between the partnership and a nonpartner. An allocation recharacterized under § 707(a)(2)(A) as a § 707(a)(1) payment is then analyzed to determine if the partnership is entitled to an immediate deduction.

The legislative history makes it clear that, in enacting § 707(a)(2)(A), Congress did not intend to reverse the general nonrecognition rule in § 721. Partners may still make a tax-free contribution of property to a partnership in exchange for a share of profits. Section 707(a)(2)(A) is targeted at a more limited category of transactions. The legislative history lists factors which help to determine whether a partner is receiving an allocation and distribution as a partner.

c. § 707(a)(2)(A) Factors

The factors in the legislative history relevant to transactions involving the use of property are: (1) risk as to amount of the payment to the partner; (2) transitory status of the partner; and (3) closeness in time between the allocation and distribution and the transfer of property. The legislative history also invited the Treasury to describe other relevant factors.

Example: Assume the same basic facts as the preceding example. Partner A plans to lease equipment to the ABC partnership for five years and the annual rental for the property would be a $10,000 per year. Instead of paying annual rent, the partnership provides a $50,000 special allocation of gross income and a distribution in the first year to A. Assume the partnership expects to have at least $50,000 of gross income during the year. In that case, it is likely the $50,000 allocation and distribution will be recharacterized under § 707(a)(2)(A) as a § 707(a)(1) payment. As recharacterized, the payment must be capitalized by the partnership as prepaid rent and deducted over the 5-year term of the lease. Consequently, the full allocation will not reduce the income taxable to the partners. Key factors in recharacterizing the allocation and distribution are: (1) the allocation is fixed in amount and it is likely the partnership will have the gross income and cash to pay A, and (2) the distribution is close in time to A's transfer of the property.

C. Guaranteed Payments: § 707(c)

Fixed payments to a partner as a return on contributed capital are guaranteed payments taxable under § 707(c). A guaranteed payment produces § 61 ordinary income and is includible by a partner in the taxable year in which the partnership's taxable year ends. §§ 706(a); 707(c). On the partnership side, a guaranteed payment is potentially deductible under § 162, subject to the capitalization requirement of § 263.

Example: The ABC limited partnership agreement provides that each limited partner annually will be paid a 10% return on the partner's capital account balance. The 10% return paid to the limited partners on their capital account balances are § 707(c) guaranteed payments. These amounts are not § 707(a)(1) payments because the 10% return is paid on contributed (not loaned) capital. The payments also are not distributive shares because they are "guaranteed," that is, not contingent on partnership profits.

D. Sales and Exchanges of Property Between Partners and Partnerships: General Rules

Under § 707(a)(1), a sale of property between a partner and a partnership generally is treated in the same manner as a sale between the partnership and a nonpartner. Several other provisions are designed to prevent tax avoidance through transactions between related parties. Section 707(b)(1) disallows losses on sales or exchanges of property between a partnership and a partner who owns, directly or indirectly, more than 50% of the capital or profits interests of the partnership. Losses are also disallowed on sales or exchanges between two partnerships in which the same persons own, directly or indirectly, more than 50% of the capital and profits interests. Under § 707(b)(2) and § 1239, gain on the sale or exchange of property between a partner and a controlled (i.e., more than 50% owned) partnership or between two controlled partnerships is characterized as ordinary income if the property: (1) is not a capital asset in the hands of the transferee or (2) is depreciable in the hands of the transferee. For purposes of § 707(b) and § 1239, ownership interests are tested taking into account the attribution rules in § 267(c), other than § 267(c)(3) (which would attribute each partner's interest to the other partners). §§ 707(b)(3); 1239(c)(2). To prevent manipulation of the installment sales, the second disposition rules in § 453(e) and the rules relating to sales of depreciable property in § 453(g) apply to certain partner/partnership transactions. See §§ 453(e); (f)(1); (g)(1), (3).

E. Disguised Sales Between Partners and Partnerships: § 707(a)(2)(B)

1. Key Factors

Section 707(a)(2)(B) is designed to prevent sales of property between a partner and partnership from being structured as nontaxable contributions and distributions under §§ 721 and 731. It provides that if there are direct or indirect transfers of money and property between a partner and a partnership and the transfers, when viewed together, are properly characterized as a sale or exchange of property, then the transfers are to be treated as a sale or exchange between the partner and partnership (or between two partners). Under the regulations, transfers of property and money constitute a sale if based on all the facts and circumstances the transfer of money would not have been made but for the transfer of property and, in the case of transfers that are not simultaneous, the subsequent transfer is not dependent on the entrepreneurial risks of the partnership. Reg. § 1.707–3(b)(1). The legislative history states that closeness in time between the "contribution" and "distribution" is a key factor and the regulations have adopted a presumption that contributions and distributions within two years of one another are related. Reg. § 1.707–3(c)(1). Transfers more than two years apart are presumed not to be related. Reg. § 1.707–3(d). Either presumption may be rebutted. Transfers of property by a partner and transfers of money or other consideration by the partnership to that partner within two years before or after the transfer of property must be reported to the Service if the partner does not treat the transfer as a sale. Reg. § 1.707–3(c)(2). The regulations also provide that the disguised sale rules apply to situations where the transferor partner receives the proceeds of certain loans secured by the property (such as by borrowing against the property on the eve of contribution) and responsibility for repaying the loan rests with the partnership. Reg. § 1.707–5(a)(1). Loans incurred within two years of transferring the property to the partnership generally are presumed to be in anticipation of the transfer. Reg. § 1.707–5(a)(7). The partnership's assumption of a loan incurred more than two years before the transfer of property is disregarded in determining whether the transfer is a sale. Reg. § 1.707–5(a)(5), (6). See Reg. § 1.707–5(f) Example 5.

2. Debt-Financed Distributions

Taxpayers have attempted to exploit a feature in the § 707(a)(2) regulations dealing with the distribution of loan proceeds. So-called "debt-financed distributions" begin with a potential seller and buyer of property forming a partnership. The seller contributes the desired asset and the partnership incurs a loan approximately equal to the "purchase price" for the asset. The partnership then distributes the loan proceeds to the seller tax free under § 731. The key to the transaction is Reg. § 1.707–5(b)(1) which generally provides that if a partner transfers property to a partnership and the partnership incurs a liability the proceeds of which are distributed with 90 days of the liability being incurred, the transfer of money to the contributing partner is only taken into account under § 707(a)(2)(B) to the extent the money received exceeds the contributing partner's share of the liability. A key to the transaction is the selling partner obtaining outside basis credit for a share of the liability. Taxation of the "sale" then is deferred until the debt is satisfied and a cash distribution occurs under § 752(b). In *Canal Corp. v. Comm'r,* 135 T.C. 199 (2010), the seller in debt-financed distribution had planned the transaction to defer $524 million of capital gain. Those expected tax benefits were upset when the court determined that the seller did not bear the economic risk of loss for the loan undertaken to finance the transaction. The court disregarded an indemnity agreement by the seller because it created no more than a remote possibility that the seller would actually be liable for payment.

F. Review Questions

1. A, a cash method taxpayer, contributes $25,000 to the ABCD partnership for a one-quarter partnership interest. A also contributes the use of office space for five years in a building owned by A to the partnership in exchange for a special allocation of the first $30,000 of partnership gross income. How will the $30,000 allocation most likely be treated for tax purposes?

2. Partner A, a cash method taxpayer, is a 50% partner in the AB partnership and has a $20,000 outside basis in his partnership interest. A owns a parcel of real estate with a fair market value of $40,000 and a basis of $5,000. Before the events below, the AB partnership has $50,000 of net income from its operations during the year. What are the tax consequences in the following alternative transactions?

    (a) A sells the real estate to the partnership for $40,000.

    (b) A makes a contribution of the real estate to the partnership and his capital account is increased by $40,000. Later in the year, the partnership makes an additional $40,000 distribution to A.

    (c) What if the distribution in (b), above, were only $20,000?

Chapter X

Sales and Exchanges of Partnership Interests

■ ANALYSIS

A.   Introduction
B.   Tax Consequences to the Selling Partner
    1.   Computation of Gain or Loss
    2.   Characterization of Gain or Loss
    3.   Related Issues
C.   Tax Consequences to the Buying Partner
    1.   Introduction
    2.   Operation of § 743(b)
D.   Review Questions

A. Introduction

Under general tax principles, a taxpayer's gain or loss on a sale or other disposition of property is equal to the difference between the amount realized on the sale and the taxpayer's adjusted basis for the property. § 1001. The character of gain or loss depends on the nature of the property (is it a capital asset?), the type of disposition (is it a sale or exchange?), and the taxpayer's holding period of the property (long-term or short-term?). §§ 64; 1221; 1222, 1223. A purchaser of property generally takes a cost basis. § 1012.

These same principles generally apply to sales and exchanges of partnership interests. A partnership interest is treated as a capital asset. A selling partner's capital gain or loss is the difference between the amount realized on a sale of the interest and the partner's outside basis at the time of sale. To prevent partners from converting ordinary income into capital gain, however, Subchapter K modifies this general rule by carving up the transaction and treating a partner as having sold her share of certain "ordinary income" assets held by the partnership.

A hybrid approach also is used on the buying partner's side of the transaction. The buyer's outside basis is her cost of acquiring the interest. If the partnership makes an election or if it has a substantial loss built into its assets, the buying partner's personal inside basis in each of the partnership's assets will be adjusted to reflect more accurately the price that she paid for her partnership interest.

This chapter examines the interaction between the Code's basic structure for taxing property dispositions and the rules in Subchapter K specifically applicable to sales and exchanges of partnership interests.

B. Tax Consequences to the Selling Partner

1. Computation of Gain or Loss

A selling partner first must determine the amount realized on a sale or exchange of his partnership interest and the adjusted basis of the interest to determine the gain or loss recognized on the transaction.

a. Amount Realized

A partner's amount realized is the sum of the cash and the fair market value of any property received for the interest. § 1001(b). In addition, § 752(d) and the principles of the *Crane* case require the selling partner to include relief from her share of any partnership liabilities in the amount realized.

b. Adjusted Basis of Partnership Interest

The selling partner's adjusted basis for her partnership interest is her outside basis determined under § 705(a) (see III.B.3.a., at page 50, *supra*), adjusted to reflect her share of partnership income or loss for that part of the partnership's taxable year up to the sale. Although the taxable year of a partnership generally does not close as a result of partner-level events (§ 706(c)(1)), it does close with respect to a partner who sells or exchanges her entire interest in the partnership (§ 706(c)(2)(A)(i)). In that situation, the selling partner includes in income her distributive share of partnership items for the short taxable year, and they are reflected in her outside basis. The portion of the partnership's income attributable to the selling partner's short taxable year is determined by taking into account the partners' varying interests in the partnership. § 706(d); see Reg. § 1.706–1(c)(4).

If a partner disposes of only a portion of her partnership interest, the taxable year of the partnership does not close even with respect to that partner. § 706(c)(2)(B). At the end of the year, however, the partners' distributive shares of partnership items must be determined by taking into account their varying interests in the partnership. § 706(d)(1); Reg. § 1.706–1(c)(4). For purposes of determining gain or loss, the selling partner's outside basis also must be adjusted as of the date of the disposition. Reg. § 1.705–1(a)(1).

2. Characterization of Gain or Loss

a. General Rule: § 741

Section 741 provides that the gain or loss recognized from the sale or exchange of a partnership interest is capital gain or loss, except as otherwise provided in § 751. If § 751 applies, it overrides the general rule in § 741. Consequently, § 751 is the starting point in characterizing a partner's gain or loss from the sale of a partnership interest.

b. Definition of § 751 Assets

Section 751(a) provides that the consideration received by a selling partner in exchange for all or part of his interest in "unrealized receivables" or inventory items, shall be considered as an amount realized from the sale or exchange of property producing ordinary income rather than capital gain. In applying § 751(a), the critical questions are: (1) does the partnership have unrealized receivables or inventory items? and (2) if so, what portion of the selling partner's gain or loss is attributable to those assets?

1) Unrealized Receivables

Unrealized receivables are rights (contractual or otherwise) to payment for goods delivered, or to be delivered (to the extent sale of the property would produce ordinary income), and services rendered or to be rendered to the extent they have not previously been included in income under the partnership's accounting method. § 751(c)(1), (2). Unrealized receivables also include the gain that would be characterized as ordinary income on a disposition of an asset for fair market value under the depreciation recapture provisions (e.g., § 1245) and other rules requiring recapture of deductions. § 751(c).

The classic unrealized receivable is a cash method partnership's accounts receivable for services performed. A similar account receivable in the hands of an accrual method partnership would not be an unrealized receivable, however, because it would have been previously included in income. The courts have construed the term "unrealized receivables" broadly. Thus, a partnership's rights in a contract or agreement to earn ordinary income in the future generally will be considered an unrealized receivable. See, e.g., *Ledoux v. Comm'r,* 77 T.C. 293 (1981), *aff'd per curiam,* 695 F.2d 1320 (11th Cir.1983), where the Tax Court held that a management agreement under which a partnership had the right to manage a dog track for 20 years was an unrealized receivable.

2) Inventory Items

"Inventory items" are defined as all property of the partnership (including § 1221(1) "dealer" property) which if sold by the partnership or the selling partner would not be considered a capital or § 1231 asset. § 751(d).

The definition of "inventory items" is broad enough to include all of a partnership's unrealized receivables since they are property which if sold by the partnership would produce ordinary income. Reg. § 1.751–1(d)(2)(ii). Even though an asset may be both an unrealized receivable and an inventory item, it will be taxed only once under § 751(a).

Example (1): Assume the ABCDE cash method, calendar year general partnership has the following balance sheet:

Assets	A.B.	F.M.V.
Cash	$ 5,000	$ 5,000
Accounts Receivable for Services	0	20,000
Dealer Property	10,000	15,000
Capital Asset	5,000	35,000
Building (no recapture)	80,000	100,000
	$100,000	$175,000

The accounts receivable are unrealized receivables. § 751(c)(2). The dealer property is an inventory item. § 751(d)(1). The accounts receivable are also considered inventory items but they are only counted once. Thus, both the accounts receivable and the dealer property are § 751 assets.

Example (2): If the dealer property in Example (1) were a capital asset to the partnership but would have produced ordinary income if sold by the selling partner (because she is a dealer in such property), it still would be an inventory item. § 751(d)(3).

Example (3): If the gain in the building in Example (1) were all § 1250 recapture income, that portion of the building would be considered a separate unrealized receivable with a $20,000 fair market value and a zero adjusted basis. Reg. § 1.751–1(c)(4), (5). The recapture gain also would be an inventory item.

Example (4): If the ABCDE general partnership in Example (1) used the accrual method of accounting, the accounts receivable would have been previously included in income and would not be unrealized receivables. The inventory items would still include the dealer property and the accounts receivable (which would have a $20,000 basis as a result of previously being included in income).

c. Computation of § 751 Gain or Loss

Once the partnership's unrealized receivables and inventory items are identified, the selling partner must determine the portions of the gain or loss characterized as ordinary under § 751(a) and capital under § 741. This is accomplished by first determining the amount of income or loss from § 751 property that would have been allocated to the selling partner if the partnership had sold all of its property in a fully taxable transaction for cash in an amount equal to the fair market value of such property. Reg. § 1.751–1(a)(2). Special allocations and allocations required under § 704(c) (including remedial allocations) are taken into account in determining the selling partner's share of income or loss from § 751 property in the hypothetical sale. Id. The gain or loss attributable to § 751 property is ordinary income or loss. The difference between the selling partner's total gain or loss and the § 751 gain or loss is § 741 capital gain or loss. It is possible for the selling partner to have a gain under § 751(a) and a loss under § 741 or vice versa. The long-term or short-term character of the § 741 portion of the sale will be determined with reference to the selling partner's holding period in the partnership interest.

Example (1):   Assume the ABCDE cash method, calendar year general partnership has the following balance sheet:

Assets	A.B.	F.M.V.
Cash	$ 5,000	$ 5,000
Accounts Receivable for Services	0	20,000
Dealer Property	10,000	15,000
Capital Asset	5,000	35,000
Building (no recapture)	80,000	100,000
	$100,000	$175,000

If A sells her one-fifth partnership interest in which she has a $20,000 adjusted basis for $35,000 cash on January 1, A's total gain would be $15,000 ($35,000 amount realized less $20,000 adjusted basis). The accounts receivable and the dealer property are § 751 assets. The accounts receivable are unrealized receivables as well as inventory items and the dealer property is an inventory item. In a hypothetical sale of all the § 751 assets for cash equal to the fair market value of those assets, A would be allocated $5,000 of income ($4,000 from the accounts receivable and $1,000 from the dealer property). Thus, A has $5,000 of ordinary income under § 751(a). The difference between A's total gain ($15,000) and A's § 751(a) gain ($5,000) would be § 741 capital gain, long-term or short-term depending on A's holding period for her partnership interest.

Example (2):   If in Example (1) A's amount realized consisted of $25,000 cash and $10,000 of liability relief instead of $35,000 of cash, under § 752(d) her total amount realized would still be $35,000 and her tax results on the sale of her partnership interest would be the same.

Example (3):   If in Example (1) A sold her partnership interest for $15,000 cash instead of $35,000 because the capital asset and building were only worth a total of $35,000, the § 751 portion of the transaction does not change. A still has a $5,000 § 751 gain (the share of income she would be allocated from the accounts receivable and dealer property). Under § 741, the difference between A's $5,000 total loss ($15,000 amount realized less

$20,000 adjusted basis) and her $5,000 § 751(a) ordinary income is $10,000, which is characterized as capital loss. This variation illustrates that a selling partner can have an overall loss on a sale of her partnership interest but still recognize ordinary income under § 751.

Example (4):   If in Example (1) A sold her entire partnership interest mid-year when her share of ABCDE income to that date was $5,000, the ABCDE taxable year will close with respect to A and she will include the $5,000 in income which will increase the basis of her partnership interest to $25,000. If the buyer now pays A $40,000 cash for her interest because he acquires her right to the $5,000, the results under § 751 and § 741 are the same. If only a portion of A's partnership interest were sold mid-year, ABCDE's taxable year would not close but a basis adjustment would have to be made to the interest sold to reflect ABCDE's tax results prior to the sale.

Example (5):   If in Example (1) A had contributed the accounts receivable to the partnership when their fair market value was $20,000 and adjusted basis was zero, she would be allocated $21,000 of income on a hypothetical sale of the § 751 assets ($20,000 from the accounts receivable under § 704(c) and $1,000 from the dealer property). Thus, A would have $21,000 of ordinary income under § 751(a). Under § 741, the difference between A's total gain ($15,000) and her § 751(a) gain ($21,000) is $6,000, which is characterized as capital loss.

d. Capital Gains Look-Through Rules

The regulations apply a "look-through rule" for determining the character of gain or loss on sales or exchanges of interests in a partnership, an S corporation, or a trust. Reg. § 1.1(h)–1. Thus, a partner who sells a partnership interest held for more than one year may recognize § 751 ordinary income, collectibles gain (taxed at up to a 28% rate), unrecaptured § 1250 gain (taxed at up to a 25% rate), and residual capital gain (generally taxed at a top rate of either 15% or 20%). Id. See § 1(h). Any gain from a partnership interest held for more than one year that is (1) attributable to unrealized appreciation in the value of the partnership's collectibles is treated as gain from the sale or exchange of a collectible, and (2) attributable to unrecaptured § 1250 gain in the partnership's assets is treated as unrecaptured § 1250 gain. The selling partner's share of collectibles gain and unrecaptured § 1250 gain is determined under a hypothetical-sale approach where you ask: how much of each type of gain would the selling partner be allocated if the partnership transferred all of those assets in a fully taxable transaction for cash equal to the fair market value of the assets immediately before the transfer of the partnership interest? Reg. § 1.1(h)–1(b)(2)(ii), (3)(ii). This determination takes into account special allocations and § 704(c) allocations (including remedial allocations). The selling partner's share of residual capital gain is equal to the amount of the § 741 long-term capital gain or loss minus the partner's shares of collectibles and unrecaptured § 1250 gains. Reg. § 1.1(h)–1(c).

e. Holding Period

A partner's holding period in a partnership interest may be part long-term and part short-term. This could result from contributions of property made to the partnership during the prior year or because a portion of the partnership interest was purchased during the prior year. Reg. § 1.1223–3(a). If a partner sells a partnership interest with a divided holding period, any capital gain or loss must be divided between long-term and short-term capital gain or loss in the same proportion as the long-term and short-term holding periods for the partnership interest. Reg. 1.1223–3(c)(1), (2)(ii). To apply the capital gains look-through rule, the regulations first identify the portions of the selling partner's § 741 capital gain or loss that are long-term or short-term gain or loss. Then a proportionate amount of any collectibles or unrecaptured § 1250 gain is deemed to be part of the long-term capital gain or loss.

If a partner sells her partnership interest, some special rules may apply to determine the holding period for the interest. If a partner makes cash contributions to and receives cash distributions from the partnership during the one-year period before the sale of her partnership interest, the partner may reduce the cash contributions made during the year by the cash distributions on a last-in-first-out basis, generally treating all cash distributions as if they were made immediately before the sale or exchange. Reg. § 1.1223–3(b)(2); see Reg. § 1.1223–3(f) Example (3). Contributions of § 751 assets (§ 751(c) unrealized receivables and § 751(d) inventory items) within one year of a sale or exchange of partnership interest generally are disregarded for holding period purposes if the partner recognizes ordinary income or loss on such § 751 assets in a fully taxable transaction (e.g., on a sale of the partnership interest or a sale by the partnership of the contributed asset). Reg. § 1.1223–3(b)(4). Thus, a contribution of § 751 assets generally will not both produce ordinary income to the contributing partner and result in a short-term holding period.

Example (1):   Assume the ABC cash method, calendar year general partnership has the following balance sheet. All partnership assets have been held long-term.

	A.B.	F.M.V.
Cash	$ 9,000	$ 9,000
Accounts Receivable	0	15,000
Capital Asset	15,000	39,000
	$24,000	$63,000

Assume A sells her one-third partnership interest in which she has an $8,000 adjusted basis for $21,000 cash on January 1 and A's holding period in the interest is 50% long-term and 50% short-term. A's total gain would be $13,000 ($21,000 amount realized less $8,000 adjusted basis). The accounts receivable are unrealized receivables and § 751 assets. In a hypothetical sale of the accounts receivable, A would be allocated $5,000 of income (one-third of $15,000). Thus, A has $5,000 of ordinary income under § 751(a). The $8,000 difference between A's total gain ($13,000) and A's § 751(a) gain ($5,000) would be § 741 capital gain. The § 741 capital gain would be 50% long-term capital gain ($4,000) and 50% short-term capital gain ($4,000).

Example (2):   Assume that in Example (1) the capital asset is two capital assets. One is a collectible with a fair market value of $9,000 and a basis of $3,000 and the other is land with a fair market value of $30,000 and a basis of $12,000. Assume A's holding period is all long-term. A would again have the same § 751(a) and § 741 gains except that all of the § 741 capital gain would be long-term capital gain. In a hypothetical sale of all the collectibles for cash equal to the fair market value of the collectibles, A would be allocated $2,000 of collectibles gain (one-third of the $6,000 of collectibles gain). Therefore, A will recognize $2,000 of collectibles gain and $6,000 of residual long-term capital gain (the difference between $8,000 of § 741 long-term capital gain and A's $2,000 share of collectibles capital gain).

Example (3):   If in Example (2) A's holding period for the partnership interest were 50% long-term and 50% short-term, then the gain attributable to the collectibles ($2,000) that is allocable to the portion of the interest sold with a long-term holding period is $1,000 (50% per holding period allocations). Thus, A would recognize $1,000 of collectibles gain, $3,000 of residual long-term capital gain, and $4,000 of short-term capital gain, in addition to $5,000 of § 751(a) ordinary income. See Reg. § 1.1(h)–i(f) Example 5.

Example (4):   If collectibles held by the partnership have a built-in loss (i.e. the basis exceeds the fair market value of the collectibles), the loss in the collectibles is ignored and not recognized at the time of the transfer of the partnership interest. See Reg. § 1.1(h)–1(f) Example 3.

3.   Related Issues

a.   Installment Sale of a Partnership Interest

An installment sale of a partnership interest raises many issues if the partnership has assets which are not eligible for installment sale reporting treatment. For example, § 453 precludes installment reporting on the sale of assets such as publicly traded stock and personal property inventory, and recapture income may not be deferred under § 453. § 453(b)(2)(B), (i), (k)(2)(A). If a partner sells an interest in a partnership under the installment method, must the gain attributable to these types of assets be recognized immediately? Congress and the Service have begun to provide guidance on this issue. Section 453(i)(2) denies installment reporting for § 1245 and § 1250 recapture income in partnership property. Thus, a partner selling an interest in a partnership which has gain subject to recapture under these provisions must recognize the gain in the year of sale. The Service has ruled that the installment method also is not available for income attributable to inventory items which would not be eligible for installment reporting if sold directly. Rev. Rul. 89–108, 1989–2 C.B. 100. The ruling concludes that the portion of any gain on the sale of a partnership interest that is attributable to "Section 751 property" may be reported under the installment method only to the extent the income could have been reported under § 453 if the asset had been sold directly. An unrealized receivable other than § 1245 or § 1250 recapture income must be separately analyzed to determine whether it was eligible for installment reporting if sold directly.

b. Exchange or Conversion of Partnership Interests

1) Exchanges of Partnership Interests

An exchange of partnership interests does not qualify for nonrecognition as a like-kind exchange. § 1031(a)(2)(D). This rule applies regardless of whether the interests exchanged are general or limited partnership interests, or interests in the same partnership or different partnerships. Reg. § 1.1031(a)–1(a)(1).

2) Conversions of Partnership Interests

A conversion of a general partnership into a limited partnership, or vice versa, is governed by §§ 721 and 731, relating to contributions to and distributions from a partnership, and is not to be treated as an exchange of partnership interests. See Rev. Rul. 84–52, 1984–1 C.B. 157.

3) Conversions into LLC or LLP Interests

The conversion of a domestic partnership into an interest in a domestic limited liability company that is classified as a partnership for tax purposes, or into a limited liability partnership, also is governed by §§ 721 and 731. Rev. Rul. 95–37, 1995–1 C.B. 130; Rev. Rul. 95–55, 1995–2 C.B. 313.

C. Tax Consequences to the Buying Partner

1. Introduction

The buyer of a partnership interest takes the interest with a cost basis. For this purpose, "cost" includes the buying partner's share of partnership liabilities attributable to the interest. §§ 742; 752(d); 1012.

At the partnership level, § 743(a) provides that the transfer of a partnership interest generally has no impact on the basis of partnership property. This rule may produce distortions in the timing and character of the buying partner's income or loss. To help remedy these potential distortions a partnership may elect under § 754 to adjust the basis of its assets pursuant to § 743(b), which is considered below.

Example: Partner A purchases a 25% interest in a cash method partnership for $50,000, the fair market value of the interest. One of the partnership's assets is a $40,000 account receivable in which the partnership has a zero basis. In the absence of a § 754 election, if the partnership collects the receivable in a later year, A's distributive share will be $10,000 of ordinary income despite the fact that A, in effect, paid $10,000 for his share of that asset. A will receive a $10,000 upward adjustment in the basis of his partnership interest which will result in a loss or less income when he sells his interest or the partnership is liquidated. But those events may not occur for many years and the loss or income offset will be capital under § 741 despite the fact that the account receivable produced ordinary income.

2. Operation of § 743(b)

a. Requirement of § 754 Election or Substantial Built-In Loss

1) General Rules

The inside basis adjustments under § 743(b) are made only if: (1) the partnership has made an election under § 754; or (2) the partnership has a "substantial built-in loss" immediately after the transfer of a partnership interest. Once made, an election applies to all subsequent taxable years of the partnership and may be revoked only with the Service's consent. A § 754 election also triggers the inside basis adjustments required by § 734 in the case of distributions of property by the partnership. See XI.B.2., at page 158, *infra*. A partnership has a substantial built-in loss and will be *required* to make inside basis adjustments if the adjusted basis in its property exceeds the fair market value by more than $250,000 immediately after the transfer of a partnership interest. § 743(b)(1) & (d)(1). The inside basis adjustments are required in order to prevent the partners from obtaining tax deferral from the built-in loss. If the partnership has a substantial built-in loss after a transfer of a partnership interest, the partnership is treated as having a § 754 election in effect for the taxable year in which the transfer occurs, but only with respect to that transfer. Prop. Reg. § 1.743–1(k)(1)(1)(iii). The IRS has authority to aggregate related partnerships and disregard acquisitions of property designed to avoid the $250,000 limit. § 743(d)(2).

2) Special Rules

An "electing investment partnership" may take advantage of a special rule that allows it to avoid the administrative inconvenience of inside basis adjustments when it has a substantial built-in loss immediately after the transfer of a partnership interest. See § 743(e)(6) for the definition of an electing investment partnership. Under § 743(e)(2), a loss limitation rule is imposed on a transferee partner in lieu of an inside basis adjustment for the partnership. Under the limit, a transferee partner's share of losses (without regard to gains) from the sale or exchange of partnership property is not allowed except to the extent it is established that such losses exceed any loss recognized by the transferor on the transfer of the partnership interest. §§ 743(e)(1), (2). An even more exotic investment vehicle, a "securitization partnership," is permitted to avoid both an inside basis adjustment and the § 743(e) loss-limitation rule. See § 743(f).

b. Adjustments to Inside Basis Under § 743(b)

1) The Overall § 743(b) Adjustment

If a partnership has a § 754 election in effect or is required to make an inside basis adjustment, § 743(b) requires that if there is a sale or exchange of a partnership interest the partnership shall: (1) increase its inside basis by an amount equal to the excess of the buying partner's outside basis over his proportionate share of inside basis, or (2) decrease its inside basis by the excess of the buying partner's share of inside basis over his outside basis.

The allocation of the total inside basis adjustment required under § 743(b) is made in accordance with the rules in § 755 and is personal to the buying partner, who will have a special basis for purposes of computing that partner's depreciation, depletion, gain or loss, and basis on distributions. § 743(c); Reg. § 1.743–1(j)(1).

The basic purpose of a § 743(b) inside basis adjustment is to give the purchasing partner the equivalent of a cost basis in his share of the partnership's assets. In a situation where there are no special allocations or § 704(c) allocations, the total amount of the § 743(b) adjustment generally is equal to the new partner's outside basis (e.g., a cost basis in the case of a purchased partnership interest or a date-of-death basis in the case of an inherited interest) and that partner's proportionate share of the partnership's inside basis. To accommodate special allocations and the complexities of § 704(c), the regulations provide a detailed formula for determining the transferee partner's share of the partnership's inside basis. Under the formula, a transferee partner's share of inside basis is equal to the sum of (1) the transferee's interest as a partner in the partnerships "previously taxed capital," plus (2) the transferee's share of partnership liabilities. The transferee partner's interest in the partnership's previously taxed capital is generally determined by considering a hypothetical, fully taxable, disposition of all the partnership's assets for cash equal to their fair market value. The transferee's interest in the partnership's previously taxed capital is equal to the cash the partner would receive on a liquidation following the hypothetical sale, increased by the amount of tax loss and decreased by the amount of tax gain that would be allocated to the transferee partner in the hypothetical sale. Reg. § 1.743–1(d)(1) and (2).

Example (1): The ABC cash method, general partnership has a § 754 election in effect and the following balance sheet:

	A.B.	F.M.V.
Accounts Receivable	$ 0	$ 30,000
Capital Asset	45,000	60,000
Depreciable Business Property (no recapture)	105,000	150,000
	$150,000	$240,000

If Nupartner purchases A's one-third interest in the partnership for $80,000 cash, her outside basis will be $80,000. Under § 743(b), Nupartner's § 743(b) total upward inside basis adjustment will be $30,000, the difference between her $80,000 outside basis and her $50,000 share of the partnership's inside basis. Under the regulations, Nupartner's share of the partnership's inside basis would equal her interest in the partnership's previously taxed capital. If there were a hypothetical cash disposition of all the partnership's assets, Nupartner would receive $80,000 of cash on the liquidation of the partnership. That amount is reduced by the $30,000 of tax gain ($10,000 in the accounts receivable, $5,000 in the capital asset, and $15,000 in the depreciable business property) that would be allocated to Nupartner in the hypothetical sale and liquidation. Thus, Nupartner's interest in the partnership's previously taxed capital and her share of the partnership's inside basis is $50,000. Note that under the formula in the regulations, Nupartner's share of the partnership's inside basis is simply her one-third proportionate share of the $150,000 total inside basis. That is because there are no special or § 704(c) allocations in the example.

Example (2):   Assume that in Example (1) A contributed the accounts receivable when they had a fair market value of $30,000 and a basis of zero. If Nupartner buys A's interest for $80,000 cash, her outside basis is again $80,000. Under § 743(b), Nupartner's § 743(b) total upward inside basis adjustment will now be $50,000, the difference between her $80,000 outside basis and her $30,000 share of the partnership's inside basis. Under the regulations, Nupartner's share of the partnership's inside basis would equal her interest in the partnership's previously taxed capital. Again, in a hypothetical sale of assets followed by a liquidation of the partnership, Nupartner would receive $80,000 cash. That amount is reduced by the $50,000 of tax gain ($30,000 in the accounts receivable, $5,000 in the capital asset, and $15,000 in the depreciable business property) that would be allocated to Nupartner in the hypothetical sale and liquidation. Nupartner, as a transferee of A steps into A's shoes with respect to the § 704(c) gain in the accounts receivable. Reg. 1.704–3(a)(7). Thus, Nupartner's interest in the partnership's previously taxed capital and her share of the partnership's inside basis in $30,000.

2)   Allocation of the Adjustment

Section 755 and its regulations set out the process for allocating the total § 743(b) adjustment to the partnership's assets. First, the partnership must determine the value of its assets. If the assets constitute a trade or business, the regulations require the valuation to be done in accordance with the rules for "applicable asset acquisitions" under § 1060 so that § 197 intangibles (e.g., goodwill and going concern value) are properly taken into account. See Reg. § 1.755–1(a)(1)–(5). Next, the partnership's assets are divided into two classes: (1) capital assets and § 1231(b) property, and (2) all other partnership property. Then the allocation is made to each of the two classes and within each class based on the allocations of income, gain, or loss (including remedial allocations under § 704(c)) that the transferee partner would receive if, immediately after the transfer of the interest, all of the partnership's property were sold for cash equal to the fair market value of such property. Reg. § 1.755–1(b). The regulations specifically allow an increase to be made to one class of property while a decrease is made to the other class. Reg. § 1.755–1(b)(1). Also, an increase can be made in the basis of one asset in a class while a decrease is made to another asset in the class. Id. Basis is first allocated to the class of all other (i.e., ordinary income) property. Keep in mind that the goal of the allocation is to produce the equivalent of a cost basis for the purchasing partner.

Example (1): Assume the same facts as Example (1) on page 145. Nupartner's $30,000 § 743(b) total inside basis adjustment will be allocated under § 755. If all of the partnership's assets were sold in a fully taxable transaction for fair market value, Nupartner would be allocated $10,000 of gain from the class of all other property (the accounts receivable) and $20,000 of gain from the class of capital assets and § 1231(b) property (capital asset and depreciable business property). Thus, the $30,000 adjustment would be allocated $10,000 to the accounts receivable and $20,000 to the capital asset and depreciable business property. Nupartner would be allocated $5,000 of gain from the capital asset and $15,000 from the depreciable business property so the $20,000 adjustment to that class would be allocated $5,000 to the capital asset and $15,000 to the depreciable business property.

Example (2): Assume the same facts as Example (2) on page 146. Nupartner's $50,000 total inside basis adjustment will again be allocated according to the allocations of income, gain, or loss Nupartner would receive in a fully taxable sale of the partnership's assets. Nupartner would be allocated $30,000 of gain from the class of all other property (accounts receivable) and $20,000 of gain from the class of capital assets and § 1231(b) property. Thus, the $50,000 adjustment would be allocated $30,000 to the accounts receivable, $5,000 to the capital asset, and $15,000 to the depreciable business property.

Example (3): The DEF cash method, general partnership has a § 754 election in effect and the following assets:

	A.B.	F.M.V.
Accounts Receivable	$ 0	$ 30,000
Capital Asset	45,000	60,000
Depreciable Business Property (no recapture)	105,000	150,000
	$150,000	$240,000

DEF also has $30,000 of partnership liabilities. If Nupartner purchases D's one-third interest in the partnership for $15,000 cash, his outside basis will be $25,000, taking into account his share of partnership liabilities under § 752(d). Under § 743(b), Nupartner's total upward inside basis adjustment will be $5,000 ($25,000 outside basis less $20,000 share of the partnership's inside basis). Nupartner's share of the partnership's inside basis would be equal to his $10,000 interest in the partnership's previously taxed capital ($15,000 cash Nupartner would receive on a sale and liquidation of the partnership, plus $10,000 share of tax loss in capital asset, minus $15,000 share of tax gain in the accounts receivable) plus his $10,000 share of partnership liabilities. The regulations permit Nupartner to make a $15,000 upward basis adjustment to the accounts receivable and a $10,000 downward basis adjustment to the capital asset so the net adjustment equals the $5,000 total § 743(b) adjustment. Reg. § 1.755–1(b)(i); see Reg. § 1.755–1(b)(2)(ii) Example 1. The regulations also permit simultaneous upward and downward basis adjustments within a class of property. Reg. § 1.755–1(b)(1)(i); see Reg. § 1.755–1(b)(3)(iii) Example 1.

c.   Effect of § 743(b) Adjustment

A basis adjustment under § 743(b) is personal to the transferee partner. The partnership's basis in its assets is not changed by the adjustment. Reg. § 1.743–1(j)(1). A partnership first computes all partnership items and each partner is allocated those items under § 704, without regard to any § 743(b) adjustments. The partnership then adjusts the transferee's distributive share of partnership items to reflect the adjustments. § 743(b) adjustments do not affect the transferee partner's capital account. Reg. § 1.743–1(j)(2). If a § 743(b) adjustment is made to a depreciable or amortizable asset, the adjustment generally is treated as being attributable to a newly purchased asset.

d.   Contributed Property with a Built-In Loss

Reg. § 1.704–3(a)(7) provides that if a partner contributes property to a partnership and later transfers the partnership interest, built-in gain or loss must be allocated to the transferee partner as it would have been allocated to the transferor partner. However, § 704(c)(1)(C), which was enacted subsequent to the issuance of that regulation, provides that in the case of property that was contributed to a partnership with a built-in loss, no other partner may be allocated that precontribution loss. Consequently, the transferee of a partnership interest may not be allocated any built-in loss that was contributed by the transferor of the partnership interest.

D. Review Questions

1.   A sells her one-third interest in ABC for $150,000. A has an adjusted basis of $100,000 in her partnership interest and has held the interest for five years. None of the partnership's assets were contributed by A. ABC is a cash method partnership and has the following assets:

	A.B.	F.M.V.
Cash	$ 65,000	$ 65,000
Accounts Receivable	0	30,000
Dealer Property	60,000	90,000
Capital Asset	25,000	85,000
Equipment (all § 1245 gain)	150,000	180,000
	$300,000	$450,000

(a)   Which of ABC's assets are § 751 assets?

(b)   What is A's § 751 income?

(c)   What is A's § 741 income?

(d)   What is the character of A's § 741 income?

2.   B sells her one-third interest in the ABC partnership for a $50,000 installment note payable in two years. B has an outside basis of $20,000. ABC has the following assets:

	A.B.	F.M.V.
Capital Asset	$ 30,000	$ 60,000
Accounts Receivable	0	30,000
Equipment (all § 1245 gain)	30,000	60,000
	$ 60,000	$150,000

Must B recognize any gain in the year of the sale?

3.   Nupartner purchases a one-third interest in the ABC cash method partnership for $30,000. ABC has the following assets:

	A.B.	F.M.V.
Cash	$ 15,000	$ 15,000
Accounts Receivable	0	15,000
Capital Asset	30,000	60,000
	$ 45,000	$ 90,000

(a)   What is Nupartner's outside basis in her partnership interest?

(b)   When the partnership collects the accounts receivable how much income will be allocated to Nupartner? Assume the partnership does not have a § 754 election in effect.

(c)   Assume the partnership has a § 754 election in effect. What is Nupartner's personal inside basis in each partnership asset?

Chapter XI

Operating Distributions

■ ANALYSIS

A. Consequences to the Partner
    1. Cash Distributions
    2. Property Distributions
    3. Dispositions of Distributed Property
B. Consequences to the Partnership
    1. Nonrecognition of Gain or Loss
    2. Impact on Inside Basis
    3. Adjustments to Capital Accounts
C. Mixing Bowl Transactions
    1. Introduction
    2. Distributions of Contributed Property to Another Partner
    3. Distributions of Other Property to the Contributing Partner
D. Distributions Which Shift the Partners' Interests in § 751 Assets: § 751(b)
    1. Purpose and Scope of § 751(b)
    2. § 751(b) Assets
    3. Operation of § 751(b)
    4. Criticisms of § 751(b)
    5. Proposed Regulations
E. Review Questions

A. Consequences to the Partner

Because partners are taxed directly on partnership income under an aggregate theory, Subchapter K has rules which generally permit partners to receive distributions of that income without being taxed again. Those rules, however, are subject to a number of provisions designed to prevent easy avoidance of tax.

1. Cash Distributions

a. In General

A partner generally does not recognize gain or loss on the receipt of a cash distribution from a partnership. § 731(a). If, however, the money distributed exceeds the partner's outside basis, the excess is recognized as gain from the sale or exchange of the partner's partnership interest. § 731(a)(1). A partner's outside basis is reduced (but not below zero) by the amount of any money distributed by the partnership. §§ 705(a)(2); 733.

These rules apply only to distributions by a partnership. So, for example, if a partnership loans money to a partner, there is no distribution but a later cancellation of the partner's repayment obligation is considered a distribution. Reg. § 1.731–1(c)(2). Advances or draws of money or property by a partner against his distributive share of income are considered distributions on the last day of the partnership's taxable year because they are contingent on the profitability of the partnership and must be repaid to the extent the partnership does not have sufficient profits. Advances and draws thus are similar to loans. Reg. § 1.731–1(a)(1)(ii). The distribution rules apply to both actual cash distributions and deemed cash distributions under § 752(b), which occur as a result of a decrease in a partner's share of partnership liabilities. A deemed distribution of money under § 752(b) is treated as an advance or draw and is taken into account at the end of the partnership taxable year. Rev. Rul. 94–4, 1994–1 C.B. 196.

Example (1): A's outside basis is $10,000. If the partnership distributes $8,000 cash to A in a pro rata distribution to all partners, he will not recognize any gain or loss and his outside basis will be reduced to $2,000. If, instead, the partnership distributed $13,000 cash to A, he would recognize $3,000 of gain from the sale or exchange of his partnership interest and his outside basis would be reduced to zero. The results would be the same if under § 752(b) the $13,000 distribution resulted from a $13,000 decrease in A's share of partnership liabilities.

Example (2): B's outside basis is $8,000. On April 1, B receives a $6,000 cash "draw" against her share of partnership profits for the year, and on October 1 she receives a second $6,000 draw. B's distributive share of partnership profits for the year is $15,000 and the other partners also receive pro rata draws in April and October. Because the $6,000 distributions are advances against B's distributive share of profits, they are treated as distributions on the last day of the partnership's taxable year. At that time B's $15,000 distributive share of partnership income increases her outside basis to $23,000 and the deemed year-end distribution reduces her outside basis to $11,000.

§ 705(a)(1)(A), (a)(2). B will not recognize gain as a result of the deemed year-end distribution because it does not exceed her outside basis. If the April and October distributions were not draws because B had no obligation to repay the amount in excess of her distributive share of profits, the October distribution would result in $4,000 of gain ($8,000 original outside basis less total of $12,000 of distributions). In addition, B would have to include in income her $15,000 distributive share of partnership profits. The characterization of the mid-year distributions as "draws" or "advances" may affect the tax results to the partners, and thus it is important to establish the partner's obligation to repay excess distributions if the partners wish a distribution to be treated as a draw or advance against partnership profits.

b. Distributions of Marketable Securities

1) General Rule

For purposes of the partnership distribution rules, "marketable securities" are treated as money to the extent of their fair market value on the date of the distribution. § 731(c)(1). This rule prevents the easy circumvention of § 731(a)(1) through the distribution of marketable securities, which are easily valued and highly liquid, instead of cash. As a result of § 731(c), a partner generally recognizes gain on a distribution of marketable securities having a fair market value, together with any cash distributed, that exceeds the partner's outside basis immediately before the distribution. The distributee partner's basis in the distributed securities is their § 732 basis (see XI.A.2.b., at page 154, *infra*), increased by the amount of gain recognized by the partner under § 731(c). § 731(c)(4)(A). Marketable securities are defined as financial instruments (e.g. stocks, bonds, options, and futures) and foreign currencies that are actively traded and include interests in mutual funds and instruments convertible into marketable securities. § 731(c)(2).

2) Reduction for Distributee's Share of Partnership Net Gain

The distributee partner reduces the amount of a § 731(c) distribution by the amount of the partner's share of the net gain in the partnership's marketable securities. § 731(c)(3)(B).

***Example*:** The ABC partnership, which is not an investment partnership, owns 300 shares of publicly traded X, Inc. stock with an adjusted basis of $3,000 and a fair market value of $30,000 and other assets, none of which are marketable securities. The partnership distributes all 300 shares of the X, Inc. stock to A, a one-third partner who has an outside basis of $5,000. Under § 731(c)(1), A is treated as receiving a $30,000 cash distribution, reduced under § 731(c)(3)(B) by $9,000 (A's one-third share of the partnership's $27,000 of net appreciation— i.e., the gain that would have passed through to A if the partnership had sold the X, Inc. stock for $30,000). A thus recognizes $16,000 of gain on the distribution ($30,000 value of X, Inc. stock less $9,000 share of net appreciation less A's $5,000 outside basis). A's basis in the X, Inc. stock is $19,000 (A's $3,000 basis determined under § 732(a) plus the $16,000 gain recognized on the distribution). § 731(c)(4)(A).

3) Exceptions

The rules in § 731(c) do not apply to: (1) distributions of marketable securities from an "investment partnership"; (2) a distribution of a security to a partner who contributed that security to the partnership; and (3) in several other very specialized situations. § 731(c)(3). For purposes of the first exception, an "investment partnership" is a partnership that never has engaged in a trade or business and substantially all of the assets of which consists of stocks, bonds, cash, currencies, and other investment-type assets. § 731(c)(3)(C)(i). For this purpose, a "trade or business" does not include the activities of investors, traders, and dealers. § 731(c)(3)(C)(ii).

2. Property Distributions

a. Recognition of Gain or Loss

When a partnership distributes property to a partner in a nonliquidating distribution, generally neither the partner nor the partnership recognizes gain or loss. § 731(a), (b). The principal exception is a distribution which is treated as a constructive sale or exchange under § 751(b). See XI.D.1., at page 164, *infra*. Additionally, if a partner contributes property to a partnership and the property is distributed to another partner within seven years, the contributing partner must recognize the precontribution gain or loss inherent in the property. § 704(c)(1)(B). See XI.C.2., at page 162, *infra*. Finally, if a partner contributes property to a partnership and the partnership distributes other property to the partner within seven years of the contribution, the partner must recognize gain as required by § 737. See XI.C.3., at page 163, *infra*.

b. Basis Consequences

1) General Rule: Transferred Basis

A partner generally takes a transferred basis in property distributed by a partnership, and the distributee partner's outside basis is reduced by the basis of the distributed property. §§ 732(a)(1); 733(2).

2) Basis Limitation

A partner's basis in distributed property may not, however, exceed the partner's outside basis less any money received in the same transaction. § 732(a)(2). For purposes of determining the amount of money distributed in a single transaction as a result of debt relief (e.g., on a distribution of encumbered property), decreases in a partner's share of partnership liabilities are offset by increases in the partner's individual liabilities (e.g., by reason of the partner's assumption of partnership liabilities). Rev. Rul. 79–205, 1979–2 C.B. 255; Reg. § 1.752–1(f).

3) Allocation of Basis

If the outside basis limitation is reached, the basis to be allocated (i.e., the partner's outside basis less cash received in the transaction) must be allocated among the various properties received by the distributee partner. First unrealized receivables and inventory items are tentatively assigned basis equal to the adjusted basis of the partnership in those assets. § 732(c)(1)(A)(i). If the partnership's basis in the unrealized receivables and inventory items is greater than the basis to be allocated, then the bases of those assets is reduced (1) by first reducing the basis of assets with built-in losses (i.e., assets with an assigned basis greater their values) in proportion to the amount of such built-in losses (and only to the extent of such losses), and (2) by then making additional reductions in basis in proportion to the remaining adjusted basis of the unrealized receivables and inventory items. §§ 732(c)(1)(A)(ii), (3). If the basis to be allocated is greater than the partnership's basis in distributed unrealized receivables and inventory items, then each other distributed asset is tentatively assigned a basis equal to the partnership's basis in those assets. § 732(c)(1)(B)(i). The partnership's bases in those assets must be reduced so that the sum of their bases equals the remaining basis to be allocated. Again, the reduction is accomplished by first reducing the basis of assets with built-in losses (in proportion to such losses), and then in proportion to the remaining adjusted bases of the properties. § 732(c)(1)(B)(ii), (3). For the definition of "unrealized receivables" and "inventory items," see X.B.2.b., at page 137, *supra*.

4) Holding Period

Because a partner generally takes a transferred basis in distributed property, the partner's holding period for such property includes, or "tacks," the partnership's holding period for the property. §§ 735(b); 1223.

Example (1): C's outside basis is $30,000 and C receives a partnership distribution of $10,000 cash and undeveloped land with a fair market value of $25,000 and a $15,000 adjusted basis. The partnership makes identical pro rata distributions to the other partners. Under § 731(a), C recognizes no gain and reduces his outside basis to $20,000 ($30,000 less $10,000 cash distribution) under § 733. Under the general rule in § 732(a)(1), the land takes a $15,000 transferred basis and C's outside basis is reduced to $5,000 under § 733.

Example (2): If C's outside basis in Example (1) were $20,000 and he received the same distribution, again he would not recognize gain and his outside basis would be reduced to $10,000 as a result of the distribution of the cash. Since C's remaining outside basis of $10,000 is less than the $15,000 transferred basis for the land, § 732(a)(2) limits C's basis in the land to $10,000. His outside basis is reduced to zero under § 733.

Example (3):   D's basis in her partnership interest is $10,000. D receives a partnership distribution of:

	A.B.	F.M.V.
Cash	$2,000	$2,000
Accounts Receivable	0	3,000
Inventory	3,000	5,000
Capital Asset	4,000	9,000

The partnership makes identical pro rata distributions to the other partners. Under § 731(a), D recognizes no gain or loss and reduces her outside basis to $8,000 ($10,000 less $2,000 cash distribution) under § 733. Under the general rule in § 732(a)(1), the accounts receivable, inventory, and capital asset take a zero, $3,000, and $4,000 transferred basis, respectively, and D's outside basis is reduced to $1,000 under § 733.

Example (4):   Assume the same facts as Example (3) except D's outside basis is $3,000. D does not recognize gain or loss and her outside basis is reduced to $1,000 as a result of the distribution of the cash. Under § 732(a)(2) and (c), D's remaining outside basis of $1,000 must be allocated to the distributed assets. First, the accounts receivable and the inventory items are assigned a basis equal to the partnership's bases in those assets (zero and $3,000 respectively). Since neither asset has a built-in loss the required $2,000 reduction is made in proportion to the remaining bases in those assets (all to the inventory). Thus, the basis in the accounts receivable is zero, the basis in the inventory is $1,000, and the basis in the capital asset is zero. D's outside basis is reduced to zero.

Example (5):   E's basis in his partnership interest is $5,000. E receives a partnership distribution of:

	A.B.	F.M.V.
Cash	$2,000	$2,000
Inventory—Lot 1	12,000	10,000
Inventory—Lot 2	5,000	18,000

The partnership makes identical pro rata distributions to the other partners. Under § 731(a), E recognizes no gain or loss and reduces his outside basis to $3,000 ($5,000 less $2,000 cash distribution) under § 733. Under § 732(a)(2) and (c), E's remaining outside basis of $3,000 is allocated between the two lots of inventory. Both lots of inventory initially are assigned a basis equal to the partnership's basis in the lots ($12,000 to Lot 1 and $5,000 to Lot 2). To apply the § 732(a)(2) basis limitation, Lot 1's basis is first reduced by the amount of built-in loss in that asset ($2,000). The remaining bases in the two lots of inventory ($15,000 total) must then be reduced to a total of $3,000 (the basis to be allocated). The $12,000 reduction is accomplished by reducing the bases of the lots in proportion to their respective remaining bases. Thus, $8,000 of the reduction (two-thirds) is made in the basis of Lot 1 and $4,000 (one-third) is made in the basis of Lot 2. Thus, Lot 1 takes a $2,000 basis and Lot 2 takes a $1,000 basis. E's outside basis is reduced to zero.

c. § 732(d) Election

Under § 732(d), a distributee partner who acquires her partnership interest in a transfer (by sale or exchange or upon the death of a partner) when there is no § 754 election in effect may elect, with respect to distributions within two years after the transfer, to treat the bases of the partnership's assets as if § 743(b) adjustments had taken place. As a result of a § 732(d) election, a distributee partner will take § 743(b) adjustments into account in determining the basis of distributed property under § 732(a) and (c). See X.C.2., at page 144, *supra,* for the operation of § 743(b). The Service may require application of § 732(d) in the case of a distribution (within two years or later) if, at the time the partner acquired her partnership interest, the fair market value of the partnership property (other than money) exceeded 110% of its adjusted basis. The regulations limit this rule to situations where there would otherwise be a shift in basis from nondepreciable to depreciable property. Reg. § 1.732–1(d)(4).

Example: B purchases a one-fourth interest in a partnership for $60,000 at a time when the partnership has not made a § 754 election. The partnership's balance sheet is as follows:

	A.B.	F.M.V.
Accounts Receivable	$ 0	$ 40,000
Nondepreciable Capital Asset	80,000	200,000
Total	80,000	240,000

Within two years of B's purchase, the partnership distributes $10,000 of the accounts receivable to each of its four partners. If B does not make a § 732(d) election, he will take a zero basis in the $10,000 of accounts receivable under § 732(a)(1) and his outside basis will continue to be $60,000. If B makes a § 732(d) election, there would be a $10,000 upward adjustment under § 743(b) and § 755 to the basis of the receivables distributed to him. See X.C.2.b., at page 144, *supra,* for the operation of § 743(b) and § 755. Under § 731(a)(1), the $10,000 basis in the receivables would carry over to B and his outside basis would be reduced to $50,000 under § 733.

3. Dispositions of Distributed Property

a. General Rules: § 735

Under § 735(a), any gain or loss recognized with respect to distributed "unrealized receivables" is characterized as ordinary, and any gain or loss recognized with respect to "inventory items" (whether or not substantially appreciated) within five years after the distribution is characterized as ordinary. See X.B.2.b., at page 137, *supra,* for the definitions of "unrealized receivables" and "inventory items." For purposes of this rule, the long-term holding period requirement in § 1231(b) is disregarded, and thus property otherwise described in § 1231(b) is not an "inventory item" even if it has not been held long-term. §§ 735(c)(1); 751(d)(2)(B). If a partner disposes of either a distributed unrealized receivable or a distributed inventory item in a nonrecognition transaction, any substituted basis property (other than C corporation stock received in a § 351 exchange) resulting from the transaction retains the taint of the distributed property. The same rule applies to a series of nonrecognition transactions. § 735(c)(2).

Example (1): Partner C receives a parcel of real property from her partnership in a pro rata distribution. The parcel is an "inventory item" because the partnership held the parcel for sale to customers in the ordinary course of its business. § 751(d)(1). If C sells the parcel within five years, any gain or loss is characterized as ordinary. After five years, gain or loss on the parcel is characterized with reference to C's activities.

Example (2): Assume C holds the parcel in Example (1) for investment and it would be a capital asset in her hands. If C disposes of the parcel in a § 1031 exchange for property of like kind, the property C receives in the exchange will retain the § 735 ordinary income taint of the distributed parcel. If the new property is sold or exchanged within five years of the distribution of the original parcel, any gain or loss is characterized as ordinary.

b. Depreciation Recapture

If a partnership distributes depreciable property which has potential recapture income under § 1245 or § 1250 to a partner, the character of that income is preserved by the definition of "recomputed basis" in § 1245 and "depreciation adjustments" in § 1250(b)(3). See §§ 1245(b)(5), 1250(d)(5).

B. Consequences to the Partnership

1. Nonrecognition of Gain or Loss

Under § 731(b), generally, no gain or loss is recognized by a partnership when it distributes property (including money) to a partner. This nonrecognition rule extends to property with potential § 1245 or § 1250 depreciation recapture income. §§ 1245(b)(3); 1250(d)(3). The principal exception is distributions which are treated as sales or exchanges under § 751(b).

2. Impact on Inside Basis

a. General Rule: No Adjustment to Inside Basis

Under § 734(a), the inside basis of the partnership's assets generally is not adjusted as a result of a property distribution by the partnership unless it has a § 754 election in effect. Section 734 may require a downward adjustment in a partnership's basis in its assets in the case of a liquidating distribution. See XII.A.2.b., at page 172, *infra*. In the absence of an inside basis adjustment, liquidating and nonliquidating distributions may create an imbalance between the partnership's total inside basis and the total outside bases of the partners' partnership interests when: (1) a partner recognizes gain under § 731(a)(1) as a result of receiving a distribution of money in excess of his outside basis, or (2) the basis of distributed property is limited under § 732(a)(2) because the partner has insufficient outside basis. Liquidating distributions also may produce an imbalance between inside and outside basis in other situations. The resulting distortions may affect the timing and character of income and loss in a manner similar to the distortions resulting when a partner purchases an interest in a partnership which does not have a § 754 election in effect.

b. § 734(b) Adjustment

Under § 734(b), if a partnership has a § 754 election in effect, it increases the inside basis of its assets by: (1) the amount of any § 731(a)(1) gain recognized by the distributee partner, and (2) if the § 732(a)(2) limitation applies, by the excess of the basis the distributed asset had to the partnership over the basis it has to the distributee partner.

c. Allocation of Basis Adjustment

An adjustment as a result of § 731(a)(1) gain recognition by the distributee partner must be allocated to capital assets and § 1231(b) property. Reg. § 1.755–1(c)(1)(ii). The basis increase as a result of a distribution of property is allocated under § 755 to the same class of property (capital assets and § 1231 property or all other property) which gave rise to the adjustment. Reg. § 1.755–1(c)(1)(i). If a basis increase is allocated within a class of property, the increase is first allocated to properties with unrealized appreciation in proportion to their appreciation. Any remaining increase is allocated in proportion to the fair market values of the properties. Reg. § 1.755–1(c)(2)(i). Decreases in the basis of partnership assets may result from a distribution that liquidates a partner's interest. See § 734(b)(2) and XII.A.2.b., at page 172, *infra*. If a basis decrease is allocated within a class of property, the decrease is allocated first to properties with unrealized depreciation in proportion to their respective amounts of unrealized depreciation before the reduction. Any remaining decrease must be allocated among the properties within the class in proportion to their adjusted bases (after adjustment for unrealized depreciation). Reg. § 1.755–1(c)(2)(ii). The basis of a property cannot be reduced below zero. Reg. § 1.755–1(c)(3). If a partnership does not have property of the character to be adjusted or if the basis of all property of like character has been reduce to zero, the adjustment carries over until the partnership acquires property of a like character to which an adjustment can be made. Reg. § 1.755–1(c)(4).

Example (1): The ABC partnership has the following balance sheet:

	Assets			Partners' Capital	
	A.B.	F.M.V.		A.B.	F.M.V.
Cash	$ 11,000	$ 11,000	A	$ 10,000	$ 11,000
Capital Asset	19,000	22,000	B	10,000	11,000
			C	10,000	11,000
Total	$ 30,000	$ 33,000		$ 30,000	$ 33,000

If A receives $11,000 in cash in liquidation of his entire interest in the partnership, he will recognize $1,000 of gain under § 731(a)(1). If the partnership does not have a § 754 election in effect, under § 734(a) there will be no adjustment to the inside basis of the capital asset and its balance sheet will be as follows:

	Assets			Partners' Capital	
	A.B.	**F.M.V.**		**A.B.**	**F.M.V.**
Capital Asset	19,000	$ 22,000	B	$ 10,000	$ 11,000
			C	10,000	11,000
Total	$ 19,000	$ 22,000		$ 20,000	$ 22,000

Because no adjustment is made under § 734(a), the partnership's asset still has $3,000 of gain potential even though A recognized $1,000 of gain on the distribution. Thus, if the partnership sold the capital asset, B and C would each recognize $1,500 of gain which would increase their outside bases to $11,500. B and C would each have $500 of potential loss built into their partnership interests which would be recognized only if they dispose of their partnership interests or if the partnership liquidates.

If the partnership had a § 754 election in effect, it would increase its inside basis by $1,000 as a result of A recognizing gain under § 731(a)(1). § 734(b)(1)(A). That $1,000 adjustment must be allocated to partnership capital assets and § 1231(b) property with unrealized appreciation in proportion to the relative appreciation in each asset. Thus, the basis of the capital asset would increase to $20,000 and the partnership's balance sheet would be as follows:

	Assets			Partners' Capital	
	A.B.	**F.M.V.**		**A.B.**	**F.M.V.**
Capital Asset	20,000	$ 22,000	B	$ 10,000	$ 11,000
			C	10,000	11,000
Total	$ 20,000	$ 22,000		$ 20,000	$ 22,000

Note that the § 734(b) adjustment brought the inside and outside bases into balance and eliminated the potential distortion which resulted from the no-adjustment rule in § 734(a). Now if the partnership sells the capital asset there will be $2,000 of gain and B and C will each recognize their $1,000 share.

Example (2): The DEF Partnership has the following balance sheet:

	Assets			Partners' Capital	
	A.B.	**F.M.V.**		**A.B.**	**F.M.V.**
Cash	$ 4,000	$ 11,000	D	$ 10,000	$ 11,000
Capital Asset # 1	11,000	5,000	E	10,000	11,000
Capital Asset # 2	15,000	24,000	F	10,000	11,000
Total	$ 30,000	$ 33,000		$ 30,000	$ 33,000

If the partnership distributes Capital Asset #1 to D, she will take a $10,000 basis in the asset under § 732(a)(2). If there is no § 754 election in effect, the loss of $1,000 of basis will again create distortions among the partners. If a § 754 election has been made, the partnership will receive a $1,000 increase in its inside basis which must be allocated to Capital Asset #2 because it is in the same class of property which gave rise to the adjustment. Thus, the basis of Capital Asset #2 would become $16,000 and the partnership's balance sheet would be:

| | Assets | | | Partners' Capital | |
	A.B.	F.M.V.		A.B.	F.M.V.
Cash	$ 4,000	$ 4,000	D	$ 0	$ 6,000
Capital Asset # 2	16,000	24,000	E	10,000	11,000
			F	10,000	11,000
Total	$ 20,000	$ 28,000		$ 20,000	$ 28,000

Note that the inside and outside bases are now in balance as a result of the § 734(b) adjustment. One problem remains. Without a special allocation, the recognition of income on Capital Asset #2 will be distorted. Originally there was $6,000 of loss in Capital Asset #1, which would have been shared equally among the partners ($2,000 each). As a result of the distribution, D would recognize $5,000 of that loss if she sold the asset ($5,000 fair market value less $10,000 adjusted basis under § 732(a)(2)). To compensate E and F for not receiving their $4,000 share of loss, D should recognize the first $4,000 of gain in Capital Asset #2. And to compensate E and F for the loss of $1,000 of basis in Capital Asset #1, D should also recognize an additional $1,000 of gain in Capital Asset #2. The remaining $3,000 of gain in Capital Asset #2 should be shared equally ($1,000 each) among the partners. Thus, the $8,000 of gain in Capital Asset #2 should be allocated $6,000 to D, $1,000 to E, and $1,000 to F. Such an allocation would not have substantial economic effect. It is not tax motivated, however, and should be recognized. For an allocation which is similar in purpose and is respected, see Reg. § 1.704–1(b)(5) Example (14)(i).

3. Adjustments to Capital Accounts

A partner's capital account is reduced by the fair market value of property received in a distribution from the partnership. Reg. § 1.704–1(b)(2)(iv)(b). In order to account for the variation between the distributed property's fair market value and its book value, the regulations require that the capital accounts first be adjusted to reflect the manner in which the unrealized gain or loss would be allocated if there were a taxable disposition of the property for its fair market value. Reg. § 1.704–1(b)(2)(iv)(e)(1).

C. Mixing Bowl Transactions

1. Introduction

Subchapter K includes two anti-abuse provisions to combat "mixing bowl transactions," an income-shifting strategy that generally involves a partner first transferring appreciated property to a partnership and the partnership later either distributing the contributed property to another partner or distributing other property to the contributing partner. The tax planning goal is to shift or defer the recognition of the contributing partner's precontribution gain by exploiting the nonrecognition rules for contributions to (e.g., § 721) and distributions by (e.g., § 731) a partnership.

2.   Distributions of Contributed Property to Another Partner

a.   The Attempted Strategy

As discussed earlier, a partner who contributes property with a built-in gain or loss to a partnership is generally allocated that gain or loss when the partnership subsequently disposes of the property. § 704(c)(1)(A). See VI.A.1. at page 90, *supra*. When first enacted, § 704(c) did not apply to distributions of contributed property. As a result, a contributing partner could avoid an allocation of precontribution gain or loss if the partnership distributed the contributed property to another partner instead of selling it. Neither the partnership nor the contributing partner normally would recognize gain or loss on the distribution, and built-in gain often was shifted to the distributee partner. This type of income-shifting is contrary to the policy of § 704(c).

b.   General Rule of § 704(c)(1)(B)

Section 704(c)(1)(B) provides that if property contributed by a partner is distributed to another partner within seven years of its contribution, the contributing partner must recognize gain or loss from the sale or exchange of the property in an amount equal to the gain or loss that would have been allocated to that partner under § 704(c)(1)(A) if the property had been sold by the partnership for its fair market value. § 704(c)(1)(B)(i). The character of the gain or loss is determined as if the partnership had sold the property. § 704(c)(1)(B)(ii). The contributing partner's outside basis is increased or decreased by the gain or loss recognized as a result of the distribution. § 704(c)(1)(B)(iii). To avoid double recognition of gain or loss, the partnership's inside basis in the distributed property is increased or decreased prior to the distribution to reflect the contributing partner's gain or loss. Id. A successor to the contributing partner (e.g., a purchaser of the partnership interest) is treated in the same manner as the contributing partner. § 704(c)(3). However, § 704(c)(1)(C) would prevent a successor partner from recognizing loss from property that was contributed with a built-in loss because the property's basis would be deemed to be equal to its fair market value at the time it was contributed to the partnership.

Example (1):   On the formation of the ABC equal partnership, A contributed Gainacre with a fair market value of $100,000 and a basis of $40,000. If the partnership distributes Gainacre to C two years later when it is worth $130,000, A recognizes $60,000 of gain (the built-in gain at the time of contribution). The character of A's gain is the same as it would have been if the partnership had sold the property. If A had sold his partnership interest to D during the two-year period, D would be treated in the same manner as A—i.e., D would recognize $60,000 gain.

Example (2):   Same facts as Example (1), except that Gainacre is worth only $80,000 when the partnership distributes it to C. If the partnership makes § 704(c) allocations using the traditional method, the ceiling rule would limit A's gain on the distribution to $40,000 because that is the gain the partnership would have recognized if it had sold Gainacre for $80,000.

c. Exceptions

The general rule of § 704(c)(1)(B) is subject to two statutory exceptions: (1) it does not apply if the contributed property is distributed back to the contributing partner or her successor (§ 704(c)(1)(B)), and (2) relief is provided to a contributing partner who receives a distribution of § 1031 like-kind property within 180 days after the contributed property is distributed to another partner, or if earlier, the due date for the contributing partner's tax return (§ 704(c)(2)). For purposes of the second exception, the contributing partner's gain or loss is reduced by the amount of built-in gain or loss in the distributed like-kind property. See § 1.704–4(d)(3) & (4) Example. The policy is that gain or loss should not be recognized under § 704(c)(1)(B) if the contributing partner would have qualified for nonrecognition if the transaction had taken place outside the partnership (e.g., with the other partner) and the gain or loss is preserved in the distributed property. The regulations also provide that § 704(c)(1)(B) does not apply if there is a constructive termination of the partnership under § 708(b)(1)(B). Reg. § 1.704–4(c)(3). See XII.B.2. at page 181, *infra*.

> ***Example (3):*** Assume in Example (1), above, that the partnership again distributes Gainacre (value, $130,000) to C two years after A's contribution. If the partnership distributes like-kind property to A that has $60,000 of built-in gain within the prescribed time limits, A does not recognize gain on the distribution of the contributed property.

3. Distributions of Other Property to the Contributing Partner

a. The Attempted Strategy

A second potential abuse identified by Congress was a transaction where a partner contributes appreciated property to a partnership and later receives a distribution of other property, with the partnership retaining the contributed property. The concern in this scenario is that, if the normal contribution and distribution rules of Subchapter K applied, a contributing partner would be able to avoid recognition of gain on a swap of properties when a similar transaction outside the partnership would not have qualified for nonrecognition.

b. General Rule of § 737

Section 737 requires a contributing partner to recognize gain if she contributes appreciated property to a partnership and within seven years of the contribution receives property other than money as a distribution from the partnership. § 737(a). The amount of the gain recognized is the lesser of: (1) the fair market value of the distributed property (other than cash) less the partner's outside basis immediately before the distribution (reduced, but not below zero, by any cash received in the distribution), or (2) the net gain that the partner would have recognized under § 704(c)(1)(B) if all of the property contributed by the partner within seven years of the current distribution had been distributed to another partner at the time of the distribution to the contributing partner ("net precontribution gain"). § 737(a), (b). In effect, § 737 requires a contributing partner to recognize precontribution gain on contributed property to the extent that the value of other property distributed by the partnership to that partner exceeds the partner's outside basis. In so doing, it permits the partner to limit potential gain recognition by netting any precontribution losses against precontribution gains.

The distributee partner's outside basis is increased by the partner's § 737 recognized gain; this adjustment is treated as occurring immediately before the distribution. § 737(c)(1). The partnership increases its inside basis in the contributed property to reflect any § 737 recognized gain. § 737(c)(2).

Example: A and B form the equal AB partnership, with A contributing Gainacre (value $40,000, basis $24,000), and B contributing $10,000 cash and Land (value and basis $30,000). Three years later, when A's outside basis is still $24,000, the partnership distributes Land (value still $30,000) to A. A recognizes $6,000 gain, which is the lesser of: (1) $6,000, the $30,000 value of Land reduced by A's $24,000 outside basis, or (2) $16,000, A's net precontribution gain. After determining the § 737 gain but immediately before the distribution, A increases his outside basis by $6,000, to $30,000. A recognizes no further gain on the distribution but reduces his outside basis by $30,000 (the partnership's inside basis in Land) to zero. The partnership's basis in Gainacre is increased by $6,000, to $30,000.

c. Exceptions

Section 737 is subject to two statutory exceptions: (1) if any portion of the distributed property consists of property contributed by the distributee partner, that property is not taken into account in determining § 737(a) gain or net precontribution gain under § 737(b), and (2) § 737 does not apply to the extent that § 751(b) applies. § 737(d). For a discussion of § 751(b), see XI.D. at page 164, *infra.* The regulations also provide that § 737 does not apply to a constructive termination of the partnership under § 708(b)(1)(B). Reg. § 1.737–2(a). See XII.B.2. at page 181, *infra.*

D. Distributions Which Shift the Partners' Interests in § 751 Assets: § 751(b)

1. Purpose and Scope of § 751(b)

Section 751(b) is designed to prevent shifts of ordinary income and capital gain among the partners through property distributions. It provides that if a partner receives in a distribution (1) unrealized receivables or substantially appreciated inventory ("§ 751 property") in exchange for some or all of her interest in other partnership property (including money), or (2) other property (including money) of the partnership in exchange for some or all of her interest in the partnership's § 751 property, then the distribution is to be treated as a sale or exchange of that property between the partner and the partnership. Section 751(b) does not apply, however, to distributions of property which the distributee partner contributed to the partnership, payments governed by § 736(a), draws or advances against the partner's distributive share, and distributions which are gifts or payment for services or the use of capital. § 751(b)(2); Reg. § 1.751–1(b)(1)(ii).

2. § 751(b) Assets

Section 751(b) generally applies to both nonliquidating and liquidating distributions that shift the partners' interests in the same types of property which § 751(a) singles out for ordinary income or loss treatment when a partner sells some or all of a partnership interest (i.e., unrealized receivables and inventory items). See X.B.2.b., at page 137, *supra,* for the definition of unrealized receivables and inventory items, and the operation of § 751(a). In the case of § 751(b), however, inventory items are treated as § 751 property only if they have "appreciated substantially in value." § 751(b)(1)(A)(ii). Inventory items are considered to have appreciated substantially in value if their fair market value exceeds 120% of their adjusted basis. § 751(b)(3)(A). Remember that the definition of inventory items is broad enough to include all of a partnership's unrealized receivables since they are property which if sold by the partnership would produce ordinary income. Reg. § 1.751–1(d)(2)(ii). The inclusion of unrealized receivables as inventory items is important for purposes of testing whether the inventory items are substantially appreciated. But if the inventory items (including the unrealized receivables) are not substantially appreciated, the unrealized receivables nevertheless retain their separate § 751 taint.

To prevent abuses, inventory acquired by a partnership with the principal purpose of avoiding the 120% test is disregarded for purposes of determining whether the inventory items are substantially appreciated in value. § 751(b)(3)(B).

3. Operation of § 751(b)

The operation of § 751(b) breaks down into four steps:

a. First, the distributee partner's interest in § 751 property and non-§ 751 property before and after the distribution must be compared to determine whether a § 751(b) exchange has occurred. If so, the amount and nature of the partnership property given up (the "exchanged" property) and the property received in the exchange (the "property received from the partnership") also must be identified. The partners are free to agree as to the composition of the exchanged property. Reg. § 1.751–1(g) Example (3)(c).

b. Second, a constructive distribution is created in which the exchanged property is distributed by the partnership to the partner. The normal rules governing partnership distributions (§§ 731, 732 and 733) apply to this constructive distribution. This step places the partner in a position to complete the fictional exchange required by § 751(b).

c. Third, after the constructive distribution, the partner is deemed to transfer the exchanged property for the property received from the partnership in a taxable transaction.

d. Finally, the tax results of the remainder of the distribution (i.e., the distributed property which is not part of the § 751(b) exchange) must be determined under §§ 731, 732, and 733.

Example: The ABC equal partnership has the following balance sheet:

Assets	A.B.	F.M.V.		Partners' Capital	A.B.	F.M.V.
Cash	$ 12,000	$ 12,000	A		$ 9,000	$ 12,000
Inventory	9,000	12,000	B		9,000	12,000
Capital Asset	6,000	12,000	C		9,000	12,000
Total	$ 27,000	$ 36,000			$ 27,000	$ 36,000

Assume A receives a distribution of the $12,000 of inventory in liquidation of her partnership interest. Before the distribution, each partner had a one-third interest in each partnership asset and would have recognized $1,000 of ordinary income if the inventory were sold and $2,000 of capital gain if the capital asset were sold. If the distribution to A were respected, A would take the $12,000 of inventory with a $9,000 basis and have $3,000 of ordinary income potential. B and C, the remaining partners, each would have $3,000 of capital gain potential in the capital asset. Thus, in the absence of § 751(b), the distribution to A would shift $2,000 of capital gain to B and C, and A would have $2,000 of additional ordinary income preserved in the inventory.

The first step in applying § 751(b) is to identify the § 751(b) exchange. Before the distribution, A had a one-third, or $4,000, interest in each of the cash, the inventory, and the capital asset. After the distribution, A has $12,000 of inventory (which is § 751(d) substantially appreciated inventory) and no interest in the cash and capital asset. As a result, a § 751(b) exchange has taken place in which A has exchanged her $4,000 interests in the cash and capital asset (non-§ 751 property) for an additional $8,000 of inventory (§ 751 property).

The second step is to set the stage for the § 751(b) exchange. The partnership constructively distributes the exchanged property ($4,000 of cash and $4,000 of the capital asset with a $2,000 basis) to A. Under § 731, A would recognize no gain or loss as a result of this constructive distribution and would receive a $2,000 transferred basis in the $4,000 capital asset under § 732. Following the constructive distribution to A, the partnership's balance sheet would be as follows:

Assets	A.B.	F.M.V.		Partners' Capital	A.B.	F.M.V.
Cash	$ 8,000	$ 8,000	A		$ 3,000	$ 4,000
Inventory	9,000	12,000	B		9,000	12,000
Capital Asset	4,000	8,000	C		9,000	12,000
Total	$ 21,000	$ 28,000			$ 21,000	$ 28,000

The third step is for A to transfer the exchanged property ($4,000 of cash and $4,000 of capital asset with a $2,000 basis) to the partnership for the property received from the partnership—the $8,000 of inventory in excess of her one-third, or $4,000 share. The $8,000 of inventory has a $6,000 basis. This exchange is taxable and A will recognize $2,000 of gain on the capital asset ($4,000 amount realized less $2,000 basis) and the partnership will recognize $2,000 of ordinary income on the inventory which is taxed $1,000 to both B and C and increases their outside basis. Reg. § 1.751–1(b)(2)(ii), (b)(3)(ii). The partnership also receives $4,000 of cash and $4,000 of capital asset with a $4,000 cost basis as a result of the exchange. After the § 751(b) exchange the partnership's balance sheet is as follows:

| | Assets | | | Partners' Capital | |
	A.B.	F.M.V.		A.B.	F.M.V.
Cash	$ 12,000	$ 12,000	A	$ 3,000	$ 4,000
Inventory	3,000	4,000	B	10,000	12,000
Capital Asset	8,000	12,000	C	10,000	12,000
Total	$ 23,000	$ 28,000		$ 23,000	$ 28,000

Finally, to complete the transaction, the partnership distributes the remaining $4,000 of inventory (her original share of that property) to A. Under § 731, neither A nor the partnership recognizes gain as a result of the distribution and A takes the $4,000 of inventory with a $3,000 basis. Following the distribution the partnership's balance sheet is:

| | Assets | | | Partners' Capital | |
	A.B.	F.M.V.		A.B.	F.M.V.
Cash	$ 12,000	$ 12,000	B	$ 10,000	$ 12,000
Capital Asset	8,000	12,000	C	10,000	12,000
Total	$ 20,000	$ 24,000		$ 20,000	$ 24,000

When the dust settles, A will have recognized $2,000 of capital gain and will hold $12,000 of inventory with an $11,000 basis, consisting of the $8,000 cost basis from the § 751(b) exchange and a $3,000 transferred basis as a result of the non-§ 751(b) distribution. B and C will have recognized their $1,000 shares of ordinary income in the inventory and have $2,000 of potential capital gain lurking in the capital asset.

In more complicated situations, the principal difficulty in applying § 751(b) is identifying the exchanged property and the property received from the partnership. The property exchanged under § 751(b) can be identified by focusing on the distributee partner's share of either § 751 property or non-§ 751 property.

4. Criticisms of § 751(b)

Section 751(b) has been criticized on a number of grounds. As the examples in the text illustrate, the section is extremely complex. And despite its complexity, § 751(b) does not reach all shifts in income among partners because it focuses on shifts in the values of § 751 property rather than shifts in the partners' shares of ordinary income. Non-pro rata distributions within a class of property (§ 751 or non-§ 751) are not reached by § 751(b). Because of these deficiencies, the American Law Institute and other commentators have called for the repeal of § 751(b).

5. Proposed Regulations

The IRS has issued proposed regulations which would fundamentally alter the approach and operation of § 751(b). Under the proposed regulations, a hypothetical-sale approach would be used to determine if a distribution alters the partners' interests in § 751(b) property. In the hypothetical sale the rules in § 704(c) and § 743 special basis adjustments apply. If there is a change in a partner's interest in § 751(b) property, the proposed regulations generally allow the partnership to determine the tax consequences under either a hypothetical sale or deemed sale approach, as long as the approach selected is consistent. See Prop. Reg. § 1.751–1.

E. Review Questions

1. A has a basis in his partnership interest of $20,000. What is A's outside basis after each of the following pro rata distributions? What gain or loss, if any, does A recognize as a result of the distributions?

    (a) The partnership distributes $15,000 cash to A.

    (b) The partnership distributes $25,000 cash to A.

    (c) The partnership distributes $15,000 cash, accounts receivable with $0 A.B. and $10,000 F.M.V., and inventory with $10,000 A.B. and $25,000 F.M.V. to A.

    (d) The partnership distributes $10,000 cash, accounts receivable with $0 A.B. and $15,000 F.M.V., inventory with $10,000 A.B. and $20,000 F.M.V., and a capital asset with a $10,000 A.B. and $20,000 F.M.V. to A.

2. If a partner receives a cash distribution and recognizes gain under § 731(a)(1), the partnership will not adjust its inside basis unless a § 754 election has been made. True or False?

3. The ABC Partnership has the following balance sheet:

    | | Assets | | | Partners' Capital | |
	A.B.	F.M.V.		A.B.	F.M.V.
Cash	$ 15,000	$ 15,000	A	$ 12,000	$ 15,000
Inventory	12,000	15,000	B	12,000	15,000
Capital Asset	9,000	15,000	C	12,000	15,000
Total	$ 36,000	$ 45,000		$ 36,000	$ 45,000

    Assume B receives a distribution of the $15,000 of inventory in exchange for his partnership interest.

    (a) *Step 1:* What is B's interest in § 751 and non-§ 751 property before and after the distribution?

    (b) *Step 2:* Determine the tax consequences of the constructive distribution by the partnership to B to set the stage for the § 751(b) exchange.

    (c) *Step 3:* Determine the tax consequences of the § 751(b) exchange.

    (d) *Step 4:* To complete the distribution, the partnership transfers the remaining inventory to B. Does B recognize any gain or loss on this distribution? What is B's total basis in the inventory?

Chapter XII

Liquidating Distributions and Terminations

■ ANALYSIS

A. Liquidation of a Partner's Interest
    1.   Introduction
    2.   § 736(b) Payments
    3.   § 736(a) Payments
    4.   Allocation and Timing of § 736 Installment Payments
    5.   Liquidation vs. Sale
B. Liquidation of the Entire Partnership
    1.   Voluntary Liquidation
    2.   Termination Forced by Statute
C. Review Questions

A. Liquidation of a Partner's Interest

1. Introduction

A partner may terminate her interest in a partnership by selling the interest to a third party and recognize capital gain except to the extent provided in § 751. See X.B., at page 136, *supra,* for the tax treatment of a sale of a partnership interest. Alternatively, the partner's interest may be liquidated. A "liquidation" is "the termination of a partner's entire interest in a partnership by means of a distribution, or series of distributions, to the partner by the partnership." § 761(d). A partner whose interest is being liquidated is often referred to as "the retiring partner." Although use of the word "retiring" may suggest that the relevant partner was active in the operations of the partnership, these provisions apply to any partner whose equity interest in the partnership is terminated.

Section 736 is the starting point for determining the tax consequences of payments in liquidation of a partner's interest in a partnership. It applies only to payments made to retiring partners or to a deceased partner's successor in interest. Reg. § 1.736–1(a)(1)(i). Section 736 classifies such payments into two broad categories, and the tax treatment of the payments is then determined under other provisions of Subchapter K. Under § 736(b), payments for a partner's interest in partnership property generally are treated as distributions by the partnership and taxed under the rules applicable to nonliquidating distributions. See generally Chapter XI, *supra.* In the case of a general partnership interest in a partnership in which capital is not a material income-producing factor, payments for the partner's share of unrealized receivables and goodwill, except to the extent the partnership agreement provides for a specific payment with respect to goodwill, are excluded from § 736(b). § 736(b)(2), (3). Under § 736(a), payments not within § 736(b) (i.e., (1) payments for unrealized receivables and "unstated goodwill" for a general partnership interest in a services partnership, and (2) "premium" payments paid to the partner in excess of her share of partnership property) are considered to be: (1) a distributive share if the amount of the payment is dependent on partnership income or (2) a § 707(c) guaranteed payment if the amount is determined without reference to partnership income.

Under general tax principles, capital is not a material income-producing factor where substantially all of the income comes from compensation for services (e.g., fees and commissions). Thus, a partnership of doctors, lawyers, architects or accountants is not a business where capital is a material income-producing factor even though the business may require a large capital investment (e.g., in equipment or a physical plant) if that investment is incidental to the professional practice.

2. § 736(b) Payments

Under § 736(b), payments to a partner for his interest in partnership property generally are treated as partnership distributions. Excluded from this treatment, however, are payments for a general partnership interest in a services partnership attributable to § 751(c) unrealized receivables and unstated goodwill. § 736(b)(2)–(3). For purposes of § 736, recapture items are not unrealized receivables and thus payments made by a partnership to a retiring partner for recapture items are § 736(b) payments. § 751(c). If a partner's interest in partnership property is determined in an arm's length agreement, that value generally is accepted as correct. Reg. § 1.736–1(b)(1).

a. Tax Consequences of § 736(b) Payments to the Partner

1) Recognition of Gain

Section 736(b) payments generally are treated like nonliquidating distributions. Gain is recognized only if the retiring partner receives cash in excess of his outside basis. § 731(a)(1).

2) Recognition of Loss

Because the liquidation of a partner's interest is a closed transaction, § 731(a)(2) provides that a partner may recognize a loss on a liquidating distribution if only cash, § 751(c) unrealized receivables, and § 751(d)(2) inventory items are distributed. In that situation, loss is recognized to the extent that the partner's outside basis exceeds the sum of the money distributed and the partner's transferred basis in the unrealized receivables and inventory items. The loss is considered as arising from the sale or exchange of a partnership interest and is thus a capital loss. These rules are designed to permit nonrecognition for the partner to the extent possible and preserve the retiring partner's share of ordinary income or loss.

3) Basis of Distributed Property: In General

The partner's basis in any property distributed by the partnership is equal to his outside basis reduced by any cash distributed in the same transaction. § 732(b).

4) Allocation of Basis

If the outside basis limitation is reached, the basis to be allocated (i.e., the partner's outside basis less cash received in the transaction) must be allocated among the various properties received by the distributee partner. First, unrealized receivables and inventory items are tentatively assigned basis equal to the adjusted basis of the partnership in those assets. § 732(c)(1)(A)(i). If the sum of the partnership's bases in the distributed unrealized receivables and inventory items exceeds the basis to be allocated, then the partnership's bases in those properties must be reduced by the amount of such excess. § 732(c)(1)(A)(ii). The reduction is achieved (1) by first reducing the basis of assets with built-in losses (i.e., assets with an assigned basis greater than their value) in proportion to the amount of such built-in losses (and only to the extent of such losses), and (2) by then making additional reductions in basis in proportion to the remaining adjusted basis of the unrealized receivables and inventory items. § 732(c)(1)(A)(ii), (3).

If the basis to be allocated is greater than the partnership's basis in the distributed unrealized receivables and inventory items, then each other distributed asset is tentatively assigned a basis in those assets equal to the partnership's basis in those assets. § 732(c)(1)(B)(i). Basis increases or decreases then must be allocated to the other distributed assets if the partner's remaining basis (after allocation to unrealized receivables and inventory items) is greater or less than the sum of the partnership's bases in those assets. § 732(c)(1)(B)(ii). If an overall increase is required, the increase is allocated (1) first among properties with unrealized appreciation in proportion to such appreciation (and only to the extent of the appreciation), and (2) then in proportion to the fair market values of the properties. § 732(c)(2). If an overall decrease is required, the decrease is allocated (1) first among properties with unrealized depreciation in proportion to such depreciation (and only to the extent of the depreciation), and (2) then in proportion to the remaining adjusted bases of the properties. § 732(c)(3). For the definition of "unrealized receivables" and "inventory items" see, X.B.2.b., at page 137, *supra*.

5) Holding Period

The distributee partner may tack the partnership's holding period in distributed property under § 735(b). Section 735(a) preserves the ordinary income character indefinitely in distributed unrealized receivables and for five years in distributed inventory items.

Example (1):   A, a retiring partner, has an outside basis of $25,000. In a liquidating distribution to which § 751(b) does not apply, A receives $15,000 cash and inventory items of the partnership which have an inside basis of $5,000. A first reduces her outside basis to $10,000 as a result of the cash distribution; $5,000 of the remaining basis is allocated to the inventory items under § 732(b) and (c)(1)(A)(i). Finally, under § 731(a)(2), A recognizes $5,000 of capital loss (the excess of her $25,000 outside basis over the sum of the $15,000 cash and $5,000 transferred basis in the inventory).

Example (2):   Assume that A in Example (1) received $15,000 cash, inventory items with a $5,000 inside basis, and a capital asset with a $2,000 inside basis. A again reduces her outside basis to $10,000 as a result of the cash distribution; $5,000 of the remaining basis is allocated to the inventory items under § 732(b) and (c)(1)(A)(i) and the remaining $5,000 basis is all allocated to the capital asset under § 732(c)(1)(B) and (c)(2). No loss is recognized. Instead, since the partner received partnership property in addition to the cash and inventory items (the capital asset), the partner's unrecognized gain or loss is preserved in that property through the basis rules.

b. Tax Consequences of § 736(b) Payments to the Partnership

1) General Rules

A partnership generally does not recognize gain or loss on a distribution of property and the distribution generally has no impact on the inside basis of the partnership's retained assets. §§ 731(b); 734(a).

2) § 754 Election

If the partnership has a § 754 election in effect, it may adjust the inside basis of its retained assets to prevent certain distortions. Under § 734(b), the partnership increases the inside basis of its retained assets by the amount of any gain recognized by the distributee partner and decreases the basis in the event the distributee partner recognizes a loss. § 734(b)(1)(A), (2)(A). These adjustments must be allocated only to capital assets or § 1231(b) property. Reg. § 1.755–1(c)(1)(ii). In addition, if the basis rules for distributed property result in a difference between the partnership's inside basis for an asset and the asset's basis in the hands of the distributee partner, the partnership adjusts the inside basis of its retained properties. § 734(b)(1)(B), (2)(B). For example, if a partner takes a distributed asset with a reduced basis because the partner has insufficient outside basis, the partnership increases its inside basis in property in the same class by the amount of the reduction. § 734(b)(1)(B); Reg. § 1.755–1(c)(1)(i). And if the basis of a distributed capital asset or § 1231(b) property is increased above its inside basis under § 732(c)(2), the partnership must reduce its inside basis in property of that class by the amount of the increase. § 734(b)(2)(B); Reg. § 1.755–1(c)(1)(i). See generally XI.B.2., at page 158, *supra,* for the operation of § 734 and allocation of § 734 adjustments under § 755.

Section 734(a) also *requires* a downward adjustment to the partnership's basis in its assets if there is a "substantial basis reduction." A substantial basis reduction occurs when the total inside basis adjustment that would have taken place if there had been a § 754 election exceeds $250,000. § 734(d). Thus, if the liquidated partner recognizes a loss greater than $250,000 or the basis of partnership assets distributed in a liquidation increases by more than $250,000, the partnership must reduce the inside basis of its assets under § 734(a).

c. Interaction of § 736 and § 751(b)

If a distribution shifts the distributee partner's interests in § 751 property and non-§ 751 property, the shift is identified and considered a sale or exchange of the property between the partner and the partnership. § 751(b). See XI.D.1., at page 164, *supra,* for a discussion of the operation of § 751(b). Because § 736(b) payments are considered a distribution by the partnership, they may trigger § 751(b). But § 736(b) does not apply to the distributee partner's share of unrealized receivables and unstated goodwill (two types of property which normally must be analyzed in applying § 751(b)) when those payments are for a general partner's interest in a services partnership. Section 751(b)(2)(B) addresses these jurisdictional questions by providing that § 751(b) does not apply to payments described in § 736(a). As a result, in the case of a general partnership interest in a services partnership, the distributee partner's pre- and post-distribution shares of unrealized receivables and unstated goodwill are ignored in applying § 751(b) to § 736(b) payments. Note, however, that unrealized receivables are still inventory items for purposes of determining whether the partnership's inventory items are substantially appreciated.

Example: The ABC partnership, which is a services partnership in which capital is not a material income-producing factor, has three equal general partners and the following balance sheet:

	Assets			Partners' Capital	
	A.B.	F.M.V.		A.B.	F.M.V.
Cash	$ 60,000	$ 60,000			
Accounts Receivable	0	15,000	A	$ 30,000	$ 60,000
Inventory	27,000	30,000	B	30,000	60,000
Capital Asset	3,000	45,000	C	30,000	60,000
Goodwill	0	30,000			
Total	$ 90,000	$ 180,000		$ 90,000	$ 180,000

Assume A's partnership interest is liquidated and A receives $60,000 cash from the partnership with no designation that $10,000 is paid for his share of partnership goodwill. A will be taxed on $15,000 of ordinary income (the amount of his share of unrealized receivables and unstated goodwill) under § 736(a). See XII.A.3., at page 175, *infra*. The inventory items of the partnership (unrealized receivables and the inventory) are substantially appreciated in value because their $45,000 fair market value exceeds 120% of the basis of those assets. While payments for the unrealized receivables are characterized under § 736(a) and thus are not considered in the § 751(b) analysis, those assets nonetheless constitute inventory items under § 751(d) for purposes of testing for the presence of substantial appreciation in the partnership's combined inventory.

A's share of § 736(b) assets (cash, inventory and capital asset) prior to the distribution is $20,000 of cash, $10,000 of inventory, and $15,000 of the capital asset. After the distribution, A has $45,000 of cash disregarding the payments under § 736(a). Thus, in the § 736(b) distribution A exchanged $10,000 of inventory and $15,000 of capital asset for $25,000 of cash. Only the inventory-for-cash exchange is governed by § 751(b) because the cash and capital asset are both non-§ 751 property. Under § 751(b), A is deemed to have received a distribution of $10,000 of inventory with a transferred basis of $9,000 which A is then deemed to have sold back to the partnership for $10,000 cash. As a result of the § 751(b) hypothetical exchange, A recognizes $1,000 of ordinary income. Additionally, the partnership will take a $10,000 cost basis in this portion of the inventory (yielding a net $1,000 increase in the partnership's inside basis in inventory).

The last step is to determine the tax results of the distribution of the remaining $35,000 of cash. A's outside basis after the § 751(b) constructive distribution and exchange is $21,000 ($30,000 less $9,000 transferred basis in inventory constructively distributed to A). The $35,000 cash distribution will reduce A's outside basis to zero and A will recognize $14,000 of capital gain under § 731. If the partnership had a § 754 election in effect, it would receive a $14,000 upward inside basis adjustment under § 734(b)(1)(A), which would be allocated to the partnership's capital asset and goodwill (the capital assets and § 1231(b) property of the partnership).

3. § 736(a) Payments

a. Definition of § 736(a) Payments

Section 736(a) payments are all liquidating payments for property not within § 736(b). This is a deceptively broad category. As a practical matter, § 736(a) only applies to payments for: (1) "premium" amounts paid in addition to the partner's share of partnership property that are in the nature of mutual insurance. Reg. § 1.736–1(a)(2), and (2) § 751(c) unrealized receivables (excluding recapture items) and goodwill, unless the partnership agreement expressly provides for payment with respect to goodwill, but only when the payments are for a general partner's interest in a partnership in which capital is not a material income-producing factor.

Only "payments" (cash or otherwise) for the retiring partner's share of § 736(a) assets are governed by § 736(a). Thus, an in-kind distribution of unrealized receivables to a retiring general partner in a services partnership is governed by § 736(b), not § 736(a). In addition, to the extent of a partner's share of inside basis in unrealized receivables and goodwill (including special basis adjustments under § 732(d) or § 734(b)), those assets are excluded from § 736(a) and treated as § 736(b) property. Reg. § 1.736–1(b)(2), (3).

b. Tax Treatment of § 736(a) Payments

Section 736(a) payments are taxed to the distributee partner as either a distributive share or a guaranteed payment, depending upon whether the amount of the payment is dependent on partnership income. § 736(a)(1), (2). If the amount of the payment is determined with regard to partnership income, the payment is considered a distributive share that will have the effect of reducing the distributive shares of other partners (which is equivalent to a deduction). Reg. § 1.736–1(a)(3)(i), (4). If the payment is determined without regard to partnership income, it is a guaranteed payment that is deductible by the partnership. Reg. § 1.736–1(a)(3)(ii), (4). The deduction in this setting is not subject to the capitalization requirement of § 263. Reg. § 1.736–1(a)(4).

c. Timing of § 736(a) Payments: In General

A § 736(a) payment characterized as a distributive share is included by the distributee partner in the taxable year within which the partnership's taxable year ends. If a § 736(a) payment is characterized as a guaranteed payment, it is included in income in the year in which the partnership is entitled to deduct the payment. Reg. § 1.736–1(a)(5). For additional timing issues when liquidating distributions are made over more than one year, see XII.A.4.b., at page 176, *infra*.

d. Special Treatment for Partnership Goodwill

Section 736(b) generally permits the distributee partner to take advantage of the nonrecognition/capital gain regime generally applicable to partnership distributions under § 731. And since § 736(b) payments are considered a distribution of partnership property, the partnership (i.e., the remaining partners) receives no deduction. Section 736(a) payments, on the other hand, produce ordinary income to the distributee partner and a reduction in the income of the other partners via either reduced distributive shares or a partnership deduction. Section 736 permits a distributee general partner and a services partnership to select which of these tax results they desire for payments with respect to partnership goodwill. Absent a provision in the partnership agreement providing for payment with respect to goodwill, such payments are taxed under § 736(a). § 736(b)(2)(B). For this purpose, the partnership agreement includes any modifications (oral or written) made up to the time for filing the partnership's return in the year of liquidation. § 761(c); Reg. § 1.761–1(c). The courts generally require that the partnership agreement specifically state that a payment is for goodwill. See *Smith v. Comm'r,* 313 F.2d 16 (10th Cir.1962). If, however, there is a statement about a payment in the partnership agreement but the statement is ambiguous, a court will attempt to ascertain the intentions of the parties concerning whether the payment is for goodwill. See *Comm'r v. Jackson Inv. Co.,* 346 F.2d 187 (9th Cir.1965).

4. Allocation and Timing of § 736 Installment Payments

a. Allocation

If liquidating distributions are made to a partner over more than one year, allocation and timing issues are raised. First, the payments made each year must be allocated between the § 736(b) portion and the § 736(a) portion. The distributee partner and the partnership may agree on the allocation provided that the total amount allocated to § 736(b) property does not exceed the value of that property at the date of retirement. Reg. § 1.736–1(b)(5)(iii). In the absence of an agreement, the regulations provide different allocation rules depending on the nature of the payments. If the payments are fixed in amount and paid over a fixed number of years, the § 736(b) portion each year is equal to the agreed fixed payment for the year, multiplied by a fraction equal to the total fixed payments under § 736(b) divided by the total fixed payments under § 736(a) and (b). The remainder of the amount received in the year is treated as a § 736(a) payment. If the total agreed payment for the year is not made, the amount actually paid is first considered to be the § 736(b) payment. Reg. § 1.736–1(b)(5)(i).

If the payments are not fixed in amount, they are first treated as § 736(b) payments to the extent of the partner's interest in partnership property and, thereafter, as § 736(a) payments. Reg. § 1.736–1(b)(5)(ii).

b. Timing

Section 736(a) payments which are considered a distributive share are included in income in the taxable year in which the partnership's taxable year ends. Section 736(a) payments which are considered a guaranteed payment are included in the year in which the partnership is entitled to a deduction. Section 736(b) payments are taken into account in the year in which they are made by the partnership. Reg. § 1.736–1(a)(5). A partner is permitted to receive actual and constructive cash distributions under § 736(b) until her outside basis is recovered before recognizing gain under § 731. Reg. § 1.731–1(a)(1). A loss is recognized in the year of the final distribution, but only if the property distributed consists only of money, unrealized receivables and inventory items. Reg. § 1.731–1(a)(2). Alternatively, a partner receiving a fixed sum may elect to report a pro rata portion of the total gain or loss as each § 736(b) payment is made. Reg. § 1.736–1(b)(6).

Example (1): The ABC general partnership, a services partnership in which capital is not a material income-producing factor, has the following balance sheet:

	Assets			Partners' Capital	
	A.B.	F.M.V.		A.B.	F.M.V.
Cash	$ 45,000	$ 45,000	A	$ 24,000	$ 40,000
Accounts Receivable	0	15,000	B	24,000	40,000
Capital Asset	12,000	24,000	C	24,000	40,000
Goodwill	15,000	36,000			
Total	$ 72,000	$ 120,000		$ 72,000	$ 120,000

Assume A receives $44,000 cash in liquidation of her partnership interest and the partnership agreement has no provision regarding goodwill. A's interest in the accounts receivable and appreciation in the goodwill is not within § 736(b). § 736(b)(2), (3); Reg. § 1.736–1(b)(2), (3). A's share of § 736(b) assets is $28,000 ($15,000 of cash, $8,000 of capital asset, and $5,000 of the basis in the goodwill). The remaining $16,000 that A receives ($44,000 less $28,000) is the § 736(a) payment which is attributable to A's $5,000 share of accounts receivable, $7,000 of appreciation in the goodwill, and $4,000 of premium payments. The $16,000 § 736(a) payment is paid without regard to partnership income and is a § 736(a)(2) guaranteed payment which will result in ordinary income to A and produce a deduction for B and C.

The $28,000 § 736(b) payment is not subject to § 751(b) because the partnership has no inventory items other than the accounts receivable which are disregarded under § 751(b)(2)(B) and § 736(a)(2). The $28,000 § 736(b) payment will result in $4,000 of capital gain to A under § 731(a)(1) ($28,000 distribution less $24,000 basis). If the partnership has made a § 754 election, it will receive a $4,000 upward inside basis adjustment which will be allocated to the capital asset and goodwill.

Example (2): If the partnership in Example (1) paid the $44,000 to A at the rate of $11,000 per year for four years, then each year's payment will have to be allocated between § 736(a) and (b) payments. Since the payments are fixed in amount for a fixed period, $28,000/$44,000 or 7/11 of each payment is treated as a § 736(b) payment. The other 4/11 of each payment is treated as a § 736(a) payment. Thus, on A's receipt of each $11,000 payment, $7,000 is treated as a § 736(b) payment and $4,000 is ordinary income under § 736(a)(2), and B and C each receive a $2,000 deduction. The $7,000 each of § 736(b) payment can be treated as all outside basis recovery in each of the first three years and A will have $4,000 of capital gain in the fourth year. Alternatively, A can elect to prorate the total $4,000 capital gain over the four $11,000 payments, $1,000 per year.

Example (3): Assume that in Example (1) A is to receive 40% of the partnership profits for four years in liquidation of her partnership interest and the profits share turns out to be $11,000 per year. Since the payments are not fixed, under the regulations they are considered to first be § 736(b) payments. Thus, the first $28,000 of payments (all of the payments in the first and second years plus $6,000 of the payment in the third year) are treated as cash distributions. A therefore will recognize $4,000 of capital gain in the third year after full recovery of her $24,000 inside basis. The remaining $5,000 of the third year payment and the full $11,000 of the fourth year payment will be a distributive share of partnership profits (characterized by the profits) which will reduce the distributive shares allocable to B and C.

Example (4):   Assume that in Example (1) A's basis in her partnership interest is $32,000 and the partnership distributes $11,000 per year for four years to A in liquidation of her partnership interest. On these facts the § 736(a) and (b) portions of each payment would still be 4/11 and 7/11, respectively. Thus, on receipt of each year's payment, A would have $4,000 of ordinary income under § 736(a)(2) and the partnership (B and C) would receive a corresponding $4,000 deduction. Under § 736(b), A would have a $4,000 capital loss under § 731(a)(2) ($32,000 adjusted basis less $28,000 § 736(b) payments). A can elect to recognize the full $4,000 of loss in the final year of the payments or recognize the loss pro rata, $1,000 per year, as payments are made.

5. Liquidation vs. Sale

a. In General

A retiring partner can structure his departure from the partnership as either a liquidation of the interest under § 736 or as a sale of the interest to the continuing partners. The choice can have a significant effect on the tax consequences to the retiring and continuing partners. The critical difference is that § 736(a) liquidating distributions generally produce ordinary income to the retiring partner and reduce the income reportable by the continuing partners, while a sale of an interest to the continuing partners produces capital gain to the retiring partner, except as provided in § 751(a), and the continuing partners must capitalize the purchase price as part of their outside bases. The partners are free to structure the transaction in whatever manner they select. In a liquidation of a general partnership interest in a services partnership, the partners can decide whether to expressly provide for payment for goodwill and can determine the allocation and timing of § 736(a) payments. When the parties disagree over the sale versus liquidation issue, the courts will characterize the transaction according to its "substance" by reviewing the partnership agreement and other relevant documents to determine the intent of the parties. See generally, *Foxman v. Comm'r,* 352 F.2d 466 (3d Cir.1965) (transaction characterized as a sale); and *Cooney v. Comm'r,* 65 T.C. 101 (1975) (transaction characterized as a liquidation of the partner's interest).

b. Abandonment of a Partnership Interest

A variation on the liquidation vs. sale issue arises when a partner abandons a worthless partnership interest. In Rev. Rul. 93–80, 1993–2 C.B. 239, the Service ruled that a loss incurred on the abandonment or worthlessness of a partnership interest results in an ordinary loss. But if there is an actual or deemed distribution to the partner, the partner recognizes a capital loss except to the extent § 751(b) provides otherwise. See XI.D.1., at page 164, *supra*. A deemed distribution for this purpose includes a decrease in the partner's share of partnership liabilities which under § 752(b) is considered a distribution of money to the partner.

B. Liquidation of the Entire Partnership

1. Voluntary Liquidation

a. In General

The tax consequences of a complete liquidation of a partnership are different from the tax consequences of liquidating a single partner's interest. The rules in § 731, § 732 and § 735 regarding partnership distributions determine the tax results of liquidating distributions to the partners. Section 736, however, does not apply to the liquidation of an entire partnership because that section contemplates payments by an ongoing partnership. But § 736 will apply to payments made to a retiring partner in a situation where termination of the partnership is contemplated at the end of the payments. Reg. § 1.736–1(a)(6). Section 751(b), however, is applicable to distributions in complete liquidation of a partnership. See XI.D.1., at page 164, *supra,* for the operation of § 751(b). If a partner receives disproportionate amounts of unrealized receivables, substantially appreciated inventory, or non-§ 751 property in a liquidation of a partnership, § 751(b) will treat that portion of the distribution as an exchange of such property between the partner and the partnership. In Revenue Ruling 77–412, 1977–2 C.B. 223, the Service ruled that in the case of a two-person partnership, § 751(b) is applied by treating the distribution as a sale or exchange between the distributee partner and the partnership even though after the distribution the partnership consisted of a single partner.

b. Incorporation of a Partnership

If partners decide to terminate their partnership and incorporate its business, the transaction may take any one of three forms: (1) the partnership may transfer its assets and liabilities to the newly formed corporation in exchange for stock and then transfer the stock to its partners, (2) the partnership may liquidate by distributing its assets and liabilities to its partners who then transfer the assets to the newly formed corporation in exchange for stock, or (3) the partners may transfer their partnership interests to the newly formed corporation in exchange for stock. Assuming the requirements of § 351 are met, the incorporation will be a nonrecognition transaction. The Service has ruled that it will follow the form of incorporation selected by the partners in applying the provisions of Subchapter K. Rev. Rul. 84–111, 1984–2 C.B. 88. This ruling permits partners to select the most favorable method of incorporating if there are differences between inside and outside basis or the holding period of partnership assets and the partners' partnership interests. The Service also has ruled that when a partnership converts into a corporation under a state law that permits the conversion without the actual transfer of assets or interests, the transaction is like an election to be classified as a corporation for federal tax purposes. The partnership is deemed to transfer its assets to a new corporation for stock and liquidate by transferring the stock to its partners. Rev. Rul. 2004–59, 2004–1 C.B. 1050. See Reg. § 301.7701–3(g)(1)(i).

c. Partnership Mergers and Divisions

1) Merger or Consolidation

If two or more partnerships merge or consolidate, the resulting partnership is considered the continuation of any merged or consolidated partnership whose members own more than 50% in the capital and profits of the resulting partnership. § 708(b)(2)(A). If the resulting partnership can be considered a continuation of more than one of the merged or consolidated partnerships under that test, it is considered a continuation of solely the partnership that contributed assets with the greatest fair market value (net of liabilities) to the resulting partnership. Reg. § 1.708–1(c)(1). Any other merged or consolidated partnership is considered terminated. If the members of none of the merged or consolidated partnerships have an interest of more than 50% in capital and profits of the resulting partnership, then all of the merged or consolidated partnerships are terminated and a new partnership results. Id.

A merger or combination of partnerships can take three forms: (1) the terminated partnership can contribute its assets and liabilities to the resulting partnership in exchange for a partnership interest and then distribute interests in the resulting partnership to its partners in liquidation (assets-over form), (2) the terminating partnership can distribute all of its assets to its partners in liquidation of the partners' interests and then the partners could immediately contribute the distributed assets to the resulting partnership in exchange for partnership interests (assets-up form), or (3) the partners in the terminating partnership can transfer their partnership interests to the resulting partnership in exchange for partnership interests and then the resulting partnership can liquidate the terminating partnership (interests-over form). The tax results of a merger of partnerships may vary depending on the form selected for the transaction. For example, the adjusted basis of the assets in the resulting partnership also may vary depending on the form of the transaction.

Under the regulations, the form selected for a merger will be respected if the partners select the assets-over or assets-up form. Reg. § 1.708–1(c)(3). If no particular form is used or if the interests-over form is selected, the merger is treated as taking the assets-over form. Reg. § 1.708–1(c)(3)(i). Increases and decreases in partnership liabilities associated with a merger are netted by the partners in the terminating and resulting partnerships to determine the effect under § 752. Reg. § 1.752–1(f); see Reg. § 1.752–1(g) Example 2. If the resulting partnership transfers cash to the terminating partnership (in addition to partnership interests) in order to buy out a partner in the terminating partnership in an assets-over transaction, the sale of the partner's interest will be respected if the parties specify (1) that the resulting partnership is purchasing an interest from a particular partner, and (2) the consideration that is transferred for each interest sold. Reg. § 1.708–1(c)(4).

In Revenue Ruling 2004–43, 2004–1 C.B. 842, the Service ruled that in a merger taking an assets-over form, the mixing bowl rules (§§ 704(c)(1)(B) and 737) apply to newly created § 704(c) gain or loss in property contributed by the transferor partnership to the continuing partnership. Revenue Ruling 2004–43 was revoked by Revenue Ruling 2005–10, 2005–1 C.B. 492, which announced that the Service would issue regulations implementing the principles of Revenue Ruling 2004–43, effective for distributions occurring after January 19, 2005. Proposed regulations implementing those principles were issued in 2007. See REG–143397–05 (Aug. 22, 2007).

2) Divisions

If a partnership divides into two or more partnerships, the resulting partnerships are considered a continuation of the prior partnership if members of the resulting partnership had an interest of more than 50% in the capital and profits of the prior partnership. § 708(b)(2)(B). Any other resulting partnership is considered a new partnership. Reg. § 1.708–1(d)(1). Partnership divisions can be accomplished through an assets-over or assets-up form. The regulations respect whichever of those two forms is selected. If no form is selected or if the assets-up form is not selected, the division is treated as taking the assets-over form. Reg. § 1.708–1(d)(3).

In a partnership division taking the assets-up form, the mixing bowl rules (§§ 704(c)(1)(B) and 737) may be triggered. In an assets-over division, the partnership interest in the resulting partnership is treated as § 704(c) property to the extent that the interest is received in exchange for § 704(c) property. Reg. § 1.704–4(d)(1). Consequently, the distribution of interests may (1) trigger § 704(c)(1)(B) to the extent interests are received by partners who did not contribute § 704(c) property, or (2) trigger § 737 if a partner who contributed § 704(c) property receives an interest in the resulting partnership that is not attributable to § 704(c) property.

2. Termination Forced by Statute

a. Sale or Exchange of 50% or More of Total Interests in Capital or Profits: § 708(b)(1)(B)

Under § 708(b)(1)(B), a partnership is considered to have terminated if within a 12-month period there is a sale or exchange of 50% or more of the total interests in partnership capital and profits. Because the interests sold or exchanged making up the 50% requirement must be different partnership interests, resales within 12 months of the same interest are not counted. Sales between partners are counted for the test but dispositions by gift, bequest, inheritance, and through liquidation of a partnership interest are not counted as "sales or exchanges." Reg. § 1.708–1(b)(2).

b. Effect of Termination

If a partnership is terminated under § 708(b)(1)(B), the partnership is deemed to contribute its assets and liabilities to a new partnership in exchange for a partnership interest. Reg. § 1.708–1(b)(4). The terminated partnership then liquidates by distributing partnership interests in the new partnership to the purchaser and the other partners. Id. The capital account of any transferee partner and the capital accounts of the other partners carry over to the new partnership and termination of the partnership is disregarded in the maintenance and computation of capital accounts. Reg. § 1.704–1(b)(2)(iv)(*l*).

If the terminated partnership has a § 754 election in effect (including one made on its final return for the year in which the sale occurs), the election applies to the incoming partner and the bases of the partnership's assets are adjusted under §§ 743 and 755 before the deemed contribution. A partner with a basis adjustment in property held by the partnership that terminates continues to have the same basis adjustment with respect to property deemed contributed to the new partnership, even if the new partnership does not make a § 754 election.

Because a § 708(b)(1)(B) termination does not result in a distribution of assets to the partners, the mixing bowl rules (§§ 704(c)(1)(B) and 737) do not apply to the termination. Reg. §§ 1.704–4(c)(3), 1.737–2(a). A new seven-year period also does not begin to run under the mixing bowl rules. Reg. §§ 1.704–4(a)(4)(ii), 1.737–2(a); see Reg. § 1.708–1(b)(4) Example. But a later distribution of § 704(c) property by the new partnership is subject to the mixing bowl rules to the same extent that a distribution by the terminated partnership would have been subject to the mixing bowl rules. Reg. §§ 1.704–4(c)(3), 1.737–2(a).

For holding period purposes, the Tax Court has held that a partner who acquired a partnership asset by way of a purchase which terminated the partnership could not tack the partnership's holding period in the asset. *McCauslen v. Comm'r*, 45 T.C. 588 (1966). The court reasoned that since the purchase terminated the partnership, the asset was acquired by purchase rather than through a distribution from the partnership.

Example (1): The equal AB partnership has the following balance sheet:

	Assets			Partners' Capital	
	A.B.	F.M.V.		A.B.	F.M.V.
Cash	$ 30,000	$ 30,000	A	$ 25,000	$ 40,000
Accounts Receivable	0	10,000	B	25,000	40,000
Capital Asset	20,000	40,000			
Total	$ 50,000	$ 80,000		$ 50,000	$ 80,000

None of the partnership's assets were contributed by A or B. On July 1 of the current year, A sells his interest to C for $40,000. Assume the partnership has never made a § 754 election. As a result of A's sale to C, the partnership will terminate under § 708(b)(1)(B). The partnership is then deemed to contribute all of its assets to a new BC partnership in exchange for an interest in the new partnership. Under § 722 the BC partnership will take the assets with the same basis as the AB partnership. Under § 723 the AB partnership will take the partnership interest with a basis of $50,000 (the basis of the contributed assets). The AB partnership will then liquidate and distribute one-half interests in the BC partnership to B and C. B will take the partnership interest with a $25,000 basis under § 732(b). C will take the partnership interest with a $40,000 basis under § 732(b). C will succeed to A's capital account and the termination will have no effect on the maintenance of capital accounts. The BC partnership will have the following balance sheet:

	Assets			Partners' Capital	
	A.B.	F.M.V.		A.B.	F.M.V.
Cash	$ 30,000	$ 30,000	B	$ 25,000	$ 40,000
Accounts Receivable	0	10,000	C	40,000	40,000
Capital Asset	35,000	40,000			
Total	$ 65,000	$ 80,000		$ 65,000	$ 80,000

Example (2): If the partnership in Example (1) had a § 754 election in effect, C would receive a $15,000 personal inside basis adjustment ($40,000 outside basis less $25,000 share of the partnership's previously taxed capital) on the purchase. That adjustment would be allocated $5,000 to the accounts receivable and $10,000 to the capital asset, which would provide C with a total personal inside basis of $5,000 in the accounts receivable and $20,000 in the capital asset. The terminated AB partnership would again contribute all its assets to the new BC partnership for an interest in the new partnership. Under § 722, the BC partnership will take the assets with the same basis (including the inside basis adjustments) as the terminated partnership. Under § 723, the AB partnership will take the partnership interest with a $65,000 basis (the basis of the contributed assets). The AB partnership will then liquidate and distribute one-half interests in the BC partnership to B and C. B will take the partnership interest with a $25,000 basis under § 732(b). C will take the partnership interest with a $40,000 basis under § 732(b). C will succeed to A's capital account and the termination will have no effect on the maintenance of capital accounts. The BC partnership will have the following balance sheet:

	Assets			Partners' Capital	
	A.B.	F.M.V.		A.B.	F.M.V.
Cash	$ 30,000	$ 30,000	B	$ 25,000	$ 40,000
Accounts Receivable	5,000	10,000	C	40,000	40,000
Capital Asset	30,000	40,000			
Total	$ 65,000	$ 80,000		$ 65,000	$ 80,000

C will continue to have a personal inside basis adjustment of $5,000 in the accounts receivable and $10,000 in the capital asset even if the BC partnership does not make a § 754 election.

C. Review Questions

1. Name the types of partnership property for which § 736(a) payments are made.

2. Section 736(a) payments are considered a distributive share if the amount is dependent on partnership income or a § 707(c) guaranteed payment if the amount is determined without reference to partnership income. True or False?

3. The ABC general partnership, which is a services partnership in which capital is not a material income-producing factor, has the following balance sheet:

| | Assets | | | Partners' Capital | |
	A.B.	F.M.V.		A.B.	F.M.V.
Cash	$ 60,000	$ 60,000	A	$ 30,000	$ 50,000
Accounts Receivable	0	30,000	B	30,000	50,000
Capital Asset	15,000	30,000	C	30,000	50,000
Goodwill	15,000	30,000			
Total	$ 90,000	$ 150,000		$ 90,000	$ 150,000

Assume A receives a $50,000 cash liquidating distribution for his partnership interest and the partnership agreement has no provision regarding payment for goodwill. Determine the tax consequences of the distribution to A.

Chapter XIII

Death of a Partner

■ ANALYSIS

A. Introduction
B. The Deceased Partner's Distributive Share in the Year of Death
C. Estate Tax, Income in Respect of a Decedent, and Basis Consequences
    1. Federal Estate Tax
    2. Income in Respect of a Decedent ("IRD")
    3. Outside and Inside Basis
D. Review Questions

A. Introduction

When a partner dies, his partnership interest may be disposed of in one of three ways: (1) it may pass to the partner's designated successor in interest who continues as a partner; (2) it may be sold at the partner's death pursuant to a preexisting buy-sell agreement; or (3) it may be liquidated pursuant to a preexisting agreement among the partners. Each of these possibilities has different tax consequences to the deceased partner and the partnership.

B. The Deceased Partner's Distributive Share in the Year of Death

When a partner dies, his taxable year closes as of the date of death. § 443(a)(2). In general, the partnership's taxable year does not close when a partner dies. § 706(c)(1). The taxable year of the partnership, however, does close with respect to a partner whose interest in the partnership terminates, whether by reason of death, liquidation, or otherwise. § 706(c)(2). Thus, a deceased partner's final tax return includes a distributive share of partnership income or loss for the portion of the partnership's taxable year prior to death.

Example: Partner B is a calendar year taxpayer and is a member of the ABC partnership, which has a taxable year ending on November 30. If B dies on September 15, 2016, his "decedent's final return" for January 1 to September 15, 2016, will include a distributive share from the partnership for its November 30, 2016 taxable year.

C. Estate Tax, Income in Respect of a Decedent, and Basis Consequences

1. Federal Estate Tax

The fair market value of the deceased partner's partnership interest, including any distributive share earned prior to death, is includible in the partner's gross estate for federal estate tax purposes. §§ 2031; 2033.

2. Income in Respect of a Decedent ("IRD")

a. In General

Property passing from a decedent generally takes a basis equal to its fair market value at the date of the decedent's death or the § 2032 alternate valuation date. § 1014(a). The "date-of-death" basis rule does not apply to property which constitutes a right to an item of "income in respect of a decedent" ("IRD") under § 691. § 1014(c). In general, IRD is a right to income which was earned by the decedent but not previously included in the decedent's gross income as a result of the decedent's method of accounting. A classic example of IRD is salary earned by a cash method taxpayer who dies before the salary is paid. The decedent's taxable year ends as of the date of death and, because the salary is not paid prior to the decedent's death, it is not included in the decedent's final income tax return. §§ 443(a)(2); 451(a). Since the right to the salary payment is IRD, it is not eligible for the date-of-death basis rule. Rather, the decedent's successor in interest includes the salary in gross income when it is paid. Other common forms of IRD are accounts receivable earned by a cash method taxpayer and installment sale obligations under § 453. But tangible property, including built-in gain (whether attributable to market appreciation or prior depreciation deductions), is not IRD and therefore is subject to the date-of-death basis rule. Accordingly, while accounts receivable of a cash method partnership is a common source of IRD in the partnership setting, IRD is not synonymous with the scope of unrealized receivables under § 751(a).

b. Distributive Share in Year of Death

A deceased partner's distributive share of income for the partnership's taxable year ending before the deceased partner's death is not IRD because it must be included in the deceased partner's final tax return. See § 706(c)(2)(A). The distributive share of partnership income attributable to the deceased partner's interest for the remaining portion of the partnership's taxable year will be taxed to the party succeeding to the deceased partner's interest.

c. Income in Respect of a Decedent in a Sale at Death or Continuing Interest

The courts have used an aggregate approach to determine whether partnership items constitute IRD. Thus, a decedent partner's share of accounts receivable of a cash method partnership is IRD. *Quick's Trust v. Comm'r*, 54 T.C. 1336 (1970), aff'd per curiam, 444 F.2d 90 (8th Cir.1971); *Woodhall v. Comm'r*, 454 F.2d 226 (9th Cir.1972).

d. Income in Respect of a Decedent in a Liquidation of a Partnership Interest

Under § 753, all § 736(a) payments (payments for a general partnership interest in a services partnership for unrealized receivables and unstated goodwill as well as premium payments made to any liquidated partner) made by a partnership to an estate or other successor in interest of a deceased partner also are IRD. If a partnership interest held by an estate or successor in interest is liquidated by the partnership, any § 736(a) payments are not eligible for a date-of-death basis. Payments for depreciation recapture are not within § 736(a) and are not IRD. An aggregate theory also could classify payments for § 736(b) property (e.g., cash method accounts receivable of a partnership in which capital *is* a material income producing factor)) as IRD.

3. Outside and Inside Basis

The basis of a partnership interest acquired from a decedent is the fair market value of the interest at the date of her death or at the alternate valuation date, increased by the successor's share of partnership liabilities and reduced by the value of IRD items. Reg. § 1.742–1. The Service has ruled that since a successor's outside basis is reduced by IRD items, § 743 cannot be applied to give the successor the benefit of an inside basis adjustment in such items. Rev. Rul. 66–325, 1966–2 C.B. 249.

If the deceased partner contributed property to the partnership with a built-in loss (i.e., the property's adjusted basis exceeded its fair market value at the time of its contribution) § 704(c)(1)(C) provides that (1) the built-in loss may only be allocated to the contributing partner, and (2) for purposes of making allocations to other partners the property is deemed to have a basis equal to its fair market value at the time of contribution. Thus, the built-in loss is eliminated when the deceased partner's partnership interest is transferred. Note that the resulting decrease in the partnership's inside basis occurs regardless of whether the partnership has a § 754 election in effect.

If the partnership has made a § 754 election, a transfer of a deceased partner's partnership interest will result in a § 743 adjustment to the basis of the partnership's assets. In addition, § 743(a) *requires* an adjustment to the basis of the partnership's assets when a deceased partner's interest is transferred if the partnership has a substantial built-in loss immediately after the transfer. The partnership has a substantial built-in loss if the adjusted basis of its property exceeds the fair market value of such property by more than $250,000. § 743(d).

Example (1):   A is an equal general partner in the ABCD services partnership which on January 1 of the current year had the following balance sheet:

	Assets			**Partners' Capital**	
	A.B.	**F.M.V.**		**A.B.**	**F.M.V.**
Cash	$ 24,000	$ 24,000	A	$ 15,000	$ 24,000
Accounts Receivable	0	12,000	B	15,000	24,000
Depreciable Property	20,000	40,000	C	15,000	24,000
(all § 1245 gain)			D	15,000	24,000
Capital Asset	16,000	20,000			
Total	$ 60,000	$ 96,000		$ 60,000	$ 96,000

Both A and the partnership are cash method, calendar year taxpayers. On June 1 of the current year A dies. In addition to the balance sheet assets listed above, the partnership earned $8,000 of income in the current year prior to June 1 of which A's share is $2,000.

For federal estate tax purposes, A's gross estate will include $26,000 as the fair market value of the partnership interest ($24,000 plus $2,000 share of income). The partnership's taxable year will close with respect to A and her $2,000 share of the partnership's income for the current year will be included in her final tax return and will not be IRD. See § 706(c)(2)(A). Under case law, A's $3,000 share of the accounts receivable is IRD. A's estate or successor in interest will take a $23,000 basis in the partnership ($26,000 fair market value less $3,000 of income in respect of a decedent). If the partnership had a § 754 election in effect, A's successor would obtain a $8,000 inside basis adjustment ($23,000 less $15,000 share of the adjusted basis to the partnership of its property) which would be allocated to the $2,000 share of this year's income, depreciable property ($5,000) and capital asset ($1,000).

Example (2):   If A's entire partnership interest in Example (1) were sold as of the date of her death pursuant to a preexisting buy-sell agreement, the partnership's taxable year would close with respect to A and she would include her $2,000 share of partnership income and that item would not be IRD. § 706(c)(2)(A). A's share of the partnership's accounts receivable is still IRD and the basis of A's partnership interest for purposes of the sale would be $23,000 ($26,000 less $3,000 of income in respect of a decedent). If the partnership had a § 754 election in effect, A's partnership interest would obtain a

$8,000 inside basis adjustment which would be allocated to the $2,000 share of this year's income, depreciable property ($5,000) and capital asset ($1,000).

Example (3): If A's entire partnership interest in Example (1) were liquidated, the partnership's taxable year closes as to A. § 706(c)(2)(A). Thus, A will include her $2,000 distributive share of the partnership's income and the distributive share will not be IRD. In addition, under § 753, the amount of § 736(a) payments will be IRD. This will include the $3,000 paid for A's share of partnership unrealized receivables ($3,000 of accounts receivable). The depreciation recapture is not an unrealized receivable for purposes of § 736. § 751(c). If the partnership had unstated goodwill or A's successor were paid a premium for the interest, those amounts also would be IRD. A's successor's outside basis will be $23,000 ($26,000 fair market value less $3,000 of income in respect of a decedent). If the partnership had a § 754 election in effect or a § 732(d) election were made, A's partnership interest would obtain a $8,000 inside basis adjustment which would be allocated to the $2,000 share of this year's income, depreciable property ($5,000) and capital asset ($1,000).

D. Review Questions

1. When a partner dies, the partnership's taxable year closes with respect to the partner regardless of the date of death. True or False?

2. If the deceased partner's partnership interest is sold at death pursuant to a buy-sell agreement, the partnership's taxable year closes with respect to the partner and the deceased partner's final return will include his distributive share of partnership income or loss for the short taxable year. True or False?

3. Which of the following is "income in respect of a decedent":

    (a) The distributive share for the partnership's taxable year ending after a deceased partner's death?

    (b) The portion of a deceased partner's interest held by a successor in interest attributable to a cash method partnership's accounts receivable?

    (c) The portion of a deceased partner's interest held by a successor in interest attributable to depreciable equipment, including depreciation recapture?

    (d) § 736(b) payments attributable to depreciation recapture?

Chapter XIV

Partnership Anti-Abuse Rule

■ ANALYSIS

A. Introduction
B. Abuse of Subchapter K Rule
   1. In General
   2. Facts and Circumstances Analysis
   3. Commissioner's Power to Recast Transactions
C. Abuse of Partnership Entity
D. Review Questions

A. Introduction

The flexible rules for taxing partnership activities provide taxpayers with considerable tax saving opportunities. That flexibility may lead to abuse if the statutory rules are applied literally. To combat improper reduction of income taxes, the Treasury promulgated Reg. § 1.701–2, which gives it the power to recast transactions that attempt to use partnerships in an abusive manner that is inconsistent with the intent of Subchapter K or the Code and regulations. The partnership anti-abuse regulation contains two main provisions. The first allows the IRS to recast a transaction as appropriate to achieve tax results that are consistent with the intent of Subchapter K. Reg. § 1.701–2(a)–(c). The second rule permits the IRS to disregard the partnership entity and treat a partnership as an aggregate of its partners (in whole or in part) as appropriate to carry out the purposes of the Code or regulations. Reg. § 1.702–2(e).

In addition to this general regulation, the IRS has included anti-abuse rules in some regulations interpreting specific Code sections. For example, the regulations under both § 704(c)(1)(B) and § 737 contain anti-abuse rules that require the Code and regulations to be applied in a manner consistent with the purpose of the statute. Reg. §§ 1.704–4(f), 1.737–4. Under those anti-abuse rules the Commissioner is given the power to recast a transaction to achieve appropriate tax results. Id. The rules for determining economic risk of loss also contain an anti-abuse provision. Reg. § 1.752–2(b)(6).

B. Abuse of Subchapter K Rule

1. In General

a. "Common Law" Requirements of Subchapter K

The partnership anti-abuse regulation acknowledges that Subchapter K is intended to permit taxpayers to conduct joint business or investment activities through a flexible economic arrangement without incurring an entity-level tax. Reg. § 1.701–2(a). Implicit in the intent of Subchapter K, however, are the following common law requirements:

1. The partnership must be bona fide and each partnership transaction must be entered into for a substantial business purpose;

2. The form of each partnership transaction must be respected under substance over form principles; and

3. The tax consequences under Subchapter K to each partner of partnership operations and transactions between the partner and the partnership must accurately reflect the partners' economic agreement and clearly reflect the partner's income. Reg. § 1.701–2(a)(1)–(3).

b. Administrative Convenience Exception

The regulation recognizes one exception to the three common law principles. Certain provisions of Subchapter K and the regulations were adopted to promote administrative convenience and other policy objectives. Thus, if the business purpose and substance over form requirements are satisfied, the clear reflection of income requirement is deemed to be met if the ultimate tax results of a transaction, taking into account all relevant facts and circumstances, are contemplated by an applicable provision of Subchapter K. Reg. § 1.701–2(a)(3).

Example: Partner withdraws from Partnership and receives a § 732(b) basis in the distributed assets, but Partnership does not make a § 754 election in order to avoid a reduction in inside basis. If the transaction does not produce a "substantial basis reduction" under § 734(d) and satisfies the business purpose and substance-over-form requirements, the clear reflection of income requirement is deemed satisfied even though distortions may result because no § 754 election is made. The § 754 election is provided for administrative convenience and the ultimate tax consequences that follow from the failure to make the election are clearly contemplated by § 754. Reg. § 1.701–2(d) Example (9). Thus, the transaction will be respected.

c. Impermissible Tax Reduction Purpose

The regulation also provides that if a partnership is formed or availed of in connection with a transaction a principal purpose of which is to reduce substantially the present value of the partners' aggregate federal tax liability in a manner inconsistent with the intent of Subchapter K, the IRS can recast the transaction to achieve appropriate tax results. Reg. § 1.701–2(b). The regulation employs an all facts and circumstances test to determine whether a partnership is formed or availed of for an impermissible purpose.

2. Facts and Circumstances Analysis

a. In General

All facts and circumstances, including a comparison of the purported business purpose for a transaction and the claimed tax benefits resulting from the transaction, are examined to determine whether a partnership is formed or availed of to reduce tax liability in a manner inconsistent with Subchapter K. The regulation provides a nonexclusive list of factors which may indicate, but do not establish, that a partnership was used in such a manner. The presence or absence of any of the listed factors also does not create a presumption that a partnership was or was not used in an impermissible manner.

b. Specific Factors

The factors listed in the regulation are:

1. The present value of the partners' aggregate federal tax liability is substantially less than had the partners owned the partnership's assets and conducted the activities directly;

2. The present value of the partners' aggregate federal tax liability is substantially less than it would be if the purported separate transactions are integrated and treated as steps in a single transaction;

3. One or more partners either have nominal partnership interests or are substantially protected from any risk of loss from partnership activity or have little or no participation in partnership profits except for a preferred return that is a payment for use of capital;

4. Substantially all of the partners (measured by number of partnership interests) are related directly or indirectly to one another;

5. Partnership allocations are inconsistent with the purpose of § 704(b);

6. The benefits and burdens of property nominally contributed to the partnership are substantially retained by the contributing partner or a related party; and

7. The benefits and burdens of partnership property are shifted to a distributee partner before or after the property is actually distributed to the partner or a related party. Reg. § 1.701–2(c).

c. Examples

The regulation illustrates the abuse of Subchapter K rules with 11 detailed examples. The examples generally suggest that the IRS will not challenge transactions designed to take advantage of the principal features of Subchapter K, such as avoidance of an entity-level tax or the ability to make special allocations with substantial economic effect under § 704(b). In contrast, transactions involving a partner with a nominal interest, a temporary partner, or a plan to duplicate losses, are viewed as not consistent with the intent of Subchapter K. Although helpful, the examples specifically state that they "do not delineate the boundaries of either permissible or impermissible types of transactions" and that the addition or deletion of any fact in an example may alter the outcome of the transaction. Reg. § 1.701–2(d). Thus, the regulation can be relied upon as guidance in specific transactions only with a great deal of caution. The examples below are illustrative of the IRS's facts and circumstances analysis.

Example (1): B, an individual, and A Corp., form a limited partnership with A Corp. having a 1% general partnership interest and B having a 99% limited partnership interest. The arrangement is properly classified as a partnership for federal tax purposes. A limited partnership was selected so that B could have limited liability without being subject to an entity-level tax. Reg. § 1.702–1(d) Example (1) concludes that the IRS will not recast this transaction.

Example (2): Corporations X and Y make equal contributions to form a bona fide partnership to make joint investments. The partnership purchases common stock of Z, an unrelated corporation which historically has paid a $6 per share dividend. The partnership allocates dividend income on the Z stock to X to the extent of an established rate for inter-bank loans on the record date applied to X's contributions and allocates the remainder of the dividend income to Y. The allocation has substantial economic effect. The purposes for the arrangement were to avoid an entity-level tax, provide X with a floating-rate return based on an established index, and permit X and Y to claim a dividends received deduction under § 243. The IRS will not recast this transaction. Reg. § 1.702–2(d) Example (5).

3. Commissioner's Power to Recast Transactions

Under the anti-abuse regulation, the Commissioner can recast a transaction to achieve tax results that are consistent with the intent of Subchapter K. The Commissioner can determine that:

a.   the purported partnership should be disregarded;

b.   one or more purported partners should not be treated as a partner;

c.   the partnership's or partner's method of accounting should be adjusted;

d.   the partnership's items of income, gain, loss, deduction, or credit should be reallocated; or

e.   the claimed tax treatment should otherwise be adjusted or modified.

Reg. § 1.701–2(b).

C. Abuse of Partnership Entity

Under the second anti-abuse rule, the Commissioner can treat a partnership as an aggregate of its partners in whole or in part as appropriate to carry out the purpose of any Code or regulation provision. Reg. § 1.701–2(e)(1). This rule is designed to prevent the use of a partnership to avoid other Code provisions and does not depend on a showing of the taxpayer's intent. An exception is made when (1) a Code section or regulation prescribes the treatment of a partnership as an entity, and (2) that tax treatment and the ultimate tax results are clearly contemplated by that provision. Reg. § 1.701–2(e)(2).

Example: Corporation X is a partner in the XYZ partnership which has conducted substantial business activities for several years. As part of its business activities, XYZ purchases shares in Corporation R which announces an extraordinary dividend under § 1059 six months later. Under § 1059(a), if a corporation receives an extraordinary dividend and it has not held the stock for more than two years before the dividend announcement date, the basis in the stock held by the corporation is reduced by the nontaxed portion of the dividend. X takes the position that § 1059(a) does not apply because XYZ is a partnership and not a corporation. Under the partnership anti-abuse rule, the IRS will treat XYZ as an aggregate of its partners. Section 1059(a) does not prescribe the treatment of a partnership as an entity for purposes of that section and the treatment of XYZ as an entity could result in corporate partners receiving dividends through partnerships contrary to the intent of § 1059. See Reg. § 1.701–2(f) Example (2).

D. Review Questions

1.   If the partnership anti-abuse regulation is violated, what remedies are available to the IRS?

2.   Will the following transaction likely be challenged by the IRS under the partnership anti-abuse regulation? A U.S. corporation and foreign corporation conduct a bona fide joint venture through a foreign partnership rather than a foreign corporation so the U.S. corporation can achieve better foreign tax credit results.

Chapter XV

S Corporations

■ ANALYSIS

A. Introduction
B. Eligibility for S Corporation Status
    1. Ineligible Corporations and Subsidiaries
    2. 100-Shareholder Limit
    3. Restrictions on Types of Shareholders
    4. One-Class-of-Stock Requirement
C. Election, Revocation, and Termination of Subchapter S Status
    1. Electing S Corporation Status
    2. Revocation and Termination of S Corporation Status
D. Tax Treatment of S Corporation Shareholders
    1. Introduction
    2. Corporate Level Determination of Tax Results
    3. Tax Consequences to Shareholders
E. Distributions to Shareholders
    1. S Corporations Without E & P
    2. S Corporations with E & P
    3. Distributions of Property
    4. Ordering of Basis Adjustments
    5. Distributions Following Termination of S Corporation Status
F. Taxation of the S Corporation
    1. § 1374 Tax on Built-In Gains
    2. § 1375 Tax on Excessive Passive Investment Income
G. Coordination of Subchapter S with Subchapter C and Other Tax Provisions
    1. Subchapter C
    2. Other Tax Provisions
    3. Employment Taxes
    4. Net Investment Income Tax
H. Review Questions

A. Introduction

Profits distributed as dividends by a C corporation to its shareholders generally are subject to tax at both the corporate and shareholder levels. A C corporation is subject to the tax under § 11 on its taxable income at rates of 15% to 35%. When the after-tax profits are distributed, noncorporate shareholders are taxed on most dividends as net capital gain at a maximum rate of 20%. §§ 1(h)(11), 61(a)(7) and 301. In contrast, a partnership is generally treated as an aggregate of its partners rather than a taxable entity. § 701. The partners are taxed directly on the income from the enterprise, and partnership distributions generally do not produce additional taxable income. §§ 702; 731.

In 1958, Congress created a method for corporations to avoid the double tax by enacting Subchapter S, which allows the shareholders of a "small business corporation" to elect to be taxed directly on corporate-level profits. The S corporation taxing scheme was substantially improved by the Subchapter S Revision Act of 1982, which adopted a simplified pass-through approach. As a result, the taxation of S corporations and their shareholders became similar, but not identical, to the taxation of partnerships and their partners, and S corporations became a more attractive legal form for operating a business enterprise. Subsequent legislation has liberalized the eligibility requirements and made S corporations more accessible vehicles for operating a closely held business.

B. Eligibility for S Corporation Status

The special tax provisions in Subchapter S are available only to an "S corporation," which is defined as a "small business corporation" which has an election under § 1362(a) in effect for the year. § 1361(a)(1). Any corporation which is not an S corporation is referred to as a "C corporation." § 1361(a)(2). Despite the use of "small business" in the definition, there are no limits on the asset size or revenue of S corporations and, although most S corporations are relatively small and many have only one shareholder, some have net assets exceeding $100 million. A "small business corporation" is defined as a domestic corporation which meets the requirements set forth in § 1361 and outlined below.

1. Ineligible Corporations and Subsidiaries

a. In General

Ineligible corporations do not qualify as small business corporations. § 1361(b)(1). The "ineligible corporation" category includes four specialized types of corporations (such as banks and insurance companies) that are subject to their own taxing regimes under the Code. § 1361(b)(2). At one time, a corporation was "ineligible" if it was a member of an affiliated group—e.g., a parent with an 80% subsidiary.

b. Wholly Owned Subsidiaries

S corporations may have 80% or more subsidiaries under certain conditions.

1. C corporation subsidiaries are generally permitted, but the S corporation parent and the C corporation subsidiary may not file a consolidated return. § 1504(b)(8).

2. Parent-subsidiary relationships between two S corporations are permitted if the parent elects to treat the subsidiary as a "qualified subchapter S subsidiary" ("QSSS"). § 1361(b)(3)(A). To be "qualified," the subsidiary must not be an ineligible corporation (see above) and 100% of the stock of such

corporation must be held by an S corporation. § 1361(b)(3)(B). If this election is made, all the assets, liabilities, income, deductions, and credits are treated as belonging to the S parent. § 1361(b)(3)(A). In effect, even though the subsidiary is a separate corporation, it is treated as a division of its parent for tax purposes. The regulations provide detailed rules for making or revoking a QSSS election. See Reg. § 1.1361–3, –4, –5.

2. 100-Shareholder Limit

An S corporation may not have more than 100 shareholders. § 1361(b)(1)(A). If stock is owned (other than by a husband and wife) by tenants in common or joint tenants, each owner is considered to be a shareholder of the corporation. Reg. § 1.1361–1(e)(1). Stock held by a nominee, guardian, custodian or agent is considered to be held by the beneficial owner of the stock. Id.

A special rule treats a husband and wife (and their estates) and all members of a "family" (and their estates) as one shareholder for purposes of the 100-shareholder limit. § 1361(c)(1)(A). A family is defined as the lineal descendants (and their spouses or former spouses) of a common ancestor who is no more than six generations removed from the youngest generation shareholder as of the later of: the date the S corporation election is made, the earliest date that a family member holds stock in the corporation, or October 22, 2004. § 1361(c)(1)(B). Adopted children and foster children are treated as children by blood. § 1361(c)(1)(C). If a husband and wife are members of a family, they are counted as part of that family (rather than separately) for purposes of the shareholder limit. § 1361(c)(1)(A)(i).

Example (1): Assume 99 of 100 outstanding shares of stock in X Corp. are owned by 99 unrelated individuals. If the remaining share is owned in joint tenancy by Herman and Wanda, who are husband and wife, X is considered to have 100 shareholders and may qualify as a small business corporation. If Herman and Wanda were brother and sister, X again would have 100 shareholders because Herman and Wanda would be members of a family that is counted as one shareholder.

Example (2): Assume again that Herman and Wanda in Example (1) are husband and wife. If Herman dies, Wanda and his estate will continue to be considered as one shareholder until distribution of the stock by the estate to a beneficiary other than Wanda and who is not part of Wanda's family. If the stock were distributed by Herman's estate to another unrelated beneficiary, X would have 101 shareholders and would no longer qualify as an S corporation. § 1362(d)(2)(A). If Herman and Wanda get divorced, X will still have 100 shareholders because former spouses are considered part of a family.

3. Restrictions on Types of Shareholders

a. In General

An S corporation may not have as a shareholder a person (other than an estate and certain trusts) who is not an individual or a § 501(c)(3) tax-exempt charitable organization or qualified pension trust. § 1361(b)(1)(B). For this purpose, the term "estate" includes the bankruptcy estate of an individual.

§ 1361(c)(3). Thus, an S corporation cannot have another corporation or a partnership as a shareholder. Reg. § 1.1361–1(f).

b. Nonresident Alien Restriction

An S corporation may not have a nonresident alien as a shareholder. § 1361(b)(1)(C).

c. Trusts as Eligible Shareholders

The following types of domestic trusts are eligible S corporation shareholders:

1. Grantor trusts—i.e., domestic trusts treated for income tax purposes as owned by an individual who is a U.S. citizen or resident. § 1361(c)(2)(A)(i). The deemed owner of the trust is treated as the shareholder. § 1361(c)(2)(B)(i). If the deemed owner of a grantor trust dies and the trust continues in existence as a testamentary trust, it continues to be a permissible shareholder for the 2-year period following the deemed owner's death. § 1361(c)(2)(A)(ii). The estate of the deemed owner is considered to be the owner of the stock. § 1361(c)(2)(B)(ii).

2. Testamentary trusts to which stock has been transferred pursuant to a will, but only for the 2-year period beginning on the day of transfer. § 1361(c)(2)(A)(iii). The testator's estate is treated as the shareholder during this period. § 1361(c)(2)(B)(iii).

3. Voting trusts—i.e., trusts created to exercise the voting power of stock. Each beneficial owner is treated as a separate shareholder. § 1361(c)(2)(A)(iv); 1361(c)(2)(B)(iv).

    Example: Assume 95 of 100 outstanding shares of stock in Y Corp. are owned by 95 individuals. If the remaining 5 shares are owned by a voting trust, Y may qualify as a small business corporation as long as the trust does not have more than 5 beneficial owners.

4. Qualified Subchapter S Trusts and Electing Small Business Trusts, discussed below.

d. Qualified Subchapter S Trusts

Section 1361(d)(1) permits the beneficiary of a "qualified Subchapter S trust" to elect to have the trust treated as a qualified shareholder for Subchapter S purposes and to be treated as the owner of the portion of the trust consisting of S corporation stock. The owner of stock in a qualified Subchapter S trust may be included in a family that elects to be treated as one shareholder. A "qualified Subchapter S trust" is a trust the terms of which require that:

1. During the life of the current income beneficiary, the trust shall have only one income beneficiary;

2. Any corpus distributed during the life of the current income beneficiary may be distributed only to that beneficiary;

3. The income interest of the current income beneficiary shall terminate on the earlier of the beneficiary's death or the termination of the trust;

4. Upon the termination of the trust during the life of the current income beneficiary, the trust shall distribute all of its assets to such beneficiary; and

5. All of the income is or must be distributed currently to one individual who is a U.S. citizen or resident. § 1361(d)(3).

e. Electing Small Business Trusts

The electing small business trust ("ESBT") was added as an eligible shareholder to provide more flexibility in estate planning for businesses operated as S corporations. An ESBT, for example, may have more than one current income beneficiary, and the trustee may have discretion over distributions of income and corpus. The requirements for an ESBT are (§ 1361(e)(1)):

1. All the beneficiaries must be individuals, estates, or tax-exempt organizations that are eligible S corporation shareholders, or charitable organizations holding contingent remainder interests;

2. No interests in the trust may have been acquired by purchase; and

3. The trustee must elect ESBT status.

Each current income beneficiary of an ESBT is treated as a shareholder for purposes of the 100-shareholder limit. § 1361(c)(2)(B)(v). A beneficiary of an ESBT who is a shareholder may be included in a family that elects to be counted as one shareholder. An ESBT's pro rata share of S corporation income is taxable to the trust at the highest marginal rates in § 1(e) (for estates and trusts), whether or not the income is distributed. § 641(d).

4. One-Class-of-Stock Requirement

a. In General

An S corporation may not have more than one class of stock. § 1361(b)(1)(D). The purpose of this rule is to simplify the allocation of income and deductions among an S corporation's shareholders. An S corporation generally is treated as having one class of stock if all of its outstanding shares confer identical rights to distribution and liquidation proceeds. Differences in voting rights are disregarded. Thus, an S corporation may issue both voting and nonvoting common stock. Reg. § 1.1361–1(*l*)(1). Distributions that take into account varying interests in stock during the taxable year do not violate the "identical rights" requirement. Reg. § 1.1361–1(*l*)(2)(iv). For purposes of this requirement, outstanding stock does not include § 83 restricted stock that is not substantially vested unless the holder made a § 83(b) election. Reg. § 1.1361–1(*l*)(1)(4)(i).

b. Buy-Sell and Redemption Agreements

Buy-sell agreements among shareholders, stock transfer restriction agreements, and redemption agreements generally are disregarded in determining whether a corporation has more than one class of stock unless a principal purpose of the agreement is to circumvent the one-class-of-stock requirement and the agreement establishes a purchase price that, at the time the agreement is entered into, is significantly higher or lower than the fair market value of the stock. Reg. § 1.1361–1(*l*)(2)(iii).

c. Obligations Treated as Equity Under General Principles

Unless the § 1361(c)(5) straight debt safe harbor applies (see XV.B.4.d., below), S corporation debt instruments or obligations treated as equity under general tax principles are treated as a second class of stock if the principal purpose of issuing the instrument is to circumvent the identical-rights-to-distributions and liquidation-proceeds rule or the shareholder-limitation rules. Reg. § 1.1361–1(*l*)(4)(ii)(A).

d. Straight Debt Safe Harbor

1) Background

At one time, S corporations with debt instruments (e.g., bonds) outstanding risked losing their S status if their debt was reclassified as equity under general debt/equity principles because the Service argued that the corporation had more than one class of stock. That threat has diminished with the enactment of the § 1361(c)(5) "straight debt safe harbor" under which "straight debt" will not be treated as a second class of stock.

2) Straight Debt Defined

"Straight debt" is any written, unconditional obligation, whether or not embodied in a formal note, to pay a sum certain on demand or on a specified date, if:

a.   The interest rate and payment dates are not contingent on profits, the borrower's discretion, the payment of dividends on common stock, or similar factors;

b.   The instrument is not convertible (directly or indirectly) into stock; and

c.   The creditor is an individual, estate or a trust that would be a permissible S corporation shareholder.

Reg. § 1.1361–1(*l*)(5)(i). The fact that an obligation is subordinated to other debt of the corporation does not prevent it from qualifying as straight debt. Reg. § 1.1361–1(*l*)(5)(ii).

3) Treatment of Straight Debt for Other Purposes

An obligation of an S corporation that satisfies the straight debt safe harbor will not be treated as a second class of stock even if it is considered equity under general tax principles. Straight debt generally will be treated as debt for other purposes of the Code (e.g., the interest deduction). But if a straight debt obligation bears an unreasonably high rate of interest, an appropriate portion of that interest may be recharacterized as a payment that is not interest. Reg. § 1.1361–1(*l*)(5)(iv). Such a recharacterization, however, does not result in a second class of stock. Id.

4) Treatment of Converted C Corporation Debt

If a C corporation has outstanding debt obligations that satisfy the straight debt safe harbor but might be classified as equity under general tax principles, the safe harbor ensures that the obligation will not be treated as a second class of stock if the C corporation elects to convert to S status. The conversion and change of status also is not treated as a taxable exchange of the debt instrument for stock. Reg. § 1.1361–1(*l*)(5)(v).

C. Election, Revocation, and Termination of Subchapter S Status

1. Electing S Corporation Status

a. In General

In order to be an S corporation, a small business corporation must make an election to which all of its shareholders consent. § 1362(a). An S election is effective for the taxable year for which it is made and for all succeeding taxable years of the corporation until it is terminated. § 1362(c). The Service may waive the effect of an inadvertent invalid election (e.g., failure to obtain all necessary shareholder consents) under certain circumstances. § 1362(f).

b. Timing and Effective Date of Election

An S election may be made for a taxable year at any time during the preceding taxable year or on or before the fifteenth day of the third month of the taxable year. § 1362(b)(1).

Example (1): Assume Z Corp. qualifies as a small business corporation under § 1361(b). If the shareholders of Z wish to elect S corporation status for calendar year 2017, they must make the election either during 2016 or before March 16, 2017.

An election made after the 15th day of the third month of the taxable year and before the same day in the following year is generally treated as made for the following year. § 1362(b)(3). If an election is made during a taxable year and on or before the 15th day of the third month of the year, but either (1) the corporation was not a small business corporation on one or more days before the election was made, or (2) one or more persons who held stock in the corporation prior to the time the election was made does not consent, then the election is treated as made for the following year. § 1362(b)(2). The Service, however, has the authority to treat a late election as timely for reasonable cause. § 1362(b)(5).

Example (2): Assume Z Corp. in Example (1) makes an election to be an S corporation on March 10, 2017. If Z had a shareholder which was a partnership during January, 2017, it could not elect S status for the 2017 taxable year, because it had an ineligible shareholder during the period of the taxable year prior to the election. The election would be treated as made for Z's 2018 taxable year.

Example (3): Assume that on January 1, 2017, W Co., which is a C corporation, had 10 shareholders. On January 15, 2017, one of W's shareholders, A, who is an individual, sells her W stock to B, who also is an individual. On March 5, 2017, W files an election to be an S corporation for its 2017 taxable year. Assuming W qualifies as a small business corporation, its election will be effective only if all of the shareholders as of March 5, 2017, as well as former shareholder A, consent to the election. If W's election were to be effective for its 2018 taxable year, A would not have to consent to the election.

2.   Revocation and Termination of S Corporation Status

a.   Revocation

An S election may be revoked with the consent of more than one-half of the shares of the stock (including nonvoting stock) of the corporation on the day the revocation is made. § 1362(d)(1)(B); Reg. § 1.1362–2(a)(1). The corporation may specify any effective date on or after the day of the revocation. If an effective date is not selected, a revocation is effective: (1) on the first day of the taxable year if made before the sixteenth day of the third month of such year, or (2) on the first day of the next taxable year if it is made after the fifteenth day of the third month of the year. § 1362(d)(1)(C), (D).

b.   Termination

1)   Ceasing to Be a Small Business Corporation

An S corporation election terminates whenever the corporation ceases to be a small business corporation. The termination is effective on and after the day of the event that terminated its small business corporation status. § 1362(d)(2). Reg. § 1.1362–2(b).

Example: If an S corporation exceeds the 100-shareholder limit, has an impermissible shareholder, issues a second class of stock, or otherwise ceases to be a small business corporation, its Subchapter S election will terminate as of the day of the disqualifying event.

2)   Passive Income Limitation for Certain S Corporations

An S corporation's election will terminate if it has Subchapter C accumulated earnings and profits (i.e., E & P from its pre-Subchapter S existence) at the close of each of three consecutive taxable years in which it was an S corporation and more than 25% of its gross receipts for each of those years consists of passive investment income. The termination is effective on the first day of the taxable year beginning after the three-year measuring period. § 1362(d)(3)(A)(i), (ii). An S corporation which has never been a C corporation or which was a C corporation but has no E & P from that period would not be concerned about a termination under this provision. "Passive investment income" generally includes gross receipts from royalties, rents, dividends, interest, and annuities but does not include gains from the disposition of property. § 1362(d)(3)(C)(i). For purposes of the overall gross receipts definition, gross receipts from sales or exchanges of stock or securities are taken into account only to the extent of gains and gross receipts from dispositions of capital assets other than stock or securities are taken into account only to the extent that capital gains from such dispositions exceed capital losses. § 1362(d)(3)(B). See also Reg. § 1.1362–2(c).

c. S Termination Year

If an S corporation's election is revoked or terminated, the corporation has an "S termination year," which consists of an S short year and a C short year. § 1362(e)(1), (4). In general, the tax results for the S termination year are assigned to the two short years on a pro rata basis unless all persons who were shareholders during the S short year and all of the shareholders on the first day of the C short year elect to make the allocation on the basis of normal tax accounting rules. § 1362(e)(2), (3). Since the C short year is subject to the full sting of the double tax on corporate profits, the corporation will be motivated to select the method which allocates the most income to the S short year. The pro rata method may not be used if there is a sale or exchange of 50% or more of the stock in the corporation during the year. § 1362(e)(6)(D). Once the allocation between the short years is made, the tax liability for the C short year is computed on an annualized basis. § 1362(e)(5). See Reg. § 1.1362–3.

d. Inadvertent Terminations

If an S corporation's election is revoked or terminated, the corporation generally is not eligible to reelect S corporation status for five years unless it receives the Treasury's consent to an earlier election. § 1362(g). Section 1362(f) provides relief for terminations that occur when the corporation ceases to be a small business corporation or violates the passive income limitation. If (1) the Treasury determines that the termination was inadvertent, (2) the corporation takes steps to rectify the problem within a reasonable period of time after discovery, and (3) the corporation and all of the persons who were shareholders during the relevant period agree to make certain adjustments required by the Treasury, then the corporation will retain its S corporation status. The fact that the terminating event was not reasonably within the control of the corporation and took place despite its due diligence tends to establish that a termination was inadvertent. Reg. § 1.1362–4(b). Section 1362(f) may also be used to obtain relief from ineffective elections to treat a subsidiary as a qualified Subchapter S subsidiary or to treat a family as one shareholder.

> *Example:* X Corporation, in good faith, determined that it had no earnings and profits, but the Service later determined on audit that X's S election terminated because X violated the passive income test for three consecutive years by having accumulated earnings and profits. If the shareholders were to agree to treat the earnings as distributed and include the dividends in income, it may be appropriate to waive the terminating event, so X's election is treated as if it never terminated.

D. Tax Treatment of S Corporation Shareholders

1. Introduction

Except in a few situations discussed later in this chapter (See XV.F., at page 218 *infra*), an S corporation is not a taxable entity. § 1363(a). Instead, the corporation's income, loss, deductions, and credits are taxed directly to its shareholders. § 1366(a). Even though aggregate principles are employed for the taxation of an S corporation's income or loss, entity principles generally are used for its computation.

2. Corporate Level Determination of Tax Results

An S corporation is required to calculate its gross income and taxable income in order to determine the tax items that pass through to the shareholders. §§ 1366(c); 1363(b). An S corporation also must file its own tax return (Form 1120S) and is subject to audit and examination by the Internal Revenue Service. § 6037.

a. Accounting Method

An S corporation generally is free to select its own accounting method. If an S corporation is a "tax shelter" as defined in § 448, however, it may not use the cash method of accounting, but the corporation is, in effect, required by § 267 to use the cash method for purposes of taking deductions on payments to persons who own stock in the corporation either directly or by way of attribution. § 267(a)(2), (e).

b. Taxable Year

1) In General

The shareholders of an S corporation are required to include in income their pro rata share of S corporation income in the taxable year in which the S corporation's taxable year ends. § 1366(a). The calendar year shareholders of a profitable S corporation would prefer the corporation to adopt a January 31 taxable year so that they could wait 14½ months (until April 15 of the following year) to pay tax on the corporation's income. To preclude this type of deferral, § 1378 requires an S corporation's taxable year to be a "permitted year," which is defined as a calendar year or an accounting year for which the corporation establishes a business purpose. Deferral of income to the shareholders is not treated as a business purpose. § 1378(b). The legislative history provides that: (1) the use of a particular year for regulatory or financial accounting purposes, (2) hiring patterns of a business, (3) administrative considerations, such as compensation or retirement arrangements with staff or shareholders, and (4) the fact that the business uses price lists, model years, etc., which change on an annual basis, ordinarily are not sufficient to satisfy the business purpose requirement. H.R.Rep. No. 99–841, 99th Cong. 2d Sess. II–319 (1986).

> ***Example:*** Assume W Corp. is an S corporation and its principal business is selling new automobiles. The fact that W's new model cars come out in late summer or fall ordinarily is not sufficient to establish a business purpose for it to use a taxable year ending at that time.

2) Natural Business Year

The business purpose standard is satisfied if the taxable year of an S corporation coincides with a "natural business year." The Service has quantified the natural-business-year concept by providing that a corporation will be deemed to have adopted a natural business year if in each of the prior three years its gross receipts for the last two months of the requested taxable year equaled or exceeded 25% of the gross receipts for the full requested year. Rev. Proc. 2006–46, 2006–2 C.B. 859. An S corporation unable to satisfy this standard still may demonstrate that a particular taxable year satisfies the business purpose standard under a facts and circumstances test. The Service, however, considers the tax consequences (i.e., deferral) of the year selected to be a fact and circumstance relevant to the question. Rev. Rul. 87–57, 1987–2 C.B. 117.

Example: Y Co. desires to use a May 31 tax year. Y's reason for the requested tax year is that due to weather conditions its business is operational only during the period of September 1 through May 1. For its 10-year business history, Y has had insignificant gross receipts for the period of June 1 through August 31. Y's facility is not used for any other purpose during those months. Despite the fact that Y was unable to satisfy the mechanical "natural business year" test, the Service ruled in Revenue Ruling 87–57 that Y established a business purpose for a May 31 tax year.

3) § 444 Fiscal Year Election

Section 444 alleviates some of the harshness of the permitted year requirement. It permits an S corporation to adopt a taxable year other than the calendar year normally required by § 1378, provided the year selected results in no more than three months of tax deferral. As a cost for this relief, the corporation must make "required payments" under § 7519 which are designed to offset the financial benefits of the tax deferral provided by § 444. A § 444 election and § 7519 payments, however, are not required if an S corporation can establish a business purpose for the taxable year it selects. § 444(e).

Example: Assume T Corp. is an S corporation which cannot establish a business purpose for using a taxable year other than a calendar year. T may elect under § 444 to select a fiscal year ending on September 30, October 31, or November 30. If it makes a § 444 election, T will have to make § 7519 required payments to, in effect, "pay back" the benefits of its shareholders being able to defer inclusion of its income for an additional one to three months. Section 7519 has a de minimis provision which would relieve T of this burden if its required payment for a taxable year is $500 or less. If T establishes a business purpose for adopting a taxable year other than a calendar year, it may adopt such a year without electing under § 444 and making § 7519 payments.

c. S Corporation Taxable Income

1) In General

An S corporation is required to compute its taxable income in the same manner as an individual except that it is not permitted certain deductions allowed only to individuals, such as personal exemptions, medical expenses, and expenses for the production or collection of income under § 212. §§ 1363(b)(2); 703(a)(2)(A), (E). Because an S corporation's losses pass through to its shareholders, the corporation is not permitted a net operating loss deduction. §§ 1363(b)(2); 703(a)(2)(D). Net operating losses from years in which the corporation was a C corporation also may not be carried over to a taxable year in which it is an S corporation. § 1371(b)(1).

2) Separately Stated Items

To preserve their unique character as they pass through to the shareholders, the corporation must separately report any item of income (including tax-exempt income) loss, deduction or credit the separate treatment of which could affect the tax liability of any shareholder. These are known as "separately stated" items. § 1363(b)(1). The characterization of items is determined at the corporate level. § 1366(b). Certain separately stated items, such as charitable contributions, foreign taxes, and depletion, are not deductible by the corporation in computing its taxable income, but they still pass through to the shareholders. §§ 1363(b)(2); 703(a)(2)(B), (C), (F). Examples of other separately stated items include: (1) capital gains and losses, so that the § 1211 limitation on capital losses may be applied at the shareholder level after consideration of each shareholder's other capital gains and losses; (2) § 1231 transactions, so the provisions of § 1231 are applied at the shareholder level taking into account all of the shareholder's § 1231 transactions; and (3) investment interest, so the § 163(d) investment interest limit is applied after taking into account each shareholder's personal tax situation. Reg. § 1.1366–1(a)(2).

3) Charitable Contributions

Unlike C corporations, S corporations are not subject to the 10% of taxable income limitation on charitable contributions. Rather, charitable contributions are categorized by the percentage limitations applicable to individuals in § 170(b) (e.g., 50% for cash contributions to public charities, 30% for contributions of long-term capital gain property) and pass through as such to the shareholders. Reg. § 1.1366–1(a)(2)(iii). Charitable contributions of appreciated capital gain property are generally deductible by the shareholders at their fair market value, subject to any reductions required by § 170(e).

Example: T Corp., which has an S election in effect, makes a charitable contribution during the year. Since T is not allowed a charitable deduction in computing taxable income, the special 10% limitation on corporate charitable deductions in § 170(b)(2) does not apply. Instead, the charitable contribution is a separately stated item which passes through to the shareholders who each combine their share of the deduction with their personal charitable deductions before applying the § 170 limits on charitable contributions by individuals.

4) No Dividends Received Deduction

Because an S corporation generally must compute its taxable income as if it were an individual, it is not allowed deductions granted only to corporations such as the § 243 dividends received deduction.

5) Organizational Expenses

An S corporation is allowed to deduct and amortize its organizational expenses under § 248. § 1363(b)(3).

d. Tax Elections

Elections affecting the determination of taxable income generally are made by the S corporation rather than its shareholders. § 1363(c)(1); Reg. § 1.1363–1(c)(1).

Example: An election to deduct and amortize organizational expenditures under § 248 must be made by the S corporation, not on a shareholder-by-shareholder basis. An election to expense the cost of § 179 property must be made by the S corporation and the dollar limitations in § 179(b) apply at both the S corporation and shareholder levels. § 179(d)(8).

3. Tax Consequences to Shareholders

a. Timing and Character of Pass-Through Items

S corporation shareholders are required to take into account their respective pro rata shares of the corporation's separately stated items and nonseparately computed income or loss (i.e., the net total of the items which are not separately stated) in the taxable year in which the S corporation's taxable year ends. § 1366(a). The separately stated items retain their character when reported by the shareholders. § 1366(b).

Example: Assume S Corp. (which is an S corporation) has properly adopted a November 30 taxable year and during its current year has the following income and expenses:

Business Income	$100,000
Salary Expense	40,000
Depreciation	10,000
Taxes	5,000
§ 1245 gain	25,000
§ 1231 gain	20,000
LTCG from stock sale	15,000
LTCL from stock sale	4,000
STCL from stock sale	6,000

Of these items, the § 1231 gain and capital gain and losses are separately stated items because their separate treatment could affect the tax liability of a particular shareholder depending on the results of the shareholder's other asset dispositions during the year. The regulations permit separate netting of long-and short-term capital gain transactions. Reg. § 1.1366–1(a)(2)(i) & (ii). Thus, S's separately stated items will be: § 1231 gain—$20,000; net LTCG—$11,000 ($15,000 of gain and $4,000 of loss); and STCL—$6,000. These items will retain their character when they are reported by the shareholders. S's nonseparately computed income will be $70,000 ($100,000 business income plus $25,000 § 1245 gain less $55,000 of deductions (salary, depreciation and taxes)). Because the

§ 1245 gain is ordinary income, its tax treatment cannot vary among shareholders so it is not a separately reported item. Each shareholder will have to take into account his or her pro rata share of the § 1231 gain, net LTCG, STCL, and $70,000 of nonseparately computed income in the taxable year in which S's November 30 taxable year ends. Calendar year shareholders would report their pro rata shares of these items on April 15 of the following year.

b. Determining Each Shareholder's Pro Rata Share

1) In General

Each shareholder's pro rata share of S corporation tax items is determined on a per share, per day basis. § 1377(a)(1).

Example: Assume Z Co. is an S corporation and has 100 shares of stock outstanding. If shareholder A owns 30 shares of Z for the full year, he will be allocated 30% of each of Z's separately stated items and its nonseparately computed income or loss. If A sells 10 of his shares to D midway through the year, he would be allocated 25% of Z's separately stated items and nonseparately computed income or loss (30% for one-half the year, or 15%, plus 20% for one-half the year, or 10%, for a 25% total).

2) Special Rule for Termination of a Shareholder's Interest

If a shareholder's interest in the corporation is terminated, all shareholders during the year may agree to elect to treat the year as if it consisted of two taxable years with the first year ending on the day of termination. § 1377(a)(2).

Example: Assume X Corp. is an S corporation and has 100 shares of stock outstanding. During the year X earns $50,000 of nonseparately computed income and under its accounting method, $40,000 of the $50,000 was earned in the first half of the year. Assume shareholder B sells all 40 of her X shares midway through the year. Under the per share, per day method of allocation, B will report $10,000 of the nonseparately computed income (40% for one-half the year, or 20% of the $50,000). Alternatively, if all of the shareholders in the corporation agree, X's books can be treated as closing as of the day of B's sale and she will report $16,000 (40% of the $40,000 earned in the first half of X's year). Presumably, B will agree to this arrangement only if she has other losses or deductions to offset the additional income or she has some other reason (maybe a family relationship?) to help the other shareholders save taxes.

3) Special Rule for a Family Group

In order to prevent tax avoidance within a family group through the use of an S corporation, § 1366(e) authorizes the Service to reallocate an S corporation's income if an individual who is a member of the "family" (defined as including a spouse, ancestors and lineal descendants) of an S corporation shareholder renders services or provides capital to the corporation and does not receive reasonable compensation. Note that the service or capital provider to whom income is reallocated does not have to be a shareholder of the S corporation. The statute only requires that a family member of the service or capital provider be a shareholder. In applying § 1366(e), the courts look to what would be paid to obtain comparable services or capital from an unrelated party. *Davis v. Comm'r,* 64 T.C. 1034 (1975).

Example: Assume W Co. is an S corporation with 100 shares of stock outstanding which are owned 20 shares by Dad, 40 shares by Daughter, and 40 shares by Son. If Dad performs $20,000 of deductible services without charge for W, the Service can step in and allocate $20,000 of W's income to Dad. The allocation would produce a $20,000 deduction for W which would reduce the income (or increase the loss) otherwise allocable to Daughter and Son.

c. Limitations on Losses

1) § 1366(d) Basis Limit

A shareholder's share of S corporation losses and deductions is limited to the shareholder's adjusted basis in the (1) stock of the corporation, and (2) indebtedness of the corporation to the shareholder. § 1366(d)(1). Losses or deductions disallowed by § 1366 carry over indefinitely and may be used when the shareholder obtains additional stock or debt basis by, for example, contributing or loaning additional funds to the corporation or buying more stock. § 1366(d)(2)(A). In the case of a transfer of stock of an S corporation to a spouse or former spouse under § 1041(a), the transferee-spouse is allowed to carry over disallowed losses or deductions until that shareholder obtains additional basis. § 1366(d)(2)(B).

Example (1): C is a shareholder in an S corporation and has a $5,000 basis in her stock. C also loaned the corporation $4,000 in exchange for a corporate note. If C's share of the corporation's nonseparately computed loss for the year is $12,000, she will be limited to a $9,000 deduction (her combined basis in the stock and note) and will have $3,000 of suspended loss which will carry over until she obtains additional basis.

If the basis limitation is exceeded by a combination of different types of losses, the limit consists of a proportionate amount of each type of loss. See Reg. § 1.704–1(d)(2), which uses this approach in the analogous partnership setting.

Example (2): D is a shareholder in an S corporation and has a $3,000 basis in his stock. D's share for the year of the corporation's long-term capital loss is $6,000 and his share of nonseparately computed operating loss is $3,000. Under § 1366(d)(1), D will be allowed a $3,000 loss deduction for the year which will be made up as follows:

$$\frac{6,000}{9,000} \times 3,000 = 2,000 \text{ LTCL}$$

$$\frac{3,000}{9,000} \times 3,000 = 1,000 \text{ OL}$$

D would have a $4,000 long-term capital loss carryover and a $2,000 operating loss carryover going into the next year. See Reg. § 1.1366–2(a)(4).

2) Basis of Indebtedness of S Corporation to a Shareholder

Treasury regulations provide general guidance on the basis of indebtedness of an S corporation to its shareholders. They provide that a shareholder receives basis credit in such indebtedness if the debt is "bona fide," a determination that is made under general tax principles and depends on all the facts and circumstances. For this purpose, relevant factors include evidence of intent to make a loan (e.g., proper documentation and adherence to a payment schedule), objective indicia of indebtedness, and economic reality (e.g., would a third party lender loan money under similar circumstances). Reg. § 1.1362–2(a)(2)(i). The facts and circumstances rule applies regardless of how the indebtedness arises. The regulations provide examples of various fact patterns, such as loans directly from a shareholder to the S corporation, back-to-back loan arrangements where one S corporation makes a loan to a shareholder and the shareholder then loans money to a different S corporation, and a loan restructuring where a sole shareholder of two S corporations receives the loan of one corporation to the other in a distribution. See Reg. § 1.1362–2(a)(2)(iii) Examples 1–3.

3) Basis Credit for Shareholder Guarantee of S Corporation Debt

The regulations provide that a shareholder does not obtain basis credit in indebtedness of an S corporation merely by guaranteeing a loan or acting as a surety, accommodation party, or in some similar capacity relating to a loan. But if a shareholder is called upon to make a payment on the corporation's indebtedness as a result of a guaranty or similar arrangement, then the shareholder may increase the basis of that indebtedness to the extent of the amount of the payment. Reg. § 1.1362–2(a)(2)(ii); see also Reg. § 1.1362–2(a)(2)(iii) Example 4. Most courts that considered this issue took the same position as the regulations. The taxpayer's argument in these cases, accepted only by the Eleventh Circuit, was that since the lender is ultimately looking to the shareholder for repayment, the transaction should be treated as a loan to the shareholder followed by a capital contribution (or loan) to the corporation. *Selfe v. United States,* 778 F.2d 769 (11th Cir.1985). The issue is important because of the § 1366(d) limitation on pass through of losses.

4) No Basis Credit for Entity Debt

Unlike partners, who generally may include their share of the partnership's indebtedness in the basis of their partnership interest, S corporation shareholders may not include debts incurred by the corporation in their stock or debt basis.

5) Use of Suspended Losses After Termination of S Corporation Status

If a shareholder's losses or deductions are disallowed because of inadequate stock basis and the corporation's status as an S corporation terminates, the loss is treated as incurred at the end of the "post-termination transition period" (a period defined in § 1377(b) as extending at least one year after the last day of the corporation's last taxable year as an S corporation). § 1366(d)(3)(A). Thus, if the shareholder has adequate stock basis (debt basis is not considered) at that time by virtue of having made an additional contribution to the corporation, the suspended loss will pass through and reduce the shareholder's personal tax liability. § 1366(d)(3)(B). A corresponding reduction is required in the basis of the stock. § 1366(d)(3)(C).

6) Related Provisions

Losses that pass through to the shareholders also may be disallowed by the at-risk rules in § 465 and the passive activity limitations in § 469. The at-risk rules are applied to an S corporation on an activity-by-activity basis, except that all activities constituting a trade or business are treated as one activity if the taxpayer actively participates in the management of the trade or business, or 65% or more of the losses are allocable to persons who actively participate in management of the trade or business. § 465(c)(3)(B). Under the passive loss limitations, if an S corporation shareholder does not materially participate in an activity, his losses from the activity will only be deductible against income from passive activities. § 469(a), (c)(1), (d)(1). Any disallowed passive activity loss may be carried forward to the next taxable year. § 469(b).

d. Basis Adjustments

The basis of each shareholder's stock in an S corporation is first increased by the shareholder's share of both separately and nonseparately computed income items and decreased, but not below zero, by distributions to the shareholder and then decreased by the shareholder's share of separately and nonseparately computed losses, deductions, and nondeductible expenses which are not capital expenditures. § 1367(a). When an S corporation makes a charitable contribution of appreciated property, the shareholders reduce basis by their pro rata share of the adjusted basis (not fair market value) of the contributed property. § 1367(a)(2), flush language. For the rules providing that basis adjustments for distributions are made before applying the § 1366(d) loss limitation for the year, see §§ 1366(d)(1)(A); 1368(d), last sentence. If losses and deductions exceed the shareholder's stock basis, they may be applied against and reduce (but not below zero) the shareholder's basis in any S corporation debt. § 1367(b)(2)(A). If debt basis is reduced under this provision, later net increases are first applied to restore that basis before being applied to increase the basis of the shareholder's stock. § 1367(b)(2)(B). Basis adjustments are made at the end of the corporation's taxable year unless during the year the shareholder disposes of the stock or the debt is wholly or partially repaid in which case the adjustments are effective immediately before the disposition or repayment. Reg. § 1.1367–1(d)(1), –2(d)(1).

Example: C is a shareholder in an S corporation who paid $5,000 for her stock and loaned the corporation $1,000 in exchange for a corporate note. During the corporation's first taxable year (Year 1), C's share of the corporation's tax items is:

LTCG	$2,000
Operating Income	$4,000
STCL	$1,000

C will report and pay tax on these items in her taxable year in which the corporate taxable year ends. At the end of Year 1 her stock basis is adjusted as follows:

$ 5,000	Original Stock Basis
+ 2,000	§ 1367(a)(1)(A)
+ 4,000	§ 1367(a)(1)(B)
− 1,000	§ 1367(a)(2)(B)
$10,000	New Stock Basis

C's basis in the corporate note remains $1,000.

In Year 2, C's share of the corporation's tax items consists of $12,000 of operating loss. Under § 1366(d), C can only deduct $11,000 of the loss (the total of her stock and debt basis in the corporation). The remaining $1,000 of loss will be suspended and carry over to Year 3. C's basis in her stock and debt will be reduced to zero under § 1367(a)(2)(C) and § 1367(b)(2)(A).

In Year 3, the corporation's business improves and C's share of the corporation's tax items consists of $5,000 of operating income. C will include the $5,000 of income in her personal tax return and will be allowed to deduct the $1,000 loss from the prior year. For basis purposes, the $5,000 increase attributable to the income will be reduced by the $1,000 loss. The remaining $4,000 of basis will first be allocated to the debt to restore it to its original $1,000 basis. § 1367(b)(2)(B).

At the end of Year 3, C's stock basis is adjusted as follows:

$ 0	Beginning Basis
+ 5,000	Income
− 1,000	Suspended Loss Deductible This Year
− 1,000	Restoration of Debt Basis
$ 3,000	New Stock Basis

e. Sale of S Corporation Stock

S corporation stock is a capital asset and historically has been treated as such for purposes of characterizing gain or loss to a selling shareholder. More recently, the regulations apply a partial and fairly narrow "look-through" rule for sales and exchanges of S corporation stock. Reg. § 1.1(h)–1. Shareholders who sell S corporation stock held for more than one year may recognize either collectibles gain (taxable at a maximum rate of 28%) or residual capital gain (taxable at a maximum rate of 20%) or loss. A selling shareholder's share of collectibles gain is the amount of "net collectibles gain" (but not loss) that would be allocated to that shareholder if the S corporation sold all of its collectibles in a fully taxable transaction immediately before the sale of the stock. The "residual" capital gain (or loss) is the amount of long-term capital gain or loss that the shareholder would recognize on the sale of the stock ("pre-look-through capital gain or loss") less the shareholder's share of collectibles gain. Reg. § 1.1(h)–1(c). It is possible for a selling shareholder who has a pre-look-through gain to end up with a collectibles gain and a residual capital loss. These look-through rules do not extend to ordinary income assets or to the 25% "unrecaptured section 1250 gain" that may be realized on the sale of depreciable real estate.

Example: A, B and C are equal shareholders in S Corp., an S corporation that invests in antique collectibles. A, who has held her S Corp. stock for more than one year and has an adjusted basis of $1,000, sells her stock to P for $1,500, recognizing $500 of pre-look-through long-term capital gain. S Corp. owned antiques which, if sold for their fair market value, would result in $3,000 of collectibles gain, of which $1,000 would be allocable to A. Therefore, on the sale of her stock, A recognizes $1,000 of collectibles gain and $500 of residual long-term capital loss. Reg. § 1.1(h)–1(f) Example 4.

E. Distributions to Shareholders

Because the shareholders of an S corporation are taxed directly on their share of the corporation's income, whether actually received or not, distributions of that income should not be taxed again. Section 1368 accomplishes that result in straightforward fashion for corporations that do not have E & P. Distributions by S corporations with E & P (for example, from prior operation as a C corporation or acquisition of a C corporation) present some additional complications.

1. S Corporations Without E & P

Distributions by S corporations with no E & P are tax free to the extent of the shareholder's adjusted basis in stock of the corporation. § 1368(b)(1). If the distribution exceeds the shareholder's stock basis, the excess is treated as gain from the sale or exchange of the stock, normally capital gain if the stock is a capital asset. § 1368(b)(2). Finally, the shareholder's stock basis is reduced by the amount of any distribution which is not includible in income by reason of the distribution rules. § 1367(a)(2)(A).

Example: D is a shareholder in an S corporation and has a $5,000 basis in his stock. If the corporation distributes $8,000 of cash to D he will be permitted to receive $5,000 tax free and $3,000 will be treated as gain from the sale or exchange of D's stock. D's stock basis will be reduced to zero as a result of the distribution.

2. S Corporations with E & P

a. In General

In order to determine the tax consequences of a distribution by an S corporation with E & P, a concept is needed to separate the results of the corporation's operations as an S corporation from its prior C corporation existence. The concept adopted for this purpose is the accumulated adjustments account (the "AAA"). To the extent of the AAA, distributions are treated in the same fashion as distributions by S corporations without E & P—first as a tax-free recovery of stock basis, then as gain from the sale or exchange of stock. If distributions during the year exceed the AAA, the AAA is proportionately allocated based on the amount of each distribution. Amounts distributed in excess of the AAA are first treated as a dividend to the extent of the corporation's E & P and then as a recovery of any remaining stock basis and gain from the sale or exchange of stock. § 1368(c). Alternatively, all shareholders receiving distributions during the year may jointly elect to have all distributions first treated as dividends to the extent of available E & P. § 1368(e)(3); Reg. § 1.1368–1(e)(2).

b. The Accumulated Adjustments Account

The AAA is an account of the corporation which is adjusted for the period since the corporation has been an S corporation (beginning in 1983) in the same general manner as adjustments are made to a shareholder's basis. § 1368(e)(1)(A). The AAA is a corporate account and is not apportioned among the shareholders. Reg. § 1.1368–2(a). The AAA is best understood as a running total of the undistributed earnings of the corporation which have been taxed to the shareholders during the time it has been an S corporation.

Example: On January 1, 2014, T Corporation elected to be an S corporation. Prior to 2014, T operated as a C corporation and at the time of its S election it had $6,000 of accumulated E & P. During 2014, T had $30,000 of operating income from its business and made no distributions to its shareholders. During 2015, T had a $10,000 LTCG, $20,000 of operating loss from its business and made no distributions. During 2016, T broke even in its business and distributed $20,000 to each of its two equal shareholders, A and B. Assume A's basis in her T stock at the beginning of 2016 is $12,000 and B's basis in his T stock is $8,000.

T's AAA is $20,000 for purposes of characterizing the distributions to A and B:

$ 30,000	2014 operating income
+ 10,000	2015 LTCG
− 20,000	2015 operating loss
$ 20,000	AAA

Thus, the first $10,000 of distributions will be treated as recovery of stock basis (to the extent thereof) and gain from the sale or exchange of stock. The next $3,000 of distributions will be a dividend as a result of T's accumulated E & P. The final $7,000 of distributions will be recovery of any remaining stock basis and gain. In summary, the results to A and B are:

A		B
$10,000	§ 1368(c)(1), (b)(1)	$ 8,000
	§ 1368(c)(1), (b)(2), (b)(1)	$ 2,000
$ 3,000	§ 1368(c)(2)	$ 3,000
$ 2,000	§ 1368(c)(3), (b)(1)	
$ 5,000	§ 1368(c)(3), (b)(2)	$ 7,000

As a result of the distributions, both A's and B's stock bases will be zero at the end of the year. § 1367(a)(2)(A). T's AAA will also be reduced to zero because it is allowed a $20,000 reduction for the amount of the distribution received by A and B tax free. §§ 1368(e)(1)(A); 1367(a)(2)(A). T's E & P will be zero at the end of the year. §§ 312(a)(1); 1371(c)(3). Since T no longer has E & P, it will be able to operate in the future without having to worry about its AAA unless it later obtains E & P—e.g., through an acquisition of a C corporation. Finally, it would not have mattered on these facts, but if the distributions had been smaller (e.g., $3,000 to each shareholder) A and B could have considered a joint election to treat the distribution as a dividend. The benefit of such an election would be to eliminate T's E & P and the need for the AAA. Elimination of E & P also would remove the threat of a termination or corporate-level tax as a result of passive investment income. See §§ 1362(d)(3) and 1375.

3. Distributions of Property

The rules in § 1368 do not distinguish between cash and property distributions at the shareholder level. The amount of a property distribution will be the fair market value of the property and a shareholder will take a fair market value basis in distributed property. § 301(b)(1), (d). The shareholder's stock basis also will be reduced by the fair market value of the distributed property. §§ 1367(a)(2)(A) and 1368.

At the corporate level, a distribution of appreciated property to a shareholder will require recognition of gain as if the property were sold. §§ 311(b)(1), 1368(a) and 1371(a)(1). The gain will be taxed directly to the shareholders like any other gain recognized by the corporation.

Example: Assume W Co. (an S corporation) has no E & P, breaks even in business during the year, and distributes appreciated land (a capital asset held long-term with a $50,000 fair market value and $20,000 adjusted basis) to C, one of its two equal shareholders. Also, assume C's basis in her W stock is $70,000 and W makes a simultaneous $50,000 cash distribution to D, its other shareholder. W will recognize $30,000 of LTCG, $15,000 of which will be taxed to each shareholder. C will receive a $50,000 tax-free distribution, and her stock basis beginning the next year will be:

$ 70,000	Stock Basis
+ 15,000	§§ 1366(a)(1)(A), 1367(a)(1)(A)
− 50,000	§§ 1368(b)(1), 1367(a)(2)(A)
$ 35,000	

4. Ordering of Basis Adjustments

A shareholder's basis is first increased by his pro rata share of income and gain for the year and then decreased (but not below zero) by distributions before any further reduction for losses. § 1368(d), last sentence. Thus, downward basis adjustments for distributions are made before applying the § 1366(d) loss limitation for the year. § 1366(d)(1)(A). This is similar to the ordering rules used by partnerships. Reg. § 1.704–1(d)(2).

Example: A is the sole shareholder of X Corp., an S corporation with no accumulated E & P. On January 1 of the current year, A's adjusted basis in her X stock is $1,000, and A holds no X debt. During the year, X recognizes a $200 LTCG, sustains an operating loss of $900, and distributes $700 cash to A. A's adjusted basis in her X stock is first increased by $200, to $1,200, to reflect the $200 LTCG. A's basis is then reduced by the distribution to $500 ($1,200 less the $700 distribution) before applying the § 1366(d)(1) loss limitation. A may deduct $500 of X's operating loss and reduces her adjusted stock basis to zero. The remaining $400 of loss may be carried forward under § 1366(d)(2).

5. Distributions Following Termination of S Corporation Status

Following termination of a corporation's S status, cash distributions during a "post-termination transition period" (a period defined in § 1377(b) as extending at least one year after the last day of the corporation's last taxable year as an S corporation) are applied against stock basis to the extent of the AAA. § 1371(e)(1). All shareholders receiving distributions during the post-termination transition period may elect to not have this rule apply. § 1371(e)(2).

F. Taxation of the S Corporation

The principal benefit of a corporation making an S election is relief from paying all corporate-level taxes. Thus, an S corporation is not subject to the § 11 tax on corporate taxable income, the corporate alternative minimum tax, and various penalty taxes such as the § 531 accumulated earnings tax and the § 541 personal holding company tax. S corporations with a prior C corporation history, however, are subject to taxation in certain limited circumstances.

1. § 1374 Tax on Built-In Gains

a. Policy of Built-In Gains Tax

When Congress repealed the remaining remnants of the *General Utilities* doctrine, it was concerned that Subchapter S might be used to avoid tax on corporate-level gain. The fear was that a C corporation seeking to liquidate or distribute a highly appreciated asset to its shareholders could make an S election prior to the contemplated distribution. Although corporate-level gain would be recognized, it would pass through to the shareholders and no corporate-level tax would be paid. The shareholders possibly would be required to recognize gain on the liquidation but only after an upward adjustment in their stock basis as a result of taking the gain into income. If permitted, this technique would reduce or eliminate the full burden of the double tax.

To curtail this strategy, Congress enacted § 1374, which applies to S corporations making an election after 1986. In keeping with its narrow purpose, § 1374 does not apply to corporations that have always been S corporations. § 1374(c)(1).

b. Operation of § 1374

Section 1374 imposes a tax (generally at the highest § 11(b) rates) on an S corporation's net recognized built-in gain for any taxable year during a 5-year "recognition period" beginning with the first day it became an S corporation. § 1374(a), (b)(1), (d)(7). An S corporation's recognized built-in gain is any gain recognized during the relevant 5-year period unless the corporation establishes that it did not hold the asset when it made its S election or the gain recognized exceeded the gain inherent in the asset at the time of the S election. § 1374(d)(3). Built-in gains subject to § 1374 include not only gains from sales or exchanges of property but also other income items, such as cash basis accounts receivable, that were earned (but not collected) when the corporation was a C corporation. § 1374(c)(5)(A). The base for the tax, "net recognized built-in gain," is the lesser of the corporation's recognized built-in gains and losses for the year or the corporation's taxable income (computed with various modifications). § 1374(d)(2). The net recognized built-in gain, however, cannot exceed the excess of the total net unrealized gain in the corporation's assets at the time of its S election over the net recognized built-in gain for prior years in the 5-year period. § 1374(c)(2).

Example: Assume S Co. was formed as a C corporation in 2015 and made an S election effective as of the beginning of the current year, when it had no E & P and the following assets:

Asset	Adjusted Basis	F.M.V.
Asset # 1	$ 40,000	$ 20,000
Asset # 2	$ 25,000	$ 50,000
Asset # 3	$ 5,000	$ 15,000
Total	$ 70,000	$ 85,000

If S sells Asset #3 for $20,000 in the first year after its S election, it has a $15,000 gain ($20,000 amount realized less $5,000 adjusted basis). Its recognized built-in gain, however, is $10,000 ($15,000 FMV less $5,000 adjusted basis), assuming it can establish the $15,000 fair market value of the asset at the time of its S election. Assuming S's taxable income (computed with the relevant modifications) is greater than $10,000, its net recognized built-in gain will be $10,000 and its § 1374 tax is $3,500 (the top § 11(b) rate of 35% times $10,000). If S's taxable income for the year were less than $10,000, the § 1374 tax would be 35% of the lesser amount. In that event, the difference between $10,000 and S's taxable income would be treated as a recognized built-in gain in S's next taxable year. § 1374(d)(2)(B).

If S sells Asset #2 for $50,000 in its next year as an S corporation, it will have a $25,000 gain ($50,000 amount realized less $25,000 adjusted basis). It also appears to have a $25,000 net recognized built-in gain. Section 1374(c)(2), however, limits the net recognized built-in gain for the year to the $15,000 of total gain potential in S's assets at the time of its election ($85,000 FMV less $70,000 adjusted basis) less the $10,000 of net recognized built-in gain in its first year. Thus, S's net recognized built-in gain for its second year is $5,000 and its § 1374(b) tax will be $1,750 (35% of $5,000), assuming its taxable income for the year is not less than $5,000.

If either of these sales had been made in the sixth or later year after the corporation's S election, they would be beyond the expiration of the recognition period and not be taxable under § 1374.

c. Treatment of Substituted Basis Properties

An S corporation may dispose of or acquire assets in a wide variety of nontaxable transactions. Section 1374(d)(6) and (8) describe the impact of these transactions under the § 1374 tax. Under § 1374(d)(6), if property held by an S corporation ("new property") has a basis determined by reference to the basis of property held by the corporation at the time of its S election ("old property"), the new property is treated as held by the corporation as of the time of the election, and if it is sold the recognized built-in gain or loss is determined with reference to the basis and value of the old property at the time of the election.

Example: If an S corporation exchanges property it held at the time of its S election ("old property") for property of like kind ("new property") in a nontaxable (or partially nontaxable) transaction under § 1031, any built-in gain in the old property will be recognized under § 1374 if the new property is disposed of in a taxable transaction during the recognition period.

Section 1374(d)(8) contains a similar rule for assets acquired by an S corporation from a C corporation in a tax-free reorganization. In that situation, the recognition period with respect to such property begins on the day the S corporation acquires the assets, not the day of its S election. § 1374(d)(8)(B)(i). The exclusion from § 1374 for corporations that have always been an S corporation does not apply if a corporation acquires assets from a C corporation in a tax-free reorganization. § 1374(d)(8)(B)(ii).

d. Installment Sales and § 1374

If an S corporation disposes of an asset with a built-in gain during the recognition period for deferred payments due after the recognition period, § 1374 continues to apply to the payments received after the recognition period. The gain in later years will be taxed to the extent it would have been taxed under § 1374 if the corporation had elected to recognize the gain in the year of sale under § 453(d). Reg. § 1.1374–4(g).

2. § 1375 Tax on Excessive Passive Investment Income

If an S corporation has E & P from Subchapter C operations and more than 25% of its gross receipts consist of "passive investment income," it is subject to a 35% tax (the highest § 11(b) rate) on its "excess net passive income." An S corporation with no E & P is not subject to § 1375. "Passive investment income" generally consists of the classic forms of investment income (dividends, interest, rents, etc., but not gains from the disposition of property) and § 1375 borrows the definitions employed in § 1362(d)(3) relating to termination of an S election for excessive passive investment income. § 1375(b)(3); see XV.C.2.b.2, at page 204, *supra*.

The regulations define "rents" as amounts received for the use of, or right to use property. But if significant services are also provided, the amounts received are not considered rents. Reg. § 1.1362–2(c)(5)(ii)(B)(2). For example, payments made to a parking lot where an attendant parks the car are not rents. Rev. Rul. 65–91, 1965–1 C.B. 431. But rents received in a mobile home community are "rents" because the services provided (utilities, garbage collection, etc.) are of the type generally provided by a landlord and, hence, not "significant." *Stover v. Comm'r,* 781 F.2d 137 (8th Cir.1986).

"Excess net passive income," the base for the tax, is a portion of the corporation's net passive income, which is generally defined as passive income less directly connected deductions for the year. § 1375(b)(1). This amount is determined by a ratio. The numerator of the ratio is the amount by which the corporation's passive investment income exceeds 25% of its gross receipts for the year and the denominator is passive investment income. Excess net passive income, however, cannot exceed the corporation's taxable income (computed with certain changes). § 1375(b)(1)(B).

The Service may waive the § 1375 tax if the S corporation establishes that it determined in good faith that it had no E & P and within a reasonable time after discovering that it did have E & P it distributed the E & P to its shareholders. § 1375(d).

Example: S Corp. (which is an S corporation) has earnings and profits from its earlier time as a C corporation. During the current year, it has $150,000 of gross receipts, $50,000 of which are passive investment income. S also has $10,000 of expenses directly connected to the production of the passive investment income. S is subject to the § 1375 tax because it has E & P and its passive investment income is at least 25% of its gross receipts ($50,000 passive investment income/$150,000 gross receipts equals 33%). S's net passive income is $40,000 ($50,000 gross receipts less $10,000 of directly connected expenses). Its excess net passive income will be $40,000 (net passive income) multiplied by a ratio having $12,500 as its numerator ($50,000 of passive investment income less 25% of gross receipts) and $50,000 as the denominator (passive investment income). Thus, S's excess net passive income is $10,000 and its § 1375 tax will be $3,500 ($10,000 × 35%). This assumes that S's taxable income as computed under § 1375(b)(1)(B) is less than $10,000.

G. Coordination of Subchapter S with Subchapter C and Other Tax Provisions

1. Subchapter C

Even though it is not subject to the corporate income tax, an S corporation is still a corporation and can engage in a wide array of corporate-shareholder transactions. Thus, an S corporation may redeem its own stock or distribute its net assets to its shareholders in a liquidating distribution. An S corporation also may participate in potentially tax-free or taxable corporate acquisitions as the purchasing corporation or the target and it is free to rearrange its structure under § 355. If various other qualification requirements are met, a § 338(h)(10) or § 336(e) election may be made on the sale or other disposition of an 80% or more controlling interest in S corporation stock, resulting in the transaction being taxed as if it were a sale or disposition of the S corporation's assets. Subchapter S provides limited guidance on the tax treatment of an S corporation and its shareholders in these Subchapter C transactions. Section 1371(a) states that Subchapter C applies to an S corporation and its shareholders, except as otherwise provided or to the extent inconsistent with Subchapter S. Section 1368 also provides that its distribution rules apply to all distributions to which § 301(c) would otherwise apply. Thus, if an S corporation redeems some of its stock in a transaction that does not qualify for exchange treatment under § 302, the distribution will be taxed under § 1368.

2. Other Tax Provisions

Section 1363(b) provides that with certain exceptions an S corporation computes its taxable income in the same manner as an individual. Thus, the tax principles throughout the Code which apply to individual taxpayers generally apply to S corporations. For purposes of fringe benefit provisions in the Code, § 1372 provides that an S corporation is to be treated as a partnership and any 2% shareholder (direct or through attribution) shall be treated as a partner. This provision has the effect of denying the tax advantages of fringe benefits such as group-term life insurance and medical reimbursement plans to disqualified shareholders.

3. Employment Taxes

a. Background

Wages received by employees are subject to federal employment (Social Security and Medicare) taxes, which are paid equally by the employer and employee at a combined rate of 15.3% on wages up to an indexed threshold ($118,500 in 2016) and at 2.9% (the Medicare portion) on all wages above the threshold. Self-employed taxpayers (including general partners) are subject to self-employment tax, using the same rates and thresholds. An additional 0.9% Medicare tax is imposed on wages and self-employment earnings of high-income taxpayers. S corporations and their owner-employees must pay Social Security and Medicare taxes on wages paid for services rendered to the corporation but, unlike partners and LLC members who are active in the business, their pro rata shares of the entity's net business income, whether or not distributed, are not subject to self-employment tax. The pro rata shares of trade or business income of S corporation owners who are active in the business also are not subject to the 3.8% tax on net investment income imposed on high-income taxpayers.

b. S Corporation Tax Avoidance Strategy

S corporation shareholders who are also service providers sometimes attempt to avoid paying federal employment taxes by converting wages into tax-free distributions. The Service may reclassify these distributions as wages to the extent that the actual wages paid do not represent reasonable compensation for the services provided by the employee-shareholder. This strategy presents significant enforcement challenges. In extreme cases, where an S corporation paid little or no salary to its principal employee and shareholder, some courts have concluded that all or part of the corporation's distributions were, in substance, wages subject to federal employment taxes. *Joseph Radtke, S.C. v. United States,* 895 F.2d 1196 (7th Cir.1990); *David E. Watson P.C. v. United States,* 668 F.3d 1008 (8th Cir. 2012).

> ***Example:*** Trial Lawyer ("TL") conducts his law practice as an S corporation (S Corp.) in which he is the sole shareholder. In the current year, the net income of the law practice was $5 million. S Corp. pays TL a salary of $500,000 for his services and distributes an additional $4.5 million to TL as a dividend. TL is seeking to avoid the Medicare portion of federal employment taxes on the amount he receives as a dividend (3.8% of $4.5 million, or $171,000). If it discovers this arrangement on an audit, the Service likely will attempt to reclassify all or part of the distribution as wages.

4. Net Investment Income Tax

a. Background

Section 1411, which applies to individuals, estate and trusts, imposes a 3.8% "net investment income tax" ("NIIT") on the lesser of a taxpayer's "net investment income" or adjusted gross income (with some specialized modifications) in excess of certain high-income thresholds ($250,000 for married filing jointly taxpayers and $200,000 for single and unmarried head of household taxpayers). "Net investment income" is generally interest, dividends, annuities, royalties, and income from a § 469 passive activity (i.e., a trade or business activity in which the taxpayer does not "materially participate").

b. Application to S Corporation Shareholders

S corporations are not subject to the NIIT. Rather, they pass through net investment income items and related expenses to their shareholders. The net business income passing through to S corporation shareholders who materially participate in the business is not subject to the NIIT. As noted above, this same income is not subject to self-employment tax unless the shareholder performs services for the corporation and the IRS attempts to reclassify all or part of the business income as wages. The ability of S corporation shareholders to avoid not only the NIIT but also employment and self-employment taxes on their share of the corporation's business income may be a significant advantage for S corporations in choice-of-entity decisions.

c. Sale of S Corporation Stock

Under proposed regulations, gains and losses on sales of S corporation stock by a shareholder who does not materially participate in any activities of the business are included in net investment income for purposes of the NIIT. If the selling shareholder materially participates in one or more of the corporation's business activities, each separate activity is deemed to have been sold for its fair market value and the shareholder's pro rata share of gains and losses from hypothetical sales of material participation activities are excluded in determining net investment income. Prop. Reg. § 1.1411–7(a)(1). An optional simplified method is available for selling shareholders with very small shares of net investment income or if the gain or loss on the sale does not exceed $250,000. Prop. Reg. § 1.1411–7(c).

H. Review Questions

1. C Corp. has one 100% owned subsidiary which has been active for several years. In 2016, C decides to elect S corporation status. May it do so?

2. C Corp.'s 150 outstanding shares are owned as follows:

F and J (a married couple)	15 shares
A and B (unrelated joint tenants)	15 shares
98 individual unrelated shareholders	120 shares

Will C qualify as a "small business corporation"?

3. Assume that in question 2 the shares owned by A and B in joint tenancy are purchased by X Partnership. Will C now qualify as a "small business corporation"?

4. S Corp. (a small business corporation) has 95 individual shareholders. One of its shareholders, M, dies and pursuant to M's will the S stock is transferred to a trust. Does M's death affect S's ability to qualify as a small business corporation?

5. C Corp. has two classes of common stock authorized. Class A is issued and outstanding. Class B has been authorized but has not been issued. Does C qualify as a small business corporation?

6. Assume that S Corp. is an S Corporation with 20 shareholders and 100 shares outstanding and that A, who owns 10 shares, wants to revoke S's status as an S corporation. How many votes are necessary for A to achieve that result?

7. In question 6, assuming revocation is achieved, when will the revocation be effective?

8. Assume that a corporation's S status has been terminated because it violates the 100-shareholder limit. On what date is the termination of S status effective?

9. Does a corporation falling under the situation in question 8 have any recourse as to the termination of its S status?

10. Assume that B, a shareholder in S Corp., an S corporation, guarantees a loan made by a lender directly to S. Will B receive a basis increase for the amount of the loan guarantee?

11. In considering the pass through of losses from an S corporation to its shareholders, what limitations besides the shareholder's basis in S stock and debt are relevant?

12. A is a shareholder in an S corporation and at the beginning of the year has a $4,000 basis in her stock. The corporation does not have any E & P. The corporation distributes $10,000 to A on July 15. A's pro rata share of the corporation's income and loss for the year is:

Nonseparately Computed Income	$8,000
Long-Term Capital Loss	$6,000

    Determine the tax results to A for the year and the results of the July 15 distribution.

13. What is the "AAA"?

14. In what situations will an S corporation be concerned with the § 1374 tax on built-in gains?

Appendix A

Answers to Review Questions

II. CLASSIFICATION

1. No. A joint undertaking merely to share expenses is not a separate entity for federal tax purposes and X and Y will not be partners. Reg. § 301.7701–1(a)(2).

2. If A and B form a limited liability company or limited partnership to conduct their business venture, the entity will be classified as a partnership. If A alone forms a limited liability company to operate the business, the entity will be treated as a disregarded entity for tax purposes—i.e., a sole proprietorship if A is an individual or as part of A if A is a corporation. In both cases an election could be made to classify the entity as a corporation.

III. FORMATION OF A PARTNERSHIP

1. **(a)** No gain or loss is recognized by A or AB. § 721(a).

   (b) A's outside basis is $70,000, the sum of the money and the adjusted basis of property contributed by A. § 722.

   (c) AB's inside basis is $15,000 in the installment obligations, $20,000 in the equipment, and $30,000 in the land. § 723.

2. **(a)** G bears the economic risk of loss for the liability. As the general partner, G is obligated to make a contribution to GL to pay the liability in the event of a doomsday liquidation.

   (b) G's outside basis is $80,000, consisting of the $20,000 contribution and the $60,000 share of partnership liabilities which is treated as a cash contribution. §§ 722, 752(a).

   (c) L's outside basis is $20,000.

3. The organization expenses under § 709 are (a), (d), and (e). The registration fees for issuing interests (b) and fees relating to the prospectus or offering materials ((c), (f) and (g)) are syndication expenses.

IV. PARTNERSHIP OPERATIONS: GENERAL RULES

1. The ABC Partnership can adopt a November 30 or August 30 taxable year. Using the mechanical rules of § 706(b)(1)(B), ABC can adopt November 30 because partners owning more than 50% of ABC's profits and capital (A and B) use a November 30 taxable year. Using the business purpose standard of § 706(b)(1)(C), ABC can adopt

an August 31 taxable year because ABC has earned more than 25% of its gross receipts in the last two months of the requested year in each of the prior three years.

2.   ABC must separately state interest income, § 1231 loss, and the charitable contributions. The interest income must be separately stated so various deduction limitations may be applied at the partner level. See, e.g., § 163(d). The § 1231 loss is separately stated so it can be combined with the partners' other § 1231 gains and losses. The partnership is not allowed a charitable deduction in determining its taxable income. § 703(b)(2)(C). But contributions pass through to the partners, who may combine their distributive share of partnership charitable contributions with their personal contributions and then apply the § 170 percentage limitations on charitable deductions. ABC's nonseparately computed income is $183,000, computed as follows:

$ 200,000	Gross Business Revenue
+ 25,000	§ 1245 Gain
− 20,000	Salary Expense
− 8,000	Depreciation Expense
− 14,000	Maintenance Expense
$ 183,000	

3.   False. Elections affecting the determination of partnership taxable income generally are made by the partnership. § 703(b).

4.   (a)   A's portion of the partnership's taxable income for the year is $35,200 (80% of $20,000 LTCG plus 80% of $24,000 nonseparately computed income). A also has $12,800 (80% of $16,000) of tax-exempt interest.

      (b)   A's outside basis is computed as follows:

$ 20,000	Beginning Basis
+ 35,200	§ 705(a)(1)(A)
+ 12,800	§ 705(a)(1)(B)
$ 68,000	

5.   AB's operations resulted in a $4,000 ordinary loss and a $12,000 capital loss. A's distributive share is $3,000 of ordinary loss (75% of $4,000) and $9,000 of capital loss (75% of $12,000). A's allowable deduction under § 704(d) is $10,000, which will be characterized as follows:

$$\frac{\$\,3,000}{\$12,000} \times \$10,000 = \$2,500 \text{ ordinary loss}$$

$$\frac{\$\,9,000}{\$12,000} \times \$10,000 = \$7,500 \text{ capital loss}$$

A's carryover loss will be characterized as follows:

$$\$\,3,000 - \$2,500 = \$500 \text{ ordinary loss}$$
$$\$\,9,000 - \$7,500 = \$1,500 \text{ capital loss}$$

B's distributive share is $1,000 of ordinary loss (25% of $4,000) and $3,000 of capital loss (25% of $12,000). Because B's basis is sufficient to accommodate the entire loss, there is no carryover.

V. PARTNERSHIP ALLOCATIONS: § 704(b)

1. **(a)** A's outside basis is $50,000 ($10,000 cash contributed plus $40,000 adjusted basis of property contributed). § 722. B's outside basis is $120,000 ($50,000 cash contributed plus $70,000 adjusted basis of property contributed). § 722.

   (b) A and B will both have a balance of $100,000 in their capital accounts. These balances reflect their interests in partnership assets and are in accordance with their agreement to be equal partners.

2. At the end of Year 3, A's capital account has a balance of $20,000 ($50,000 beginning balance less $30,000 of cost recovery deductions), while B's capital account has a balance of $50,000. The $70,000 ($20,000 proceeds from the sale of the asset plus $50,000 cash) must be distributed in accordance with positive capital account balances, $20,000 to A and $50,000 to B.

3. Yes. The regulations provide that partnership agreements with allocations that fail to have economic effect will be deemed to have economic effect if, when interpreted according to state law, a liquidation would produce the same economic results as if The Big Three were satisfied. Reg. § 1.704–1(b)(2)(ii)(i); see Reg. § 1.704–1(b)(5) Example 4(ii).

4. **(a)** No, the economic effect of the allocation is not substantial. At the time the allocation was considered, there was a strong likelihood that tax-exempt interest and dividends realized would not substantially differ. As a result, the net increases and decreases in A's and B's capital accounts would be the same with the allocation as without the allocation, while the total taxes of A and B would be reduced as a result of the allocation.

   (b) The amount will be reallocated to A and B in proportion to the net increases in their capital accounts due to the allocations of these items:

   Allocations Per the Partnership Agreement

To A:	90% of $10,000	=	$ 9,000
	10% of $5,000	=	$ 500
			$ 9,500

To B:	10% of $10,000	=	$ 1,000
	90% of $5,000	=	$ 4,500
			$ 5,500

   Reallocations as Follows:

   To A: $\dfrac{9,500}{15,000} \times \$10,000 = \$6,333$ tax exempt interest

   $\dfrac{9,500}{15,000} \times \$5,000 = \$3,167$ dividends

   To B: $\dfrac{5,500}{15,000} \times \$10,000 = \$3,667$ tax exempt interest

   $\dfrac{5,500}{15,000} \times \$5,000 = \$1,883$ dividends

VI. PARTNERSHIP ALLOCATIONS: INCOME-SHIFTING SAFEGUARDS

1. **(a)** If AB sells the parcel of land for $70,000, the tax gain is $50,000 ($70,000 amount realized less $20,000 adjusted basis), and the book gain is $20,000 ($70,000 amount realized less $50,000 book value). The $30,000 difference between the tax gain and the book gain is allocated to A under the traditional method. § 704(c)(1)(A). The remaining $20,000 gain is divided equally between A and B according to the partnership agreement.

   (b) If AB sells the parcel of land for $40,000, the tax gain is limited by the ceiling rule to $20,000 ($40,000 amount realized less $20,000 adjusted basis), and the book loss is $10,000 ($40,000 amount realized less $50,000 book value). The $20,000 tax gain is allocated to A. The $10,000 of book loss is allocated equally between A and B. The book loss only results in a book adjustment to capital accounts. See Reg. § 1.704–1(b)(5) Example 14(iii). The distortions created by the ceiling rule could be corrected through a curative allocation or by use of the remedial method.

2. **(a)** The amount of depreciation in Year 1 for book purposes is $10,000 ($50,000 book value/5-year useful life). The amount of depreciation in Year one for tax purposes is $4,000 ($20,000 book value/5-year useful life).

   (b) Book depreciation is allocated equally between A and B, $5,000 each. The $4,000 of tax depreciation is allocated entirely to B, the noncontributing partner, under the traditional method. Even though B is entitled to receive $5,000 of depreciation deductions (an amount equal to his share of book depreciation), the ceiling rule limits the allocation to $4,000 (the actual amount of tax depreciation).

   (c) A's outside basis in his partnership interest will remain at $70,000, while B's outside basis will be reduced to $96,000 ($100,000 beginning balance less $4,000 tax depreciation allocation).

   (d) A's and B's capital accounts will be $95,000 at the end of Year 1 ($100,000 beginning balance less $5,000 of book depreciation).

3. **(a)** The receivables are "unrealized receivables" in the hands of A and the $50,000 of income realized would be allocated to A and would be characterized as ordinary income. §§ 704(c)(1)(A); 724(a); 751(c).

   (b) Same answer as in (a) above. Gain or loss on the disposition or collection of the receivables will always be treated as ordinary income.

4. **(a)** The $40,000 of tax gain ($100,000 amount realized less $60,000 adjusted basis) will be allocated entirely to A. § 704(c)(1)(A). The gain will be characterized as ordinary gain because the cars were "inventory items" in the hands of A. § 724(b).

   (b) The $40,000 of tax gain again is allocated to A. § 704(c)(1)(A). The gain will be characterized as long-term capital gain because the disposition was made more than five years after A's contribution and, therefore, is characterized at the partnership level. § 724(b).

5. A, B and C will all be allocated $10,500 of income. They each held a one-third interest for one-half of the year and a one-quarter interest for one-half of the year. The pro rata income interest is calculated as follows: (1/3 × 1/2 × $36,000) + (1/4 × 1/2 × $36,000) = $10,500. D will be allocated $4,500 of income. D held a one-quarter

interest for one-half of the year. D's pro rata income interest for the year is calculated as follows: 1/4 × 1/2 × $36,000 = $4,500.

VII. PARTNERSHIP LIABILITIES

1. AB is considered to have assumed the $60,000 nonrecourse loan upon B's contribution of the property. Therefore, B's individual liabilities decrease by $60,000. The partners' shares of nonrecourse liabilities will be determined under Reg. § 1.752–3. First, there is no partnership minimum gain because partnership minimum gain is computed using book value rather than tax basis. Next, under the traditional method for § 704(c) allocations, B is allocated $40,000 of the liability (the § 704(c) gain realized if the property was disposed of for full satisfaction of the debt). Finally, the remaining liability ($20,000) is allocated between A and B in accordance with their shares in partnership profits. Presumably, that is 50% each, but see Example 2, at page 111, *supra,* for possible alternative allocations. Assuming B is allocated $10,000 of the remaining liability, the net decrease in B's liabilities is $10,000 ($60,000 decrease in individual liabilities and a $50,000 increase in share of partnership liabilities).

B's outside basis is:

$ 20,000	basis of property contributed
− 10,000	§ 752(b) distribution (net decrease in liabilities—see §§ 731(a)(1), 733)
$ 10,000	Outside Basis

A's outside basis is:

$100,000	basis of property contributed
+ 10,000	§ 752(b) distribution (net increase in liabilities—see § 722)
$110,000	Outside Basis

2. No. Because L is subrogated to the rights of the lender, L would have the right to recover from the general partner. Therefore, L does not bear the risk of loss. See Reg. § 1.752–2(f) Example 4.

VIII. COMPENSATING THE SERVICE PARTNER

1. **(a)** If the amount is a distributive share, A will recognize $10,000 of income, $8,000 of which is ordinary income and $2,000 of which is long-term capital gain. The partnership will have $72,000 of ordinary income and $18,000 of long-term capital gain to be divided among the partners. The income will be included by the partners in the taxable year in which the partnership's taxable year ends.

(b) If § 707(a)(1) applies, A, as a cash-method taxpayer, will not have any income until payment or constructive receipt of the $10,000. If A's services are ordinary and necessary (not a capital expenditure), the partnership potentially gets a $10,000 deduction. Under § 267(a)(2) and (e), the partnership will not receive a deduction for A's services until A includes the amount in income. That leaves $80,000 of ordinary income and $20,000 of long-term capital gain to be divided among all the partners and a potential $10,000 deduction when A is paid.

(c) If the $10,000 is a § 707(c) guaranteed payment, A will have $10,000 of income and the partnership will receive a $10,000 § 162 deduction, assuming A's services are not a capital expenditure. The timing of the guaranteed payment is determined by the year in which the partnership accrues the guaranteed payment. Thus, even if it is not paid, A is taxed when the partnership accrues the guaranteed payment. Assuming the guaranteed payment is deductible to the partnership under § 162, the partnership ends up with $70,000 of ordinary income and $20,000 of long-term capital gain.

2. **(a)** D recognizes $100,000 of income in Year Five when the property is no longer subject to a substantial risk of forfeiture. § 83(a).

    (b) ABC will recognize $90,000 of gain ($100,000 fair market value less $10,000 basis) on the transfer of the 25% capital interest to D.

    (c) D recognizes $25,000 of income (the fair market value of 25% of the assets) in Year One. § 83(b).

    (d) D is not entitled to a deduction when the partnership interest is forfeited. § 83(b).

    (e) In part (a), D's outside basis is $100,000. In part (c), D's outside basis is $25,000.

IX. PROPERTY TRANSACTION BETWEEN PARTNERSHIPS AND PARTNERS

1. The allocation of the first $30,000 of partnership gross income to A most likely will be classified as a § 707(a)(1) transaction between the partnership and a nonpartner under § 707(a)(2)(A). There is a transfer of property (use of the office space) and an allocation which, in effect, should be treated as prepaid rent assuming a distribution accompanies the allocation. Short-lived gross income allocations are particularly suspect. If the allocation and distribution are characterized as prepaid rent, A will have gross income and the partnership will have to amortize the payment over the five-year period that it uses the office space.

2. **(a)** The sale is treated under § 707(a)(1) as a transaction between unrelated parties. A will have a taxable gain of $35,000 and the partnership will take the real estate with a $40,000 cost basis. A's gain would be characterized according to how A holds the real estate. Assuming the real estate is a capital asset held long-term, A's gain will be long-term capital gain.

    (b) If the contribution and distribution are treated as separate, A has no gain on the contribution under § 721 and A's outside basis is increased by $5,000 to $55,000. The partnership takes the real estate with a $5,000 basis. When the $40,000 is distributed to A, the distribution will be tax free and A's outside basis will be reduced to $15,000. Instead of a currently taxable gain of $35,000, A will have a tax-free contribution and distribution that reduces outside basis. Likely, § 707(a)(2)(B) will frustrate A's tax goal. The transfer of the real estate is likely related to the transfer of money, and the two steps will be treated as a disguised sale in which A recognizes a $35,000 gain. Closeness in time between the two steps is a key factor in classifying the events as a sale and the regulations provide a rebuttable presumption that a contribution and distribution occurring within a two-year period constitutes a sale.

    (c) If A receives only partial consideration in the distribution, the transaction could be converted into a part-sale, part-contribution under § 707(a)(2)(B). There would be a sale of $20,000/$40000, or one-half of the real estate with an adjusted basis of $2,500, resulting in $17,500 of gain. The contributed part of the real estate would be the other one-half with a $2,500 basis.

X. SALES AND EXCHANGES OF PARTNERSHIP INTERESTS

1. **(a)** The accounts receivable and the § 1245 recapture are unrealized receivables. The accounts receivable, § 1245 recapture and dealer property are inventory items. Thus, the accounts receivable, § 1245 recapture and dealer property are all § 751 assets.

    (b) A's § 751 ordinary income is $30,000, which is equal to the amount of income that would be allocated to A if the partnership sold all of its § 751 assets in a fully taxable sale for cash in an amount equal to the fair market value of such property. In such a sale, A would be allocated $10,000 of gain from the accounts receivable, $10,000 of gain from the dealer property, and $10,000 of the § 1245 recapture.

    (c) A's § 741 capital gain is $20,000, the difference between A's $50,000 total gain ($150,000 amount realized less $100,000 adjusted basis) and her $30,000 § 751(a) ordinary income.

    (d) A's capital gain will be characterized as long-term because she has held the partnership interest for 5 years.

2. In the year of sale, B must recognize $10,000 of gain attributable to the § 1245 recapture income. § 453(i). The $10,000 of gain attributable to the accounts receivable must also be recognized under an aggregate theory. Cf. Rev.Rul. 89–108, 1989–2 C.B. 100.

3. **(a)** Nupartner's outside basis in his one-third partnership interest is $30,000. § 1012.

    (b) $5,000 of ordinary income is allocated to Nupartner even though Nupartner paid $5,000 for his share of the receivables and has no economic gain.

    (c) Nupartner's total § 743(b) inside basis adjustment is $15,000 ($30,000 outside basis less her $15,000 share of the partnership's inside basis). Nupartner's $15,000 share of inside basis is equal to her interest in the partnership's previously taxed capital ($30,000 cash received on a hypothetical sale of assets followed by a liquidation of the partnership, minus Nupartner's $15,000 share of tax gain in the accounts receivable and capital asset). Under § 755, the $15,000 adjustment would be allocated between the accounts receivable and the capital asset according to the allocations of income, gain, or loss to Nupartner from a fully taxable sale of those assets for cash equal to the fair market value of those assets. Thus, $5,000 of the adjustment would be allocated to the accounts receivable and $10,000 would be allocated to the capital asset. These adjustments give Nupartner a personal inside basis of $5,000 in the accounts receivable and $20,000 in the capital asset.

XI. OPERATING DISTRIBUTIONS

1. **(a)** A's outside basis would be reduced to $5,000 and A recognizes no gain or loss. §§ 731(a)(1); 733.

    (b) A's outside basis would be reduced to zero and A would recognize $5,000 gain from the sale or exchange of his partnership interest. §§ 731(a)(1); 733.

    (c) A's outside basis is reduced to $5,000 by the cash distribution and A recognizes no gain or loss. §§ 731(a)(1); 733. The remaining basis ($5,000) must be allocated to the accounts receivable and inventory. First, those assets are each tentatively assigned a basis equal to the partnership's adjusted basis in those assets (zero in accounts receivable and $10,000 in the inventory). Since neither asset has a built-in loss, the basis of the inventory must be reduced by $5,000—i.e., according to the remaining inside basis of the accounts receivable and inventory. Thus, A's basis in the accounts receivable is zero and A's basis in the inventory is $5,000.

(d) A's outside basis is reduced to $10,000 by the cash distribution and A recognizes no gain or loss. §§ 731(a)(1); 733. The remaining basis ($10,000) must be allocated to the accounts receivable, inventory, and capital asset. First, the accounts receivable and inventory are each tentatively assigned a basis equal to the partnership's adjusted basis in those assets (zero in accounts receivable and $10,000 in inventory). Since there was sufficient basis to be allocated to those assets, A's basis in the accounts receivable is zero and A's basis in the inventory is $10,000. Since there is no remaining basis to be allocated, A's basis in the capital asset is zero.

2. True. § 734(a).

3. **(a)** Before the distribution, B had a one-third interest in each partnership asset as follows:

	A.B.	F.M.V.
Cash	$ 5,000	$ 5,000
Inventory	$ 4,000	$ 5,000
Capital Asset	$ 3,000	$ 5,000

After the distribution, B has the following interest in each partnership asset:

	A.B.	F.M.V.
Cash	$ 0	$ 0
Inventory	$ 12,000	$ 15,000
Capital Asset	$ 3,000	$ 0

Thus, as a result of the distribution, B exchanged $5,000 of cash and $5,000 of capital asset for $10,000 of inventory.

(b) The partnership constructively distributes B's interests in cash and the capital asset that B has given up as a result of the exchange. Cash in the amount of $5,000 and a capital asset with a $3,000 A.B. and $5,000 F.M.V. are constructively distributed to B.

Under 731(a), B would not recognize any gain or loss as a result of the deemed distribution. A would take a $3,000 transferred basis in the capital asset and A's outside basis would be reduced to $4,000 ($12,000 beginning basis less $5,000 cash and $3,000 basis in capital asset).

The partnership's balance sheet after the deemed distribution is as follows:

	Assets			Partners' Capital	
	A.B.	F.M.V.		A.B.	F.M.V.
Cash	$ 10,000	$ 10,000	A	$ 12,000	$ 15,000
Inventory	12,000	15,000	B	4,000	5,000
Capital Asset	6,000	10,000	C	12,000	15,000
Total	$ 28,000	$ 35,000		$ 28,000	$ 35,000

(c) B transfers his interest in cash and the capital asset to the partnership in exchange for the $10,000 of excess inventory. The exchange is taxable and B will recognize a $2,000 capital gain on the capital asset ($5,000 amount realized less $3,000 adjusted basis). The partnership recognizes $2,000 of ordinary income on the inventory ($10,000 amount realized less $8,000 adjusted basis) which is taxed to A and C.

(d) B's remaining outside basis is $4,000. Under § 731, B does not recognize any gain on the transfer of the remaining $5,000 of inventory. B takes a $4,000 transferred basis in that portion of the inventory and has a $14,000 total basis in the inventory ($10,000 cost basis plus $4,000 transferred basis).

XII. LIQUIDATING DISTRIBUTIONS AND TERMINATIONS

1. The types of partnership property are: 1) "premium" amounts paid in addition to the partner's share of partnership property which are in the nature of mutual insurance; and 2) unrealized receivables as defined in § 751(c) (excluding depreciation recapture), and goodwill, unless the partnership agreement expressly provides for payment of goodwill, when the payments are for a general partnership interest in a partnership where capital is not a material income-producing factor.

2. True. See § 736(a).

3. A's share of § 736(b) assets is $35,000 ($20,000 cash, $10,000 capital assets and $5,000 basis in goodwill). A's § 736(a) payment is $15,000 which is attributable to A's $10,000 share of accounts receivable and $5,000 share of appreciation in goodwill. The $15,000 § 736(a) payment is paid without regard to partnership income and will be a guaranteed payment. § 736(a)(2). The guaranteed payment will result in ordinary income to A and a deduction for B and C.

Section 751(b) does not apply because the partnership has no inventory items other than the accounts receivable. § 751(b)(2)(B). The § 736(b) payment will result in $5,000 of capital gain under §§ 731(a)(1) and 741 since the payment is $35,000 and A's outside basis is $30,000.

XIII. DEATH OF A PARTNER

1. True. The partnership's taxable year does close with respect to a partner whose interest terminates by reason of death. § 706(c)(2)(A).

2. True. The taxable year of a partnership closes with respect to a partner who sells or exchanges his entire interest in a partnership. § 706(c)(2)(A).

3. The only item which is income in respect of a decedent is (b).

XIV. PARTNERSHIP ANTI-ABUSE RULE

1. Under the partnership anti-abuse regulation, the Service can disregard the purported partnership; treat a purported partner as a nonpartner; adjust the partnership's accounting method; reallocate items of partnership income, gain, loss, deduction or credit; or otherwise adjust or modify the claimed tax treatment. Reg. § 1.701–2(b).

2. The transaction likely will not be challenged under the partnership anti-abuse regulation. This problem is based on Reg. § 1.701–2(d) Example (3). The example concludes that the decision to organize the partnership to take advantage of the look-through rules for foreign tax credit purposes is consistent with the intent of

Subchapter K to permit taxpayers to conduct joint business activity through a flexible economic arrangement without incurring an entity-level tax.

XV.   S CORPORATIONS

1. Yes. Under current law, C corporation subsidiaries are permitted.

2. No. C has 101 shareholders and therefore does not satisfy the 100-shareholder limit in § 1361(b)(1)(A). F and J are counted as one shareholder since they are husband and wife. A and B are unrelated joint tenants and therefore are considered to be two separate shareholders.

3. No. Although C now satisfies the 100-shareholder limit, a small business corporation may not have a partnership as a shareholder. § 1361(b)(1)(B).

4. A trust which has stock transferred to it pursuant to a will can be a shareholder in a small business corporation but only for a two-year period beginning on the day of transfer. § 1361(c)(2)(B)(iii).

5. According to the regulations, the second class of authorized but unissued stock will not cause C to be in violation of the one class of stock requirement of § 1361(b)(1)(D). Therefore, assuming C meets all of the other requirements, it would qualify as a small business corporation.

6. A majority of shares of stock must vote in favor of revocation. § 1362(d)(1)(B). Thus, A will need 41 additional votes to revoke the election.

7. Any effective date on or after the date of revocation may be selected. If a date is not selected, then the revocation is effective on the first day of the taxable year if made before the sixteenth day of the third month of such year or on the first day of the next taxable year if it is made after the fifteenth day of the third month of the year. § 1362(d)(1)(C), (D). Thus, if S's taxable year ends on December 31, 2016 and the revocation is approved on March 10, 2016, if no prospective effective date is selected the revocation will be effective on January 1, 2016. Alternatively, if the revocation is approved on June 10, 2016, the revocation will be effective on January 1, 2017.

8. The termination is effective on the date it acquired its 101st shareholder and terminated its S corporation status. § 1362(d)(2).

9. Yes. The corporation may argue that the termination was inadvertent under § 1362(f). If the Treasury agrees that the termination was inadvertent, the corporation takes steps to correct the terminating event within a reasonable period, and the corporation agrees to make any adjustments required by the Treasury, the corporation will be treated as continuing to be an S corporation.

10. Reg. § 1.1362–2 provides that loan guarantees do not result in basis credit to the shareholder until the shareholder makes an economic outlay pursuant to the guarantee. The vast majority of the cases decided before issuance of the regulation also took this position.

11. Even if a loss pass-through is allowed because it is less than the shareholder's adjusted basis in the corporation's stock and debt, the at-risk limitations in § 465 and the passive loss limitations in § 469 may limit the amount of loss that is currently deductible by the shareholder.

12. A will include her pro rata share of income and capital loss for the year and the basis of her S stock will be:

$$\begin{array}{r} \$\ 4{,}000 \\ +\ 8{,}000 \\ \hline \$12{,}000 \end{array}$$ § 1367(a)(1)(B)

Since S has no earnings and profits, the $10,000 distribution will be considered recovery of stock basis, and A's stock basis will be reduced to $2,000. A may deduct $2,000 of the long-term capital loss, and the remaining $4,000 of loss may be carried forward under § 1366(d)(2).

13. The accumulated adjustments account (otherwise known as the "AAA") is relevant to characterizing distributions by an S corporation with E & P. The AAA is a running total of the undistributed earnings of the corporation which have been taxed to its shareholders since it became an S corporation. Distributions are treated as recovery of stock basis and gain from the sale or exchange of the stock to the extent of the corporation's AAA. § 1368(c).

14. The § 1374 tax on built-in gains generally is relevant to an S corporation which was once a C corporation. Section 1374 imposes a corporate level tax on the appreciation in a corporation's assets which arose while it was a C corporation, but which is recognized within five years of its S election. The tax is designed to reduce the incentive for C corporations to elect S status to avoid corporate-level tax on pre-election gains. The tax does not apply to a corporation which has always been an S corporation except to the extent the corporation acquires assets from a C corporation with a transferred basis. § 1374(c)(1), (d)(8).

Appendix B

Practice Examination

FACT PATTERN

X, Y and Z are equal general partners in the XYZ Services Partnership. On December 31, 2016, the XYZ Partnership will have the following balance sheet:

	Basis	FMV
Cash	$150	$150
Accounts Receivable	0	60
Inventory	45	90
Land (held for investment and subject to a $60 mortgage)	60	120
TOTAL	$255	$420

Partner X has decided to leave the partnership at the end of 2016 and is considering various transactions to achieve that result. On December 31, 2016, X will have a $85 basis in her partnership interest. The XYZ Partnership has made a § 754 election.

QUESTION ONE

X is considering selling her interest to Buyer for $120 cash. X has requested that you evaluate all of the tax consequences to the proposed sale.

QUESTION TWO

Instead of a sale, the partnership is willing to transfer $140 cash to X in liquidation of her partnership interest. Y and Z will continue to operate the partnership. X has requested that you evaluate all of the tax consequences to the proposed liquidation. X also would appreciate any advice you may have on how to improve her personal tax results.

ANSWER TO QUESTION ONE

Tax Consequences to X: On the sale of her partnership interest, X will have $55 of gain:

$140	Amount Realized ($120 cash plus $20 of debt relief)
− 85	Adjusted Basis
$ 55	Gain Recognized

The character of the gain will be determined under §§ 751(a) and 741. The accounts receivable are § 751(c) unrealized receivables. The accounts receivable and inventory are § 751(d) inventory items. In a hypothetical sale of all of the partnership's property, X would be allocated $35 of income from the accounts receivable and inventory. Thus, $35 of X's gain is ordinary and the remaining $20 of gain is capital gain under § 741. X's capital gain is long-term or short-term depending on the holding period for her partnership interest. None of X's § 741 gain is attributable to partnership collectibles or unrecaptured § 1250 gain.

Tax Consequences to Buyer: Since the partnership has a § 754 election in effect, Buyer will obtain a § 743(b) upward inside basis adjustment equal to $55, which is the difference between Buyer's outside basis ($140) and his $85 share of the adjusted basis to the partnership of its property. Buyer's interest in the partnership's previously taxed capital is $65 ($120, the amount of cash Buyer would receive if the partnership liquidated after a hypothetical sale of its assets, minus $55 of the gain in the accounts receivable, inventory, and land from the hypothetical sale). Buyer's share of the adjusted basis to the partnership of its property is $85 ($65 share of previously taxed capital, plus $20 share of the partnership's liabilities).

The next step is to allocate the $55 adjustment under § 755. If the partnership sold all of its assets in a fully taxable transaction at fair market value immediately after the transfer of the partnership interest to Buyer, the total amount of ordinary income that would be allocated to Buyer is equal to $35 ($20 gain from the accounts receivable and $15 gain from inventory). Buyer would also be allocated $20 of gain from the partnership's capital assets (the land). The amount of the adjustment that is allocated to the ordinary income property thus is $35 and the amount of the adjustment allocated to the land is $20. The final step is to allocate the $35 adjustment to the ordinary income property between the accounts receivable and the inventory according to the amounts of gain that would be allocated to Buyer from those assets: $20 to the accounts receivable and $15 to the inventory. These basis adjustments are personal to Buyer.

ANSWER TO QUESTION TWO

Characterization of Payments: The total distribution to X is $160 which includes relief of her $20 share of liabilities. The § 736(b) payment is $120 and is for X's share of the cash ($50), inventory ($30), and land ($40). The remaining $40 of the distribution is a § 736(a) payment. The § 736(a) payment is $20 for X's share of unrealized receivables and the $20 premium paid to X in excess of the value of the partnership's assets.

Consequences to X of the § 736(b) Payment: The § 736(b) payment is subject to § 751(b). Here X exchanges her $30 share of inventory for $30 of cash. That exchange is taxable under § 751(b). The § 751(d) inventory items include both the inventory and the accounts receivable and those assets are substantially appreciated since the fair market value ($150) exceeds 120% of their basis ($54). To set the stage for the exchange, X is deemed to receive $30 of inventory with a $15 basis from the partnership in a distribution and then exchange the inventory with the partnership for $30 of cash. That exchange produces $15 of ordinary income for X and gives the partnership a $30 basis in that portion of the inventory so its total basis in the inventory becomes $60. The remaining $90 of § 736(b) payment exceeds X's $70 outside basis ($85 outside basis less $15 attributed to the § 751(b) inventory distribution) by $20 which is capital gain under § 731(a).

Consequences to X of the § 736(a) Payment: The $40 § 736(a) payment will be considered a guaranteed payment to X which will produce a $40 deduction for Y and Z.

Consequences to the Partnership: Since X recognized $20 of gain under § 731(a)(1) on the § 736(b) payment, the partnership will be entitled to a $20 increase in inside basis under § 734(b)(1)(A). That increase will be allocated to the land since it is a capital asset.

Advice to X: X was paid $20 more than her share of the fair market value of the balance sheet assets. If the partnership agreement stated that the $20 was a payment with respect to partnership goodwill, X would have $40 of capital gain on the § 736(b) payment and $20 less of ordinary income.

Appendix C

Glossary

This glossary is intended to provide the reader with brief definitions of some of the terms frequently encountered in a course covering the taxation of partnerships and S corporations. More comprehensive definitions of many of these terms are included in the body of the outline.

A

Accumulated Adjustments Account (AAA): An account of the corporation which is adjusted for the period since the corporation has been an S corporation (beginning in 1983) in the same manner as adjustments are made to a shareholder's basis. The AAA is employed to characterize distributions by S corporations with E & P and, in general, represents the earnings of an S corporation previously taxed to the shareholders.

Aggregate Concept: An approach to taxing business organizations under which the organization is viewed as a collection of its individual owners rather than a separate taxable entity.

Alternate Economic Effect Test: A widely used test in the regulations under which a partnership allocation will be respected even though the partners are not unconditionally obligated to restore capital account deficits. For allocations to be respected under this test, the partnership agreement must contain a "qualified income offset."

Association: An unincorporated entity with sufficient corporate attributes to be classified and taxed as a corporation.

B

The Big Three: A shorthand description of the basic test to determine whether a partnership allocation has economic effect. This test requires the partnership agreement to provide for proper maintenance of capital accounts, liquidating distributions to be made in accordance with positive capital account balances, and an unconditional obligation by each partner to restore a deficit capital account balance.

Built-In Gain or Loss: The difference between the fair market value and the adjusted basis of an asset (or assets)—i.e., the unrealized appreciation or depreciation inherent in an asset at a given point in time. The concept is employed for purposes of the § 1374 tax on S corporations, the carryover of tax attributes following a corporate acquisition, and partnership allocations with respect to contributed property under § 704(c).

Business Purpose Doctrine: A judicial doctrine that may be applied to deny tax benefits when a transaction has no substance, purpose or utility apart from tax avoidance.

C

C Corporation: A corporation fully subject to the provisions of Subchapter C (§§ 301–385) of the Internal Revenue Code that has not made an S election. See S Corporation.

Capital Account: An account on a partnership's balance sheet which represents a partner's share of partnership capital. The regulations include specific requirements for maintenance of capital accounts for partnership allocations to be respected.

Capital Interest: An interest held by a partner in partnership capital—i.e., the amount the partner would be entitled to receive if all partnership assets were sold, all liabilities were paid, and the net proceeds were distributed in complete liquidation of the partnership.

Ceiling Rule: A limitation on a partnership's ability to make allocations (e.g., of gain or loss or depreciation) with respect to contributed property under § 704(c).

D

Distribution: Used broadly, a term that refers to any kind of payment (of cash, property, debt obligations) by a corporation to shareholders with respect to their stock, or a transfer of cash or property by a partnership to a partner.

Distributive Share: The portion of a partnership's income, gain, loss or deduction that passes through to a partner and is reported on the partner's tax return. A partner's distributive share generally is determined in the partnership agreement unless the allocation does not have substantial economic effect.

Double Tax: The result of the entity approach employed by Subchapter C, under which profits of C corporations are first taxed to the corporation when earned and taxed again to the shareholders when earnings are distributed as dividends.

E

Economic Effect Equivalence: A test in the regulations under which partnership allocations which do not have economic effect under The Big Three or the alternative economic effect test are deemed to have economic effect if a liquidation of the partnership would produce the same results to the partners as The Big Three.

Economic Risk of Loss: A standard used for allocating partnership liabilities. A partner bears the economic risk of loss for a partnership liability to the extent that the partner would bear the economic burden of discharging the liability if the partnership were unable to do so.

Electing Small Business Trust: A trust that may make an election in order to become a permissible shareholder of an S corporation. The current beneficiaries of such a trust must otherwise be eligible S corporation shareholders.

Entity Concept: An approach to taxing business organizations under which the organization is considered to be an entity that is separate and distinct from its owners.

Equity: An ownership interest evidenced by shares of stock (if a corporation) or a partnership or membership interest (if a partnership or a limited liability company).

F

Family Partnership Rules: A term historically used to refer to rules in § 704(e) that are designed to prevent the shifting of income among partners who may not be dealing at arm's length, such as family members and other donees of partnership interests.

G

General Utilities Doctrine: A doctrine, named after an early Supreme Court case, under which a corporation did not recognize gain or loss on distributions of property to its shareholders and on certain sales of property pursuant to a plan of complete liquidation. The doctrine was repealed in the Tax Reform Act of 1986.

Guaranteed Payment: Fixed payments to a partner for services performed as a partner or as a return on contributed capital.

H

Hypothetical-Sale Approach: An approach used for various purposes (e.g., determination of the character of gain or loss on the sale of a partnership interest) in the partnership tax regulations. The approach assumes that a partnership sold all of its assets at their fair market value for cash and assumption of liabilities.

I

Inside Basis: A term used to refer to a partnership's basis in its assets.

Interim Closing of the Books: An accounting method used to apportion partnership items when a partnership's taxable year closes or interests in the partnership change during the year. Under this method, the portions of partnership items attributable to different periods in the partnership's taxable year are determined under the partnership's accounting method rather than simply prorated on a daily basis throughout the year.

Inventory Item: A category of § 751 asset that generally consists of property which, if sold by a partnership or a selling or distributee partner, would not be a capital or § 1231 asset.

L

Limited Liability Company: A legal form of business entity that provides limited liability for each of its owners, who are usually known as "members." Limited liability companies with more than one member are usually classified as partnerships for federal tax purposes.

Limited Partnership: A partnership that has a general partner and at least one limited partner—i.e., one partner who is not liable for partnership debts beyond the partner's contributed capital.

Liquidation: A transaction in which a corporation ceases to be a going concern and its activities are merely for the purpose of winding up its affairs, paying its debts and distributing any remaining balance to its shareholders. When used in connection with a partnership, a "liquidation" may connote a winding up of the entire partnership or simply a liquidation of the interest of a particular partner.

M

Minimum Gain: A term used in the regulations governing allocations with respect to nonrecourse liabilities of a partnership. Partnership "minimum gain" with respect to a nonrecourse liability is the amount of gain which would be realized by the partnership if it disposed of the partnership property subject to the liability in full satisfaction of the liability and for no other consideration.

Minimum Gain Chargeback: A provision that must be inserted in a partnership agreement in order for allocations of nonrecourse deductions to be respected. Under a minimum gain chargeback, if there is a net decrease in partnership minimum gain for a partnership taxable year, each partner must be allocated items of income and gain for the year in proportion to, and to the extent of, the greater of: (1) the partner's portion of the net decrease in minimum gain allocable to the disposition of partnership property subject to nonrecourse liabilities, or (2) the deficit in the partner's capital account at the end of the year before any allocation for the year.

Mixing Bowl Transaction: A strategy used in the partnership setting to shift or defer recognition of precontribution gain on property contributed to a partnership by utilizing the nonrecognition rules for contributions and distributions. Mixing bowl transactions are now largely foreclosed by §§ 704(c)(1)(B) and 737.

N

Net Investment Income Tax: A 3.8% tax imposed by § 1411 on high-income individuals and trusts on the excess of "net investment income" (e.g., dividends, interest, capital gains, and most forms of income from passive activities) over a threshold amount.

Noncompensatory Option: An option to acquire a partnership interest that is not issued in connection with the performance of services.

Nonrecourse Deductions: A technical term of art used in the § 704(b) allocation regulations. A partnership's nonrecourse deductions for the year equal the excess of the net increase in partnership minimum gain for the year over the aggregate of distributions during the year of proceeds of a nonrecourse liability that are allocable to an increase in partnership minimum gain.

Nonrecourse Liabilities: Any partnership liability (or portion thereof) for which no partner bears the economic risk of loss.

O

Organizational Expenditures: Fees and expenses of organizing a corporation or partnership that normally would have to be capitalized but which may be deducted up to certain dollars limits and then amortized over 180 months if a corporation makes a § 248 election or a partnership makes a § 709 election.

Outside Basis: A partner's basis in her partnership interest.

P

Partner's Interest in the Partnership: The default standard used to allocate partnership items based on all the facts and circumstances when a partnership agreement fails to provide for the partners' distributive shares or an allocation made in the agreement does not have substantial economic effect.

Passive Activity: A term used to describe trade or business activities in which a taxpayer does not materially participate and most rental activities. In general, for taxpayers affected by the passive activity loss limitations, losses from passive activities are currently deductible only to the extent of income from such activities.

Previously Taxed Capital: A concept used in the formula to determine an elective § 743(b) basis adjustment. A transferee's share of a partnership's "previously taxed capital" equals: (1) the amount of cash the partner would have received on liquidation of the partnership immediately following a hypothetical sale of the partnership's assets at fair market value, increased by (2) the amount of tax loss that would be allocated to the transferee from the hypothetical sale, and decreased by (3) the amount of tax gain that would have been allocated to the transferee from the hypothetical transaction.

Profits Interest: A partnership interest in which the partner is entitled to receive a specified share of future profits (including capital appreciation) but not any partnership capital existing at the time the profits interest is received.

Proration Method: An accounting method used to apportion partnership items when a partnership's taxable year closes or interests in the partnership change during the year. Under this method, the portions of most partnership items attributable to different periods in the partnership's taxable year are prorated on a daily basis throughout the year.

Publicly Traded Partnership: A partnership whose interests are traded on an established securities market or are readily tradable on a secondary market. Publicly traded partnerships generally are classified as corporations for tax purposes.

Q

Qualified Dividend: A dividend received by a noncorporate shareholder from domestic or some foreign corporations that meets a holding period requirement. Qualified dividends are taxed as net capital gain under § 1(h)(11).

Qualified Income Offset: Boilerplate language that must be included in a partnership agreement in order for a partnership allocation to be respected under the alternate test for economic effect. A qualified income offset requires that if a partner has a deficit capital account balance as a result of certain unexpected events (e.g., a distribution), that partner will be allocated items of income or gain in an amount and manner sufficient to eliminate the deficit as quickly as possible.

Qualified Subchapter S Trust: A type of irrevocable trust that may elect to be a qualified shareholder of an S corporation.

R

Recourse Liability: A partnership liability to the extent that any partner bears the economic risk of loss for the liability.

Remedial Method: A method authorized by the regulations for making allocations with respect to contributed property under § 704(c) that seeks to remedy book/tax disparities created by the ceiling rule.

S

S Corporation: A corporation that qualifies to make an election to be treated as a pass-through entity subject to the provisions of Subchapter S (§§ 1361–1379) of the Code and which consequently avoids the double tax imposed on earnings of C corporations.

Section 336(e) Election: An election made jointly by the buyer (which need not be a corporation) and seller to treat a sale, exchange or distribution of 80% or more of the stock of the target corporation within a 12-month period as a sale of the target's assets.

Section 338 Election: An election that may be made by a purchasing corporation following a purchase of 80% or more of a target's stock within a 12-month acquisition period. The election triggers a deemed sale of all of the target's assets.

Section 704(c) Allocation: An allocation of tax items with respect to property contributed by a partner to a partnership that takes into account the variation between the inside basis of the property and its fair market value at the time of the contribution. The most common § 704(c) allocations relate to precontribution gain or loss and cost recovery deductions on property contributed to a partnership.

Section 732(d) Adjustment: An adjustment under which a distributee partner who acquired her partnership interest by a transfer when there is no § 754 election in effect may elect, with respect to distributions, within two years after the transfer, to adjust the bases of the partnership's assets as if a § 743(b) adjustment had taken place.

Section 734(b) Adjustment: An adjustment to the inside basis of partnership assets that is triggered by certain partnership distributions if a partnership has a § 754 election in effect and is required in certain other cases where there would be a substantial (more than $250,000) basis reduction.

Section 743(b) Adjustment: An adjustment made following a transfer (by sale or exchange, or death of a partner) of a partnership interest if a partnership has a § 754 election in effect or in certain other cases where the partnership has a substantial (more than $250,000) built-in loss immediately after the transfer. The adjustment increases or decreases the inside basis of the partnership's assets by the difference between the transferee's outside basis and the transferee's proportionate share of inside basis.

Section 751 Assets: A category of assets described in § 751 that consists of a partnership's unrealized receivables and substantially appreciated inventory. Section 751 assets are sometimes referred to as "hot assets."

Section 754 Election: If made by a partnership, a § 754 election triggers basis adjustments under § 734(b) (in the case of distributions) and § 743(b) (in the case of transfers of a partnership interest).

Single-Member LLC: A limited liability company with only one member (which could be an individual, corporation, partnership, or another LLC). A single-member LLC is treated as a disregarded entity for tax purposes unless it elects to be taxed as a corporation.

Subchapter C: Sections 301–385 of the Code. Subchapter C adopts an entity concept by treating corporations as separate taxpaying entities. When Subchapter S does not provide a specific rule, Subchapter C also may apply to S corporations and their shareholders.

Subchapter K: Sections 701–761 of the Code. Subchapter K is a pass-through taxing model under which partnerships are not treated as separate taxpaying entities, and partnership income and deductions pass through to the partners.

Subchapter S: Sections 1371–1379 of the Code. Subchapter S governs the tax treatment of S corporations and their shareholders.

Substantial Economic Effect: A standard for testing partnership allocations of income, deductions, etc., that is imposed by the Code and amplified by extensive regulations.

Substantially Appreciated Inventory: "Inventory items" of a partnership are "substantially appreciated" if their fair market value exceeds 120% of the adjusted basis of such property. Inventory acquired with a principal purpose of avoiding the 120% standard is disregarded for purposes of determining whether inventory items are substantially appreciated in value.

Syndication Expenses: Expenses connected with issuing and marketing of interests in a partnership. Syndication expenses are not deductible and may not be amortized as organizational expenses under § 709.

T

Tax-Book Disparity: The disparity (sometimes called "book-tax disparity") between the inside basis of an asset contributed to a partnership and the book value used to establish and maintain the partners' capital accounts. A tax-book disparity is often relevant in connection with allocations of gain, loss and cost recovery deductions with respect to contributed property under § 704(c).

Target Allocation: A term used to describe provisions in a partnership agreement providing that tax items shall be allocated among the partners as necessary so that their capital accounts will be equal to the amounts each partner would be entitled to receive if the partnership sold all its assets, paid its liabilities, and liquidated.

Tiered Partnership: An ownership structure where all of part of the interests in an entity taxed as a partnership (the "lower tier" partnership) are owned by one or more other partnerships (the "upper tier" partnership).

Traditional Method: A method authorized by the regulations for making allocations with respect to contributed property under § 704(c). Ceiling rule distortions resulting from the traditional method may be corrected by using the traditional method with curative allocations or the remedial method.

U

Unrealized Receivables: A category of § 751 assets that includes any rights to payment for goods or services that have not yet been included in income under the partnership's accounting method.

Table of Cases

Allison v. Commissioner, 39

Armstrong v. Phinney, 117

Campbell v. Commissioner, 124

Canal Corp. v. Commissioner, 133

Cooney v. Commissioner, 178

Court Holding Co., Commissioner v., 35

Culbertson, Commissioner v., 39, 100

David E. Watson P.C. v. United States, 222

Davis v. Commissioner, 211

Demirjian v. Commissioner, 60

Diamond v. Commissioner, 124

Esmark, Inc. v. Commissioner, 35

Foxman v. Commissioner, 178

Gaines v. Commissioner, 119

Gefen v. Commissioner, 64

Hale v. Commissioner, 124

Hempt Brothers, Inc. v. United States, 50

Hubert Enterprises v. Commissioner, 64

Jackson Inv. Co., Commissioner v., 176

Joseph Radtke, S.C. v. United States, 222

Kingbay v. Commissioner, 62

Larson v. Commissioner, 42

Ledoux v. Commissioner, 137

Littriello v. United States, 42

Madison Gas & Electric Co. v. Commissioner, 39

McCauslen v. Commissioner, 182

McDougal v. Commissioner, 123

Morrissey v. Commissioner, 42

Orrisch v. Commissioner, 70

Pratt v. Commissioner, 117

Pritchett v. Commissioner, 64

Quick's Trust v. Commissioner, 187

Rice's Toyota World v. Commissioner, 36

Selfe v. United States, 212

Smith v. Commissioner, 176

Stover v. Commissioner, 220

Tufts, Commissioner v., 83

Wheeler v. Commissioner, 41

Woodhall v. Commissioner, 187

Table of Internal Revenue Code Sections

1(e)..............................201
1(h) 140
1(h)(11) 198, 245
11 ....32, 198, 218
11(b)............218, 219, 220
49(a)(1)(D)(iv)............63
61..............11, 48, 116,
   119, 121, 122, 131
61(a)(7) 198
64 136
83................11, 48, 121,
   122, 124, 125, 126, 201
83(a)...............122, 230
83(b)..........122, 123, 125,
   127, 128, 201, 230
83(b)(1) 122
83(c)............................122
83(h)...............122, 125
162................11, 39, 120,
   122, 125, 131, 229, 230
163(d)..........................226
165.............................54
170 ....208, 226
170(b)...............61, 208
170(b)(2) 208
170(e)..........................208
179....................38, 61, 209
179(b)...............61, 209
179(d)(8) 38, 61, 209
197............................146
212....................60, 207
243............................208
248.....................209, 244
263 ....11, 120, 131, 175
267............................206
267(a)..........................116
267(a)(2)..............206, 229
267(c)..........................132
267(c)(3)........................132
267(e)...........116, 206, 229
301............................198
301(b)(1) 217
301(c) 221
301(d)..........................217
301–317 32
301–385 ....32, 241, 246
302...........................221
311(b)(1) 217
312(a)(1) 217

331–346 32
336(e)..........................221
338(h)(10) 221
351......48, 50, 98, 158, 179
351(e)(1) 49
351–384 32
355...........................221
367(a)(2)(C) 214
385............................32
443(a)(2) 186
444....................59, 207
444(e)..................59, 207
448....................58, 206
448(a)...........................58
448(b)(1) 58
448(b)(2) 58
448(b)(3) 58
448(c)..........................58
451(a)..........................186
453.........26, 142, 143, 186
453(b)(2)(B) 142
453(d)..................60, 220
453(e)..........................132
453(f)(1) 132
453(g)..........................132
453(g)(1) 132
453(g)(3) 132
453(i) 142, 231
453(i)(2) 142
453(k)(2)(A) 142
453B 6, 48
465......21, 63, 65, 213, 235
465(a)(1) 63
465(a)(2) 65
465(b)(1) 63
465(b)(2) 63
465(b)(3) 63
465(b)(4) 63
465(b)(5) 65
465(b)(6)(B)(ii)...............63
465(b)(6)(B)(iv)...............63
465(b)(6)(D)(i)...............63
465(b)(6)(D)(ii)...............63
465(b)(6)(E)(ii)...............64
465(c)(2)(A) 63
465(c)(2)(B) 63
465(c)(3)(B)............63, 213
469................21, 65, 66,
   67, 213, 223, 235

469(a).....................65, 213
469(a)(2)(A) 65
469(b)...................67, 213
469(c)(1)................65, 213
469(c)(7)........................65
469(d)(1) 65, 213
469(e)(1) 65
469(e)(3) 65
469(g)(1) 67
469(h) 41
469(h)(1) 66
469(h)(2) 66
469(h)(5) 41
469(i)...........................65
469(l)(3) 65
501(c)(3).......................199
531...........................218
541...........................218
641(d) 201
691............................186
701.....................58, 198
701–709 32
701–761 246
701–777 32
702....................61, 198
702(a)..............60, 70, 102
702(a)(1)–(a)(6) 60
702(a)(7) 60
702(a)(8) 60
702(b)......38, 60, 61, 98, 99
702(c)...........................58
703(a)...................58, 62
703(a)(2)(A) 60, 207
703(a)(2)(B) 208
703(a)(2)(C) 62, 208
703(a)(2)(D) 60, 207
703(a)(2)(E) 60, 207
703(a)(2)(F) 208
703(b)....38, 41, 58, 60, 226
703(b)(2)(C) 226
704...........................86, 148
704(a)....................70, 101
704(b)...............60, 80, 83,
   84, 102, 108, 122, 123,
   194, 244
704(b)(1) 70
704(b)(1)(B) 15
704(b)(2) 70

704(c) 9, 10, 50, 60, 90, 91, 92, 93, 94, 95, 96, 97, 98, 104, 109, 110, 111, 112, 113, 114, 139, 140, 145, 146, 162, 167, 181, 182, 229, 241, 242, 245, 246, 247
704(c)(1)(A) 8, 9, 15, 90, 92, 94, 98, 99, 100, 162, 228
704(c)(1)(B)......19, 98, 154, 162, 163, 181, 182, 192, 244
704(c)(1)(B)(i) 98, 162
704(c)(1)(B)(ii) 162
704(c)(1)(B)(iii) 162
704(c)(1)(C)..........100, 148, 162, 187
704(c)(2) 163
704(c)(3) 162
704(d) 62, 63, 64, 106, 226
704(e) 9, 100, 242
704(e)(1)................100, 101
704(e)(2)........................101
705 ....61, 67
705(a)........51, 62, 106, 136
705(a)(1)(A) 62, 153, 226
705(a)(1)(B) 62, 226
705(a)(2) 62, 152
705(a)(2)(B) 62
706 ....58, 59
706(a)................38, 58, 61, 116, 119, 131
706(b)................................59
706(b)(1)(A) 58
706(b)(1)(B) 225
706(b)(1)(B)(i) 58
706(b)(1)(B)(ii)...............58
706(b)(1)(B)(iii)..............58
706(b)(1)(C) 59, 225
706(b)(3) 58, 120
706(b)(4)(A) 58
706(c)(1)........101, 136, 186
706(c)(2)........................186
706(c)(2)(A)..........187, 188, 189, 233
706(c)(2)(A)(i) 136
706(c)(2)(B)...........101, 137
706(d)............102, 103, 137
706(d)(1) 101, 102, 137
706(d)(2) 10
706(d)(2)(A) 102, 103
706(d)(2)(B) 103
706(d)(2)(C)(i)...............103
706(d)(2)(C)(ii)..............103
706(d)(2)(D) 103
706(d)(3) 103
707 ....116, 130
707(a)..............................116
707(a)(1) 11, 12, 116, 117, 118, 119, 127, 130, 131, 132, 229, 230
707(a)(2) 133

707(a)(2)(A) 11, 12, 117, 118, 127, 130, 131, 230
707(a)(2)(B) ...13, 132, 133, 230
707(b)....................120, 132
707(b)(1) 132
707(b)(2) 132
707(b)(3) 132
707(c) 11, 12, 119, 120, 127, 130, 131, 170, 184, 229
708(b)..............................120
708(b)(1)(B) ...17, 163, 164, 181, 182
708(b)(2)(A) 180
708(b)(2)(B) 181
709 ....54, 55, 60, 117, 225, 244, 246
709(a)................................54
709(b)................................54
709(b)(1)(A) 54
709(b)(1)(B) 54
709(b)(2) 54
709(b)(3) 54
721.......5, 6, 13, 48, 49, 50, 51, 121, 123, 124, 130, 131, 132, 143, 161, 230
721(a)..............................225
721(b)........................49, 50
721–724 32
722 ....10, 48, 50, 51, 52, 71, 106, 182, 183, 225, 227, 229
723 ....48, 50, 51, 71, 182, 183, 225
724 ....9, 50, 98
724(a)......................98, 228
724(b)......................99, 228
724(c) 99
724(d)(1) 98
724(d)(2) 99
731 ....13, 17, 98, 113, 120, 132, 133, 143, 161, 165, 166, 167, 174, 175, 176, 179, 198, 233
731(a)............14, 152, 154, 155, 156, 232, 238
731(a)(1) 39, 51, 106, 152, 153, 157, 158, 159, 160, 168, 171, 177, 229, 231, 232, 233, 238
731(a)(2) 171, 172, 178
731(b)......14, 154, 158, 172
731(c) 153, 154
731(c)(1)........................153
731(c)(2)........................153
731(c)(3)........................154
731(c)(3)(B)..................153
731(c)(3)(C)(i) 154
731(c)(3)(C)(ii) 154
731(c)(4)(A)...........153, 154
731–736 32
732 ....17, 153, 165, 166, 179
732(a)....................154, 157

732(a)(1) 154, 155, 156, 157
732(a)(2) 154, 155, 156, 159, 160, 161
732(b)....171, 172, 183, 193
732(c) 156, 157
732(c)(1)(A)(i) 155, 171, 172
732(c)(1)(A)(ii) 155, 171
732(c)(1)(B)..................172
732(c)(1)(B)(i) 155, 171
732(c)(1)(B)(ii) 155, 171
732(c)(2)................172, 173
732(c)(3)........155, 171, 172
732(d)...........157, 175, 189
733 ....7, 51, 62, 106, 113, 152, 155, 156, 157, 165, 229, 231, 232
733(2)............................154
734 ....144, 158, 173
734(a)............15, 158, 159, 160, 172, 173, 232
734(b)..........159, 160, 161, 172, 175, 246
734(b)(1)(A) 160, 173, 174, 238
734(b)(1)(B) 173
734(b)(2) 159
734(b)(2)(A) 173
734(b)(2)(B) 173
734(d)....................173, 193
735 ....17, 158, 179
735(a).............14, 157, 172
735(b)....................155, 172
735(c)(1)........................158
735(c)(2)........................158
736.................16, 17, 170, 176, 178, 179, 189
736(a)................16, 17, 18, 164, 170, 173, 174, 175, 176, 177, 178, 184, 187, 189, 233, 238
736(a)(1) 175
736(a)(2) 175, 177, 178, 233
736(b).............16, 17, 170, 171, 173, 174, 175, 176, 177, 178, 187, 189, 233, 238, 239
736(b)(2) 170, 177
736(b)(2)(B) 176
736(b)(2)–(b)(3).............170
736(b)(3) 170, 177
737.....15, 19, 98, 154, 163, 164, 181, 182, 192, 244
737(a)....................163, 164
737(b)....................163, 164
737(c)(1)........................164
737(c)(2)........................164
737(d)............................164
741 ....13, 51, 106, 137, 138, 139, 140, 141, 142, 143, 149, 231, 233, 237, 238
741–743 32

742 143
743 ....18, 167, 182,
187, 188
743(a)............14, 143, 188
743(b)............14, 143, 144,
145, 146, 147, 148, 157,
231, 238, 244, 245, 246
743(b)(1) 144
743(c) 145
743(d)...........................188
743(d)(1) 144
743(d)(2) 144
743(e) 144
743(e)(1) 144
743(e)(2) 144
743(e)(6) 144
743(f) 144
751 ....13, 16, 137,
138, 139, 140, 141, 142,
148, 149, 164, 165, 166,
167, 168, 170, 173, 174,
179, 231, 243, 246, 247
751 et seq. 32
751(a)..........137, 138, 139,
140, 141, 142, 165, 178,
187, 231, 237
751(b)................14, 15, 16,
17, 154, 158, 164, 165,
166, 167, 168, 172, 173,
174, 177, 179, 233, 238
751(b)(1)(A)(ii)..............165
751(b)(2) 164
751(b)(2)(B) 173, 177,
233
751(b)(3)(A) 165
751(b)(3)(B) 165
751(c) 16, 17, 98,
137, 141, 170, 171, 175,
189, 228, 233, 237
751(c)(1).......................137
751(c)(2)...............137, 138
751(d)...........138, 141, 166,
174, 237, 238
751(d)(1) 138, 158
751(d)(2) 99, 171
751(d)(2)(B) 158
751(d)(3) 138
752 ....32, 51, 64,
108, 109, 113, 114, 180
752(a)..................6, 10, 51,
52, 106, 225
752(b)..................6, 10, 51,
106, 133, 152, 179, 229
752(c) 53, 111
752(d)....136, 139, 143, 147
753 ....187, 189
754 ...14, 15, 143, 144, 145,
147, 149, 157, 158, 159,
160, 168, 172, 173, 174,
177, 182, 183, 188, 189,
193, 237, 238, 245, 246
755 ....14, 103, 145,
146, 147, 157, 159, 173,
182, 231, 238
761(a)..................39, 40, 41

761(b)...........................100
761(c) 70, 101, 176
761(d)...........................170
761(f) 41
1001 ....120, 136
1001(a)............................48
1001(b)...........................136
1001(c) 34, 48
1012 ....136, 143, 231
1014(a)...........................186
1014(c) 186
1031 ....26, 40, 158,
163, 220
1031(a)(2)(D) 143
1032(a)..........................123
1033 60
1041(a)...........................211
1059 195
1059(a)..........................195
1060 146
1202 60
1211 208
1221 136
1221(1)....................99, 138
1222 136
1223 ....136, 155
1223(1)............................50
1223(2)......................50, 51
1231 ....6, 21, 50, 60, 61,
67, 81, 82, 99, 138, 159,
208, 209, 210, 226, 243
1231(b).........146, 147, 157,
158, 159, 160, 173, 174
1239 132
1239(c)(2)......................132
1245 ....50, 54, 61,
67, 100, 137, 142, 143,
148, 149, 158, 188, 209,
210, 226, 231
1245(a)............................50
1245(a)(2) 51, 100
1245(b)(3) 48, 50, 158
1245(b)(5) 158
1250 .....100, 138, 140, 141,
142, 143, 158, 215, 238
1250(b)(3) 100, 158
1250(d)(3) 48, 158
1250(d)(5) 158
1361 198
1361(a)(1) 198
1361(a)(2) 32, 198
1361(b)...........................203
1361(b)(1) 198
1361(b)(1)(A) 199, 234
1361(b)(1)(B) 199, 234
1361(b)(1)(C) 200
1361(b)(1)(D) 201, 234
1361(b)(2) 19, 198
1361(b)(3)(A) 198, 199
1361(b)(3)(B) 199
1361(c)(1)(A)................199
1361(c)(1)(A)(i) 199
1361(c)(1)(B)................199
1361(c)(1)(C)................199
1361(c)(2)(A)(i) 200

1361(c)(2)(A)(ii) 200
1361(c)(2)(A)(iii)...........200
1361(c)(2)(A)(iv) 200
1361(c)(2)(B)(i) 200
1361(c)(2)(B)(ii) 200
1361(c)(2)(B)(iii)..........200,
234
1361(c)(2)(B)(iv) 200
1361(c)(2)(B)(v) 201
1361(c)(3)......................200
1361(c)(5)......................202
1361(d)(1) 200
1361(d)(3) 201
1361(e)(1) 201
1361–1379 ....32, 245
1362(a)...........19, 198, 203
1362(b)(1) 203
1362(b)(2) 203
1362(b)(3) 203, 220
1362(b)(5) 203
1362(c)...........................203
1362(d)(1)(B) 204, 234
1362(d)(1)(C) 204, 234
1362(d)(1)(D) 204, 234
1362(d)(2) 204, 234
1362(d)(2)(A) 199
1362(d)(3) 217, 220
1362(d)(3)(A)(i)............204
1362(d)(3)(A)(ii)...........204
1362(d)(3)(B) 204
1362(d)(3)(C)(i)............204
1362(e)(1) 205
1362(e)(2) 205
1362(e)(3) 205
1362(e)(4) 205
1362(e)(5) 205
1362(e)(6)(D) 205
1362(f) 203, 205, 234
1362(g)..........................205
1363(a)..........................205
1363(b)..................206, 221
1363(b)(1) 208
1363(b)(2) 207, 208
1363(b)(3) 209
1363(c)(1)......................209
1366 211
1366(a).........205, 206, 209
1366(a)(1)(A) 217
1366(b).................208, 209
1366(b)(1) 217
1366(c)...........................206
1366(d) 212, 213, 214,
217
1366(d)(1) 211, 218
1366(d)(1)(A) 211, 213,
217
1366(d)(2) 218, 235
1366(d)(2)(B) 211
1366(d)(3)(A) 213
1366(d)(3)(B) 213
1366(d)(3)(C) 213
1366(e)..................210, 211
1367(a)..........................213
1367(a)(1)(A) 214, 217
1367(a)(1)(B) 214, 235

1367(a)(2) 213
1367(a)(2)(A) 215, 216, 217
1367(a)(2)(B) 214
1367(b)(2)(A) 213, 214
1367(b)(2)(B) 213, 214
1368 ....215, 217, 221
1368(a)..........................217
1368(b)(1) 215, 216
1368(b)(2) 215, 216
1368(c) 216, 235
1368(c)(1)......................216
1368(c)(2)......................216
1368(c)(3)......................216
1368(d)..............213, 217
1368(e)(1)(A).........216, 217
1368(e)(3).....................216
1371(a)..........................221
1371(a)(1) 217
1371(b)(1) 208
1371(c)(3)......................217
1371(e)(1)......................218
1371(e)(2)......................218
1371–1379 246
1372.............................221
1374 ....22, 218, 219, 220, 224, 235, 241
1374(a)..........................218
1374(b)..........................219
1374(b)(1) 218
1374(c)(1)..............218, 235
1374(c)(2)......................219
1374(c)(5)(A) 219
1374(d)(2) 219
1374(d)(2)(B) 219
1374(d)(3) 218
1374(d)(6) 219
1374(d)(7) 218
1374(d)(8) 219, 220, 235
1374(d)(8)(B)(i).............220
1374(d)(8)(B)(ii)...........220
1375 ....22, 217, 220, 221
1375(b)(1) 220
1375(b)(1)(B) 221
1375(d).........................221
1377(a)(1) 210
1377(a)(2) 210
1377(b)................213, 218
1378 ....206, 207
1378(b).........................206
1504(b)(8) 198
2031 186
2032 186
2033 186
6031 ....38, 58
6037 206
6072(b)...........................58
6221–35 58
6222 61
6662(a)............................36
6662(b)(6) 36
6662(i)............................36
7519 ....59, 207
7701(a)(3) 42
7701(o)............................36

7704(a)............................44
7704(b)..............5, 44, 125
7704(c) 44

Table of Treasury Regulations

§ 1.1(h)–1............. 140, 214
§ 1.1(h)–1(b)(2)(ii) 140
§ 1.1(h)–1(b)(3)(ii) 140
§ 1.1(h)–1(c).........140, 215
§ 1.1(h)–1(f) Ex. 3.........142
§ 1.1(h)–1(f) Ex. 4.........215
§ 1.1(h)–i(f) Ex. 5..........142
§ 1.83–1(e) 126
§ 1.83–6(a)(4).................122
§ 1.83–6(b)....................123
§ 1.108–8(a)....................49
§ 1.108–8(b)....................49
§ 1.351–1(c) 49
§ 1.453–9(c)(2) 48
§ 1.701–2 ....35, 192
§ 1.701–2(a) 192
§ 1.701–2(a)(1)–(3) 192
§ 1.701–2(a)(3)...............192
§ 1.701–2(a)–(c)...........192
§ 1.701–2(b)........193, 195, 234
§ 1.701–2(c) 194
§ 1.701–2(d) 194
§ 1.701–2(d) Ex. (3) 234
§ 1.701–2(d) Ex. (9) 193
§ 1.701–2(e)(1)...............195
§ 1.701–2(e)(2)...............195
§ 1.701–2(f) Ex. (2).......195
§ 1.702–1(a)(1)..............61
§ 1.702–1(a)(2)..............61
§ 1.702–1(a)(8)(i) 60
§ 1.702–1(a)(8)(ii)...........60
§ 1.702–1(d) Ex. (1) 194
§ 1.702–2(d) Ex. (5) 194
§ 1.702–2(e) 192
§ 1.704–1(b)(1)(i) 70
§ 1.704–1(b)(2)(i)............70
§ 1.704–1(b)(2)(ii)(a)......70, 72
§ 1.704–1(b)(2)(ii)(c).......74
§ 1.704–1(b)(2)(ii)(d) 74, 75
§ 1.704–1(b)(2)(ii)(h) 72
§ 1.704–1(b)(2)(ii)(i) 76, 227
§ 1.704–1(b)(2)(iii)(a) 77, 80
§ 1.704–1(b)(2)(iii)(b) 78
§ 1.704–1(b)(2)(iii)(c).....79, 80
§ 1.704–1(b)(2)(iv) 72
§ 1.704–1(b)(2)(iv)(b).....72, 91, 161

§ 1.704–1(b)(2)(iv)(d)......91
§ 1.704–1(b)(2)(iv)(e)(1)..........................161
§ 1.704–1(b)(2)(iv)(f) 97
§ 1.704–1(b)(2)(iv)(g)......91
§ 1.704–1(b)(2)(iv)(g)(3)..........................94
§ 1.704–1(b)(2)(iv)(h).....73
§ 1.704–1(b)(2)(iv)(l).....182
§ 1.704–1(b)(3)(i) 80
§ 1.704–1(b)(3)(ii)...........81
§ 1.704–1(b)(3)(iii)..........81
§ 1.704–1(b)(4)(i) 97
§ 1.704–1(b)(4)(ii)..........82
§ 1.704–1(b)(5) 76
§ 1.704–1(b)(5) Ex. (13)(i)....................91
§ 1.704–1(b)(5) Ex. (14)(i)...........97, 161
§ 1.704–1(b)(5) Ex. (14)(iv) 97
§ 1.704–1(b)(5) Ex. (4)(ii)....................77
§ 1.704–1(b)(5) Ex. (5)(i) 78
§ 1.704–1(b)(5) Ex. (6) 82
§ 1.704–1(b)(5) Ex. (7)(i) 79
§ 1.704–1(b)(5) Ex. (7)(iii)...................79
§ 1.704–1(b)(5) Ex. 14(iii) 228
§ 1.704–1(b)(5) Ex. 4(ii) 227
§ 1.704–1(d)(2) 62, 211, 217
§ 1.704–1(e)(1)(v) 121
§ 1.704–2(b)(1)................83
§ 1.704–2(c) 83, 85, 86, 87
§ 1.704–2(d)(1) 83
§ 1.704–2(d)(3) 83, 111
§ 1.704–2(e) 84
§ 1.704–2(f)(1) 84
§ 1.704–2(g)(1).........84, 87
§ 1.704–2(g)(2)...............84
§ 1.704–2(h)(1) 87
§ 1.704–2(m) Ex. (1)(i)..................86
§ 1.704–2(m) Ex. (1)(ii)....................86

§ 1.704–2(m) Ex. (1)(ii) & (iii) 110
§ 1.704–2(m) Ex. (1)(iii)....................86
§ 1.704–2(m) Ex. (1)(vi)....................86
§ 1.704–3(a)(1) 90, 91
§ 1.704–3(a)(10) 91
§ 1.704–3(a)(11) 82
§ 1.704–3(a)(2) 91
§ 1.704–3(a)(3)(i) 90
§ 1.704–3(a)(6) 97
§ 1.704–3(a)(7) 146, 148
§ 1.704–3(b)(1) 91, 94
§ 1.704–3(b)(2) Ex. 1(ii) 95
§ 1.704–3(c)(1) 93
§ 1.704–3(c)(3)(i) 93
§ 1.704–3(c)(3)(ii) 93
§ 1.704–3(c)(3)(iii) 93
§ 1.704–3(c)(4) Ex. 1 95
§ 1.704–3(d)(1) 93
§ 1.704–3(d)(2) 96
§ 1.704–3(d)(3) 94
§ 1.704–3(d)(5) Ex. 1......96
§ 1.704–4(a)(4)(ii) 182
§ 1.704–4(c)(3)......163, 182
§ 1.704–4(d)(1) 181
§ 1.704–4(d)(3) 163
§ 1.704–4(d)(4) Ex. 163
§ 1.704–4(f)...................192
§ 1.705–1(a)(1) 137
§ 1.706–1(b)(2)(C) 58
§ 1.706–1(b)(3)(i) 59
§ 1.706–1(c)(4) 137
§ 1.706–4(a)(3)(iii)........102
§ 1.706–4(b)(1) 102
§ 1.706–4(b)(2) 102
§ 1.706–4(c) 102
§ 1.706–4(f)...................102
§ 1.707–1 130
§ 1.707–1(a)..................117
§ 1.707–1(c) 120, 122
§ 1.707–3(b)(1) 132
§ 1.707–3(c)(1)..............132
§ 1.707–3(c)(2)..............132
§ 1.707–3(d)..................132
§ 1.707–5(a)(1) 132
§ 1.707–5(a)(5) 133
§ 1.707–5(a)(6) 133
§ 1.707–5(a)(7) 133
§ 1.707–5(b)(1) 133
§ 1.707–5(f) Ex. 5 133

§ 1.708–1(b)(2).............181
§ 1.708–1(b)(4).............182
§ 1.708–1(b)(4) Ex. 182
§ 1.708–1(c)(1).............180
§ 1.708–1(c)(3).............180
§ 1.708–1(c)(3)(i)..........180
§ 1.708–1(c)(4).............181
§ 1.708–1(d)(1).............181
§ 1.708–1(d)(3).............181
§ 1.709–2(a)...................54
§ 1.709–2(b)...................54
§ 1.721–1(a).....................48
§ 1.721–1(b)(1)........48, 122
§ 1.721–1(b)(2).............122
§ 1.721–1(d)(1)...............49
§ 1.721–1(d)(2)...............49
§ 1.721–2(a)...................49
§ 1.721–2(b)...................49
§ 1.721–2(c)...................49
§ 1.721–2(f)...................49
§ 1.721–2(g)(1)...............49
§ 1.731–1(a)(1)..............176
§ 1.731–1(a)(1)(ii)..........152
§ 1.731–1(a)(2)..............176
§ 1.731–1(c)(2)..............152
§ 1.732–1(d)(4).............157
§ 1.736–1(a)(1)(i) 170
§ 1.736–1(a)(2).............175
§ 1.736–1(a)(3)(i) 175
§ 1.736–1(a)(3)(ii) 175
§ 1.736–1(a)(4).............175
§ 1.736–1(a)(5)......175, 176
§ 1.736–1(a)(6).............179
§ 1.736–1(b)(1).............170
§ 1.736–1(b)(2)......175, 177
§ 1.736–1(b)(3)......175, 177
§ 1.736–1(b)(5)(i) 176
§ 1.736–1(b)(5)(ii) 176
§ 1.736–1(b)(5)(iii) 176
§ 1.736–1(b)(6).............176
§ 1.737–2(a) 164, 182
§ 1.737–4 192
§ 1.742–1 187
§ 1.743–1(d)(1).............145
§ 1.743–1(d)(2).............145
§ 1.743–1(j)(1).......145, 148
§ 1.743–1(j)(2).............148
§ 1.751–1(a)(2).............139
§ 1.751–1(b)(1)(ii) 164
§ 1.751–1(b)(2)(ii) 167
§ 1.751–1(b)(3)(ii) 167
§ 1.751–1(c)(4) 138
§ 1.751–1(c)(5) 138
§ 1.751–1(d)(2)(ii) 138,
   165
§ 1.751–1(g)
   Ex. (3)(c)..................165
§ 1.752–1(a)(1).......52, 106,
   108
§ 1.752–1(a)(2)........52, 106
§ 1.752–1(a)(4)...............51
§ 1.752–1(e) 53
§ 1.752–1(f)...........53, 113,
   154, 180
§ 1.752–1(g) Ex. 1...........53

§ 1.752–1(g) Ex. 2.........180
§ 1.752–1(i)..................113
§ 1.752–2(a) 52, 53, 106,
   108
§ 1.752–2(b)(1).......52, 106,
   108
§ 1.752–2(b)(3)(i)–(iii) ...52,
   106
§ 1.752–2(b)(3)(ii) 108
§ 1.752–2(b)(4)........52, 106
§ 1.752–2(b)(5)........52, 106
§ 1.752–2(b)(6).........52, 64,
   106, 192
§ 1.752–2(f) Ex. 1 109
§ 1.752–2(f)
   Ex. 1 & 2 107
§ 1.752–2(f) Ex. 3 64
§ 1.752–2(f)
   Ex. 3 & 4 108
§ 1.752–2(f) Ex. 4 229
§ 1.752–2(f) Ex. 5 107
§ 1.752–3 111
§ 1.752–3(a) 52, 106
§ 1.752–3(a)(1).............109
§ 1.752–3(a)(2)......109, 111
§ 1.752–3(a)(3).............109
§ 1.752–3(b) Ex. (1) 111
§ 1.755–1(a)(1)–(5) 146
§ 1.755–1(b)..................146
§ 1.755–1(b)(1).............146
§ 1.755–1(b)(1)(i) 148
§ 1.755–1(b)(2)(ii)
   Ex. 1 148
§ 1.755–1(b)(3)(iii)
   Ex. 1 148
§ 1.755–1(b)(i) 148
§ 1.755–1(c)(1)(i)..........159,
   173
§ 1.755–1(c)(1)(ii) 159,
   173
§ 1.755–1(c)(2)(i)..........159
§ 1.755–1(c)(2)(ii) 159
§ 1.755–1(c)(3) 159
§ 1.755–1(c)(4) 159
§ 1.761–1(c) 176
§ 1.1031(a)–1(a)(1) 143
§ 1.1223–3(a) 141
§ 1.1223–3(b)(1).............50
§ 1.1223–3(b)(2)............141
§ 1.1223–3(b)(4)............141
§ 1.1223–3(c)(1)............141
§ 1.1223–3(c)(2)(ii) 141
§ 1.1223–3(e) 50
§ 1.1223–3(f) Ex. (3).....141
§ 1.1245–1(e)(2)............82
§ 1.1245–1(e)(2)(i) 82
§ 1.1245–1(e)(2)(ii) 82
§ 1.1250–1(f).................82
§ 1.1361–1(e)(1)...........199
§ 1.1361–1(f).................200
§ 1.1361–1(l)(1)............201
§ 1.1361–1(l)(1)(4)(i).....201
§ 1.1361–1(l)(2)(iii).......201
§ 1.1361–1(l)(2)(iv) 201
§ 1.1361–1(l)(4)(ii)(A)...202

§ 1.1361–1(l)(5)(i) 202
§ 1.1361–1(l)(5)(ii).......202
§ 1.1361–1(l)(5)(iv).......202
§ 1.1361–1(l)(5)(v) 203
§ 1.1361–3 199
§ 1.1361–4 199
§ 1.1361–5 199
§ 1.1362–2 234
§ 1.1362–2(a)(1)............204
§ 1.1362–2(a)(2)(i) 212
§ 1.1362–2(a)(2)(ii).......212
§ 1.1362–2(a)(2)(iii)
   Ex. 1–3 212
§ 1.1362–2(a)(2)(iii)
   Ex. 4........................212
§ 1.1362–2(b) 204
§ 1.1362–2(c) 204
§ 1.1362–2(c)(5)(ii)
   (B)(2) 220
§ 1.1362–3 205
§ 1.1362–4(b) 205
§ 1.1363–1(c)(1) 209
§ 1.1366–1(a)(2)............208
§ 1.1366–1(a)(2)(i) 209
§ 1.1366–1(a)(2)(ii).......209
§ 1.1366–1(a)(2)(iii).....208
§ 1.1366–2(a)(4)...........212
§ 1.1367–1(d)(1)...........213
§ 1.1367–2(d)(1)...........213
§ 1.1368–1(e)(2)...........216
§ 1.1368–2(a) 216
§ 1.1374–4(g) 220
§ 301.7701–1(a)...............39
§ 301.7701–1(a)(1)...........38
§ 301.7701–1(a)(2)...........39,
   40, 41, 225
§ 301.7701–2(a) 43
§ 301.7701–2(a)(1)..........42
§ 301.7701–2(b)(1)..........43
§ 301.7701–2(b)(7)..........43
§ 301.7701–2(b)(8)..........44
§ 301.7701–3(b)(2)(i) 44
§ 301.7701–3(b)(3)(i) 44
§ 301.7701–3(c)(1)(iii) 44
§ 301.7701–3(c)(1)(iv).....44
§ 301.7701–3(c)(2) 44
§ 301.7701–3(g)(1)(i) 180
§ 301.7701–4(a) 44
§ 301.7701–4(b) 44
§ 301.7701–2(c)(1) 43
§ 301.7701–2(c)(2) 43
§ 301.7701–3(a) 43
§ 301.7701–3(b)(1)(i) 43
§ 301.7701–3(b)(1)(ii) 43
Prop. Treas. Reg.
   § 1.83–1(l) 126
Prop. Treas. Reg.
   § 1.453B–1(c) 48
Prop. Treas. Reg.
   § 1.469–5(e)(2) 66
Prop. Treas. Reg.
   § 1.469–5(e)(3) 66
Prop. Treas. Reg.
   § 1.469–5(e)(3)(ii) 66

Prop. Treas. Reg.
§ 1.707–1(c) Ex. 2 121
Prop. Treas. Reg.
§ 1.721–1(b)(1) 123, 124
Prop. Treas. Reg.
§ 1.721–2(h) Ex 49
Prop. Treas. Reg.
§ 1.743–1(k)
(1)(1)(iii) 144
Prop. Treas. Reg.
§ 1.751–1 168
Prop. Treas. Reg.
§ 1.752–2(b)(3)(ii) 109
Prop. Treas. Reg.
§ 1.752–3 229
Prop. Treas. Reg.
§ 1.752–3(a)(3) 113
Prop. Treas. Reg.
§ 1.1411–7(a)(1) 223
Prop. Treas. Reg.
§ 1.1411–7(c) 223
Prop. Treas. Reg.
§ 301.7701–1
(a)(5)(i) 43
Temp. Treas. Reg.
§ 1.469–4T 66
Temp. Treas. Reg.
§ 1.469–4T(a)(3)(ii) 66
Temp. Treas. Reg.
§ 1.469–4T(a)(4)(i) 66
Temp. Treas. Reg.
§ 1.469–5T(a)
(1)–(3) 66

Table of Revenue Rulings and Procedures

Rev. Rul. 65–91............220
Rev. Rul. 66–325.........187
Rev. Rul. 68–79.............60
Rev. Rul. 69–184.........117
Rev. Rul. 75–374...........40
Rev. Rul. 77–309.........114
Rev. Rul. 77–412..........179
Rev. Rul. 79–205..........154
Rev. Rul. 83–151..........107
Rev. Rul. 84–52...........143
Rev. Rul. 84–111.........179
Rev. Rul. 87–57......59, 207
Rev. Rul. 87–111............54
Rev. Rul. 88–4...............54
Rev. Rul. 88–77.............51
Rev. Rul. 89–11.............54
Rev. Rul. 89–108.........142, 231
Rev. Rul. 93–80............179
Rev. Rul. 94–4..............152
Rev. Rul. 95–37...........143
Rev. Rul. 95–41....112, 113
Rev. Rul. 95–55............143
Rev. Rul. 2002–69.........44
Rev. Rul. 2004–43........181
Rev. Rul. 2004–59........180
Rev. Rul. 2005–10........181
Rev. Rul. 2007–40........120
Rev. Proc. 93–27 ....121, 124, 125, 126
Rev. Proc. 2001–43 125
Rev. Proc. 2002–1 40
Rev. Proc. 2002–22 40
Rev. Proc. 2006–46 ....59, 206

Index

ALLOCATIONS: SECTION 704(b)
Generally, 70
Capital accounts, maintenance of, 70–71
Credits, 82
Depreciation recapture, 82
Economic effect, 72–77
Alternate test, 74–75
Basic test, 72–74
Economic effect equivalence, 76–77
Nonrecourse liabilities, 83–87
Minimum gain chargeback requirement, 86
Nonrecourse deductions, 83
Partnership minimum gain, 83
Refinancing and distributions, 86–87
Safe harbor test, 84
Partner's interest in the partnership, 80–82
Substantial economic effect concept, 70
Substantiality, 77–80
Fair market value presumption, 80
Shifting allocations, 79–80
Transitory allocations, 79
Target allocations, 83

ALLOCATIONS WHERE INTERESTS VARY DURING YEAR
Generally, 101
Allocable cash basis items, 102–103
Allocation methods, 101–102
Items attributable to periods not within taxable year, 103
Tiered partnerships, 103

ANTI-ABUSE RULE
See Partnership Anti-Abuse Rule

ASSIGNMENT OF INCOME
Partnership interests acquired by purchase from family member, 100–101
Partnership interests created by gift, 100–101

AT-RISK LIMITATIONS, 63–65

BASIS
Adjustments, to partnership assets, 144–148, 158–161
Allocation of basis adjustments, 146–148, 159–161
Contributed property, to partnership, 50
Death of a partner, 187–189
Distributed property, 154–157
Impact of partnership liabilities, 51
Inside vs. outside basis, partnerships, 50
Partnership operations, effect of, 61–62
Property distributions, 154–155
S corporations, 213–214, 217–218

BUSINESS ORGANIZATIONS, FORMS OF
Corporation, 30
Limited liability company, 31
Partnership, 30–31
Sole proprietorship, 30
Taxing models, 31

CHOICE OF ENTITY, 45–46

CLASSIFICATION OF BUSINESS ENTITIES
Generally, 38, 42
"Check-the-box" regulations, 43–45
Election out of partnership status, 40–41
Foreign entities, 44
Husband-wife qualified joint venture, 41
Limited liability companies, 43
Series LLCs, 43
Partnership defined, 100
Partnership vs. corporation, 42
Partnerships vs. other relationships, 41–42
Publicly traded partnerships, 44
Separate entity, existence of, 39–40

Single-member entities, 43
Trusts, 44–45

COMPENSATING THE SERVICE PARTNER
Carried interests, policy issues, 126–127
Disguised payments for services, 117–119
Management fee waivers, 119
Guaranteed payments, 119–121
Partnership equity issued for services, 121–127
Capital and profits interest defined, 122
Capital interest for services, 122–123
Profits interest for services, 124–126
Services rendered in nonpartner capacity, 116–117

CONTRIBUTED PROPERTY
Allocations with respect to contributed property, 90–96
Ceiling rule, 91
Remedial method, 93–94, 96
Traditional method, 91–93, 94–95
Traditional method with curative allocations, 93, 95
Built-in loss property, anti-abuse rules, 100, 148
Characterization of gain or loss on disposition, 98–100
Distributions of contributed property, 98, 162–163
Encumbered property, 53
Entry of new partner, allocation of preexisting gain or loss, 97–98
Formation of a partnership, generally, 48–51
Revaluations, 97–98

DEATH OF A PARTNER
Generally, 186
Basis consequences, 187–189

Deceased partner's
distributive share, year of
death, 186
Estate tax consequences, 186
Income in respect of a
decedent, 186–187

DISTRIBUTIONS
See Liquidating Distributions;
Operating Distributions

**FAMILY PARTNERSHIP
RULES**
See Assignment of Income

**FORMATION OF A
PARTNERSHIP**
See also, Compensating
the Service Partner;
Contributed Property
Generally, 48
Basis, 50
Contributions of property, 48–
51
Contributions of services, 121–
127
Debt-for-equity exchange, 49
Holding period, 50–51
Investment partnerships, 49
Liabilities, treatment of, 51–
53
Classification of liabilities,
51–52
Economic risk of loss, 52–53
Impact on outside basis, 51
Property encumbered by
recourse debt,
contributions of, 53
Noncompensatory options, 49
Organization and syndication
expenses, 54

**GUARANTEED
PAYMENTS**
See Compensating the Service
Partner; Partner-
Partnership Property
Transactions

HOLDING PERIOD
Partnership interest, 50–51
Property distributed by a
partnership, 155
Sales or exchanges of
partnership interests, 141–
142

JUDICIAL DOCTRINES
Generally, 34
Business purpose, 36
Economic substance, 36
Sham transactions, 36
Step transactions, 35–36
Substance over form, 35

LIABILITIES
Generally, 106
Basis of partnership interest,
impact on, 51

Contributions of property
subject to recourse debt, 53
Economic risk of loss, 52–53,
106–109
Nonrecourse liabilities,
allocations with respect to,
109–110
Part recourse, part
nonrecourse liabilities,
113–114
Tiered partnerships, 114

**LIQUIDATING
DISTRIBUTIONS**
Generally, 170
Abandonment, 179
Allocation and timing issues,
176–178
Liquidation vs. sale, 178
Section 736(a) payments, 175–
176
Goodwill, 175–176
Premium payments, 175
Section 736(b) payments, 170–
174
Interaction with § 751(b),
pp. 173–174
Partnership, tax
consequences to, 172–
173
Retiring partner, tax
consequences to, 171–
172

**LIQUIDATION OF A
PARTNERSHIP**
Terminations, 181–183
Voluntary liquidations, 179–
181
Incorporation of a
partnership, 179–180
Mergers and divisions,
180–181

**MIXING BOWL
TRANSACTIONS,** 161–
164

**OPERATING
DISTRIBUTIONS**
Basis of distributed property,
154–157
Capital accounts, adjustments
to, 161
Cash distributions, 152–153
Contributed property,
distribution of, 98
Distributed property,
dispositions of, 157–158
Distributee partner,
consequences to, 152–158
Distributions altering
interests in ordinary
income property (§ 751(b)),
pp. 164–168
Inside basis adjustments, 158–
161
Marketable securities, 153–
154

Mixing bowl transactions,
161–164
Partnership, consequences to,
158–161
Property distributions, 154–
157
Section 732(d) election, 157

**OPERATIONS OF A
PARTNERSHIP**
Accounting method, 58
Aggregate vs. entity concept,
58
Limitations on losses, 62–67
At-risk limitation, 63–65
Basis limitation, 62–63
Passive activity loss
limitations, 65–67
Partners, tax treatment of,
60–62
Tax elections, 60
Taxable income, 60
Taxable year, 58–59

**ORGANIZATION AND
SYNDICATION
EXPENSES**
See Formation of a
Partnership

**PARTNER-PARTNERSHIP
PROPERTY
TRANSACTIONS**
Generally, 130
Disguised payments, services
or property, 130–131
Disguised sales, 132–133
Guaranteed payments, 131
Partner acting as a
nonpartner, 130
Sales and exchanges, 132

**PARTNERSHIP ANTI-
ABUSE RULE**
Generally, 192
Abuse of partnership entity,
195
Abuse of Subchapter K, 192–
195

**PASSIVE ACTIVITY LOSS
LIMITATIONS,** 65–67

**PUBLICLY TRADED
PARTNERSHIPS,** 44

S CORPORATIONS
Generally, 198
Accounting method, 206
Accumulated adjustments
account, 216–217
Basis adjustments, stock, 213–
214, 217–218
Distributions to shareholders,
215–218
Election of S corporation
status, 203–204
Eligibility, 198–203
Ineligible corporations, 198

Limit on number of shareholders, 199
One-class-of-stock requirement, 201–202
Passive investment income, 204
Straight debt safe harbor, 202–203
Subsidiaries, 198–199
Trusts as eligible shareholders, 200–201
Employment tax issues, 222
Loss limitations, basis, 211–213
Net investment income tax, 222–223
Revocation of election, 204
Sale of S corporation stock, 214–215, 223
Shareholders, taxation of, 205, 209–211
Subchapter C, relationship to, 221
Tax elections, 209
Taxable income, 207–209
Taxable year, 206–207
Taxation of, 218–221
Built-in gains, tax on, 218–220
Excess passive investment income, 220–221
Termination of S corporation status, 204–205

SALES AND EXCHANGES OF PARTNERSHIP INTERESTS
Generally, 136
Buying partner, consequences to, 143–148
Contributed property with built-in loss, 148
Cost basis, 143
Sale vs. liquidation, 178
Section 743(b) inside basis adjustments, 144–148
Section 754 election, 143–144
Selling partner, consequences to, 136–143
Capital gain look-through rules, 140
Characterization of gain or loss, 137
Computation of gain or loss, 136–137
Exchange or conversion, 143
Holding period, 141
Installment sales, 142–143

SECTION 751 ASSETS
Definition, 137–138
Inventory items, 138
Unrealized receivables, 137
Distributions that alter partners' interests, 164–168
Liquidation of retiring partner's interest, 173–174

Sales and exchanges of partnership interest, 138–140

SECTION 732(d) ELECTION, 157

SECTION 754 ELECTION, 143–144, 158–159

SHAM TRANSACTIONS
See Judicial Doctrines

SPECIAL ALLOCATIONS
See Allocations: § 704(b)

STEP TRANSACTIONS
See Judicial Doctrines

SUBCHAPTER S
See S Corporations

SUBSTANCE OVER FORM DOCTRINE
See Judicial Doctrines

SYNDICATION EXPENSES
See Organization and Syndication Expenses

TAXABLE YEAR
Partnerships, 58–59
S corporations, 206–207

TERMINATION OF A PARTNERSHIP
See Liquidation of a Partnership

UNREALIZED RECEIVABLES
See Section 751 Assets